The
Reference Shelf®

Faith and Science

Edited by
Paul McCaffrey

The Reference Shelf
Volume 84 • Number 5
H. W. Wilson
A Division of EBSCO Publishing, Inc.
Ipswich, Massachusetts
2013

The Reference Shelf

The books in this series contain reprints of articles, excerpts from books, addresses on current issues, and studies of social trends in the United States and other countries. There are six separately bound numbers in each volume, all of which are usually published in the same calendar year. Numbers one through five are each devoted to a single subject, providing background information and discussion from various points of view and concluding with an index and comprehensive bibliography that lists books, pamphlets, and articles on the subject. The final number of each volume is a collection of recent speeches. Books in the series may be purchased individually or on subscription.

Library of Congress Cataloging-in-Publication Data

Faith & science / edited by Paul McCaffrey.
   p. cm. — (The reference shelf ; v. 84, no. 5)
   Includes bibliographical references and index.
   ISBN 978-0-8242-1119-6 (issue 5, pbk.) — ISBN 978-0-8242-1249-0 (volume 84)
1.Religion and science. I. McCaffrey, Paul, 1977– II. Title: Faith and science.
   BL240.3.F35 2012
   201'.65—dc23

                          2012025906

Cover: Injection of human embryonal stem cells into egg © Halaska,Jacob/Index Stock/ Corbis

Visit: www.salempress.com/hwwilson

Printed in the United States of America

Contents

Preface: Faith and Science   ix
By Joseph L. Spradley

1

Common Ground Between Faith and Science?

"And Yet, It Moves": The Conflict Between Faith and Science   3
By Paul McCaffrey

Religion and Science   7
By Albert Einstein, *The New York Times Magazine*, November 9, 1930

Science at the Crossroads   10
By Tenzin Gyatso, the Dalai Lama, DalaiLama.com, November 12, 2005

White Lies of Dover   16
By Eugene W. Harper, Jr., *Commonweal*, October 10, 2008

God vs. Science   20
By Dean Nelson, *The Saturday Evening Post*, September 2011

Einstein's Religious Awakening   24
By William Berkson, *Reform Judaism*, December 1, 2010

2

Is Your Brain Hardwired for Religion?

"It's Just All One": Neurotheology, Religion, and the Brain   31
By Paul McCaffrey

The Biology of Belief   35
By Jeffrey Kluger, *Time*, February 12, 2009

Divided Minds, Specious Souls   42
By David Weisman, *Seed Magazine*, September 1, 2010

How I Learned To Stop Worrying and Love the Brain   45
By David A. Hogue, *Religious Education*, May 2011

Does Analytic Thinking Erode Religious Belief?   49
By Andrew Aghapour, *Religious Dispatches Magazine*, May 29, 2012

Science and Religion: Reality's Toolkit   52
By Jessica Hahne, *Yale Scientific*, May 10, 2012

Neuorononsense   56
By Roger Scruton, *ABC: Australian Broadcast Company*, May 9, 2012

3

The Politics of Religion and Science

The Bible, the Beaker, and the Ballot Box: Faith,
    Science, and American Politics   63
By Paul McCaffrey

Unholy Alliance   67
By Jonathan Cohn, *The New Republic*, February 22, 2012

New Poll: Even Religious Voters Overwhelmingly Want
    Candidates to Debate Science   72
By Shawn Lawrence Otto, *Neorenaissance*, April 3, 2012

How Science Can Lead the Way   76
By Lisa Randall, *Time*, October 3, 2011

A Day in Heaven   78
By Joe Murphy, *The Humanist*, May 2011

Some Ojibwe Tribal Members Object to Wolf Hunting, Trapping   83
By Tom Robertson, *Minnesota Public Radio*, March 13, 2012

4

Evolution and Public Education

Evolution in the Classroom: From Monkey Laws to Intelligent Design   87
By Paul McCaffrey

A Spiritual Approach to Evolution   91
By Michael Lerner, *Tikkun Magazine*, November 2010

Intelligent Design or Intelligible Design?   97
By Frederick Grinnell, *The Chronicle of Higher Education*, January 9, 2009

Religion Doesn't Belong in Public Schools, but Debate Over
    Darwinian Evolution Does   101
By Casey Luskin, *The Christian Science Monitor*, December 16, 2010

Evolution Still Debated on Religious Grounds in the Public Domain 104
By Susan Barreto, *Covalence Magazine*, March 2012

The Light of the World   108
By Michael Reiss, *New Statesman*, April 5, 2010

Faith and the Cosmos   112
By Ila Delio, *America Magazine*, April 4, 2011

5

The Greening of Faith

Silent Spring: Faith and the Environment   119
By Paul McCaffrey

Environment and the New Humanism   123
By Edward O. Wilson, *Humanist*, November 2007

Environmentalism as Religion   128
By Joel Garreau, *New Atlantis: A Journal of Technology & Society*, Summer 2010

The Emerging Alliance of World Religions and Ecology   140
By John Grim and Mary Evelyn Tucker, *Carnegie Ethics Online*, September 2, 2009

Stewards of the Earth   147
By Jim E. Motavalli, *E: The Environmental Magazine*, November 2002

Making the Climate a Part of the Human World   159
By Simon D. Donner, *Bulletin of the American Meteorological Society*, October 2011

6

Creation, the Cosmos, and the Origin of the Universe

The Origins of the Universe: Faith and the Big Bang   171
By Paul McCaffrey

The Testimony of Faith to the Ultimate Origin   176
By Hans Küng, Translated by John Bowden, *Tikkun Magazine*, March/April 2010

Science on Faith   180
By Elaine Howard Ecklund, *Chronicle of Higher Education*, February 2, 2011

Let's Get a Big Bang Out of Science   184
By Richard Malloy, *U.S. Catholic*, January 17, 2011

Physics of the Divine   188
By Zeeya Merali, *Discover*, March 1, 2011

A God of Creativity   194
By Stuart Kauffman, *New Scientist*, May 10, 2008

Bibliography   197
Web Sites   199
Index   201

Preface: Faith and Science

The relation between religious faith and natural science is complex, changing, and diverse. This dynamic relationship is evident throughout history, having sometimes enriched and sometimes impeded both scientific and religious traditions. Religion has often provided scientists with motivation, moral insight, and faith in a created order; science has opened new horizons for faith, revealing the greatness of creation, and has attempted to analyze and understand religion. These interactions have often spilled into political disputes, influenced educational policies, and shaped attitudes toward the environment. They have provided multiple perspectives on and insights into the origin and evolution of life and the universe.

In the ancient and medieval world, science emerged from various cultural and religious traditions. Cooperation between faith and science was especially evident in the scientific revolution of the sixteenth and seventeenth centuries, an era in which virtually all European scientists shared a strong Christian faith and were motivated by a desire to reveal the glory of God in nature and improve human welfare. The success of science during this period led to the Enlightenment of the eighteenth century and a trend toward separating science from religion. Although many nineteenth-century scientists were devout Christians, some began to provide nonreligious explanations for the origins of life. Some nineteenth-century observers began to perceive a conflict between science and religion; however, historical studies in the twentieth century have challenged this idea, even as some conservative religious traditions have fought against scientific advances.

The Ancient and Medieval World

Much of what is now thought of as science developed out of the polytheistic religions of the ancient Egyptian and Babylonian civilizations. Egyptian worship of the sun and stars led observers to track their motions and eventually discover the 365-day solar calendar. In a similar fashion, the ancient Babylonian priests carefully recorded the motions of their planetary deities and are believed by some scholars to have created a seven-day week, with each day dedicated to and named for one of the seven visible bodies: the sun, the moon, Mars, Mercury, Jupiter, Venus, and Saturn (matching the names for the days of the week in most modern Romance languages).

In the monotheistic tradition of the ancient Hebrews, Abraham was called out of the Babylonian culture and received a new revelation of one God who created all things. This new view of the unity of God's creation reinterpreted the days of the week as a seven-day ritual that celebrates a different function of God's creation on each day. This historical understanding of the seven-day week avoids creationist literalism, which interprets the seven days of the creation account in the book of Genesis as consecutive days of creation that occurred a few thousand years ago and leads some believers to reject scientific evidence of the earth's age. The biblical story of creation teaches that nature is God's handiwork, to be appreciated and studied rather than worshipped, and that humans are responsible for its care and protection. It emphasizes the reality and goodness of nature, which later provided the motivation for experimental science in the Christian era. A similar emphasis on the order and intelligibility of creation encouraged theoretical science, and the purpose and meaning associated with creation supported applied science and care for the environment.

Around 600 BCE, Greek natural philosophers began a similar shift from nature worship to rational and natural explanations. In the Ionian region of Asia Minor, Thales reinterpreted Babylonian myths of creation out of watery chaos, suggesting that water in its various solid, liquid, and gaseous forms is the principle of all things and that the earth floats on water. His followers suggested other basic elements to explain matter, including air, earth, and fire, and proposed that the earth hangs unsupported at the center of space. Around 550 BCE, Pythagoras and his followers emigrated from Ionia to southern Italy, where they developed mathematics as the basis of reality in a religious community that emphasized mind over matter. Their religious beliefs led them to suggest that the earth has the perfect symmetry of a sphere.

The material and mathematical approaches of the Ionians came together in Athens beginning in about 450 BCE. There, the Ionian philosopher Anaxagoras claimed that the sun and moon are material objects made of fire and earth and that the moon reflects the light of the sun. He also explained the phases and eclipses of the moon by examining the geometric relations between the two. His view that the sun and moon are not deities led to one of the first clashes between science and religion, resulting in his being charged with impiety and banished from Athens. Plato and Aristotle tried to resolve this conflict by proposing that the universe is composed of an unchanging realm of celestial perfection in the heavens and an imperfect, earth-centered terrestrial realm extending to the moon. This cosmology dominated Greek science after the center of scientific inquiry shifted from Athens to Alexandria in the third century BCE. Philosopher Aristarchus challenged this cosmology with his proposal of a heliocentric (sun-centered) universe, but his challenge was unsuccessful, and Aristotelian cosmology continued on to become the primary influence on both Islamic and medieval Christian science.

In the sixth century CE, John Philoponus, one of the last Alexandrian philosophers and one of the first known scientists to adopt the Christian faith, criticized Aristotle's deification of the heavens and proposed new ideas on motion that eventually influenced Italian astronomer Galileo Galilei. Meanwhile, with the rise of Islam in the seventh century, Aristotelian science was further developed and largely integrated with Islamic theology. Latin translations of Greek and Arabic texts introduced this science to Europe beginning in about the twelfth century; by the middle of the thirteenth century, Italian theologian Thomas Aquinas achieved a comprehensive integration of Aristotelian science with Christian theology. This medieval Thomistic synthesis later became the official theology of the Roman Catholic Church and stood as the supreme example of convergence between Christian faith and science. The Protestant Reformation began a critique of Thomistic theology that reached a crisis with the Copernican revolution and the promotion of the heliocentric system by Galileo and others.

The Scientific Revolution and the Enlightenment

After the fall of Constantinople in 1453, original Greek manuscripts became available in Europe, prompting a resurgence of interest in Greek science and philosophy. Polish astronomer Nicolaus Copernicus, a canon in the Catholic Church, was influenced by Pythagoras, Aristarchus, and others and devoted his life to developing the heliocentric system. Two Lutheran scholars, Georg Joachim Rheticus and Andreas Osiander, assisted him in publishing his work in 1543. However, few accepted his idea of a moving earth because it contradicted official theology and required an annual shift in the positions of the stars (parallax), which astronomers had not yet observed. Copernicus explained this lack of stellar parallax by claiming the stars are too far away for it to be detected and suggested that such a vast increase in the size of the universe is consistent with the greatness of God.

The first English account of the Copernican system was published in 1576 by Thomas Digges, who suggested that the universe is infinite and that the space between the planets and the nearest stars is the "habitacle for the elect," a Puritan version of heaven. Giordano Bruno, an Italian monk, recognized that the stars must be comparable to the earth's sun and thus have their own planets, and he proposed the existence of an infinite number of populated planets. Because he was accused of unrelated heresies by the Catholic Church and burned at the stake in 1600, he is often wrongly referred to as the first martyr to science.

Among the few Copernican astronomers by 1600 were Galileo and German scientist Johannes Kepler, who also accepted a moving earth on the basis of faith because they were unable to detect parallax even with the aid of telescopes. As a devout Lutheran, Kepler saw the sun, the earth, and the intervening space as a symbol of the Christian Trinity and viewed his new planetary laws as evidence of God's creative plan. As a faithful Catholic, Galileo also believed he was viewing God's handiwork with the telescope, but he found enough evidence supporting Copernicus to be of concern to the church. At his 1632 trial for heresy, he was forced to recant his assertion that the earth moves, and he spent the remaining ten years of his life under house arrest.

Building on Kepler's laws, English scientist Isaac Newton developed a complete explanation for the motions of the earth and other planets based on his three laws of motion and his law of universal gravitation. His work was so successful in describing a self-sufficient mechanical system that it convinced many scientists that God either is not needed in the operation of the universe (deism) or does not exist at all (atheism). The eighteenth-century Enlightenment was dominated by faith in this mechanical view of the universe, even though there was still no evidence of stellar parallax. By the time that parallax was finally measured in the nineteenth century, the Catholic Church had removed Copernicus's writings from its index of forbidden books and established a more cooperative and accepting approach toward science. However, the success of Newton's laws and the mechanical worldview led to a belief in determinism that denied not only the providential acts of God but also the existence of human free will.

The Nineteenth and Twentieth Centuries

Challenges to the mechanical view of isolated objects and forces began in the nineteenth century with the development of relational concepts such as energy, electromagnetism, and evolution, which revealed a unified and interconnected world of active processes, fields, and organisms. The energy concept extended beyond mechanics to other forms of energy, such as chemical, thermal, electrical, biological, and nuclear. The electromagnetic field concept of British scientists Michael Faraday and James Clerk Maxwell, both devout Protestants, is based on electric charges that permeate all space and connect all objects. Faith in Maxwell's prediction of electromagnetic waves led German physicist Heinrich Hertz to perform groundbreaking experiments with radio waves. The evolutionary ideas of British scientists Charles Darwin and Alfred Russel Wallace led to the recognition that all life is related through common ancestry and continual change. Although these relational concepts suggest an underlying unity consistent with religious perceptions, evolutionary ideas conflict with some forms of biblical literalism and creationism. Nevertheless, several conservative theologians, including James Orr and Benjamin Warfield, argued that evolution could be viewed as God's method of creation.

In the twentieth century, the relational worldview expanded to encompass new concepts associated with relativity theory, quantum mechanics, and molecular biology. The theories of relativity revealed connections among space, time, matter, and energy, leading to the formulation of new theories about the origin and age of the observable universe. Some creationists reject such theories, even though they support the religious idea of a temporal creation. Quantum theory opened up a complex world within the atom and challenged mechanistic determinism with the introduction of German physicist Werner Heisenberg's uncertainty principle. Some theologians have found support for human freedom and God's action in the world in the idea of alternate possibilities at the quantum level governed by statistical rules. Deciphering the genetic code and mapping the human genome have confirmed evolutionary theory and revealed a detailed record of the interconnectedness of all life. From the perspective of faith, this genetic information can be seen as the "language of God."

Many discoveries associated with the expansion of the universe and the forces that act within it suggest a finely tuned balance within narrow limits that have produced the conditions for life. The slightest change in the expansion rate, fundamental forces, or particle masses would cause a collapse of the universe, prevent the formation of stars, or limit the synthesis of the elements and molecules needed for life. This "Goldilocks universe" has been the subject of much speculation, leading many to conclude that the universe is the result of a cosmic accident, is one of a multitude of universes with a range of different cosmic constants, or was designed to be congenial for life in a providential act of creation. If this latter faith in intelligent design includes a belief in divine intervention in natural events, it can impede the progress of science by limiting further research into natural causes; a belief in a system of intelligent design in which God acts as a "random designer" in and through natural laws, however, can maintain the integrity of both faith and science.

Joseph L. Spradley, PhD
August 2012

1

Common Ground Between Faith and Science?

Regarded as the most important theoretical physicist of the twentieth century, Albert Einstein held a profound philosophy of religion. He defined cosmic religious feeling as a religious feeling that is beyond dogma and church, experienced as the highest form of spiritual pursuit, and the basis for the noblest scientific research.

"And Yet, It Moves": The Conflict Between Faith and Science

By Paul McCaffrey

The challenge of reconciling faith and science is an age-old human dilemma. Throughout history, scientific inquiry has led to conclusions that run counter to accepted religious beliefs, calling into question the veracity of Scripture, and often generating a backlash from the faithful. These periodic conflicts have led many to conclude that the natural dynamic between science and religion is one of opposition. In the words of Yale psychologist Paul Bloom, "Religion and science will always clash." One of the most storied of these clashes took place several hundred years ago when scientists discovered evidence that the earth revolved around the sun rather than vice versa. By championing this heliocentric model, the astronomer Galileo Galilei endured a legendary confrontation with the Roman Catholic Church. More than four centuries later, this incident continues to serve as a symbol of the conflict between faith and science.

Galileo was not the first to propose a sun-centered model of the earth's galaxy. The ancient Greek astronomer Aristarchus of Samos had articulated such a system over 1,500 years before, in the third century BCE. Aristarchus endured accusations of impiety for his efforts, and his scholarship was ignored. In the ancient world, the consensus of both science and religion was that the earth lay at the center of the universe. In the second century AD, the Alexandrian astronomer Claudius Ptolemy developed an earth-centered, or geocentric, model of the cosmos that formed the foundation of astronomy for the next 1,300 years. Heliocentrism was not revived again in earnest until the sixteenth century, when in 1543 the Polish astronomer Nicolaus Copernicus published *De revolutionibus orbium coelestium* (*On the Revolutions of the Heavenly Spheres*) in which he presented mathematical evidence for heliocentrism. Though Copernicus was a cleric, the church did not respond favorably to his work, and the volume was banned. Still, his challenge to the Ptolemaic vision was widely circulated among scientists of the era and the so-called Copernican revolution was set in motion as other researchers began to build on his findings.

Christian religious authorities, whether Roman Catholic or otherwise, dismissed the Copernican theory as antithetical to Scripture. They believed a geocentric system was referenced in the Bible, lending the model divine support. The King James Bible reads, "And the sun stood still, and the moon stayed, until the people had avenged themselves upon their enemies. Is not this written in the book of Jasher? So the sun stood still in the midst of heaven, and hasted not to go down about a whole day" (Joshua 10:13)—in other words, the sun normally moves, but on this occasion stood still. Isaiah 40:22 declares, "It is he that sitteth upon the circle of the earth, and the inhabitants thereof are as grasshoppers; that stretcheth out the heavens as a curtain, and spreadeth them out as a tent to dwell in." However, the objections to the Copernican model of the universe went deeper than biblical citations. If scientists proved the earth was not the center of the universe, church leaders feared that its connection to the planet, humanity, and God would be threatened and diminished.

Born in Pisa, Italy, in 1564, Galileo initially made his name as an inventor and physics pioneer, exploring the dynamics of motion. In a famous experiment, he is alleged to have dropped different-sized cannonballs from the Leaning Tower of Pisa, finding that they fell at the same speed. In his early life, astronomy was not his primary area of focus, but based on his own observations of the tides, he accepted the Copernican model while still a young man. In early 1609, he started building his own telescopes and using them to study the skies, making a number of important discoveries, among them the moons of Jupiter. After publishing his findings in the 1610 treatise *Sidereus Nuncius* (*Sidereal Messenger*), Galileo was recognized by his contemporaries as one of the great scientists of the era.

In 1613, in a letter to a former student, mindful of the supposed contradictions between Copernican theory and Holy Scripture, Galileo sought to reconcile the two. He observed, "Holy Scripture can never lie or err, and . . . its declarations are absolutely and inviolably true. I should have added only that, though Scripture cannot err, nevertheless some of its interpreters and expositors can sometimes err in various ways." Then, taking up the verse from Joshua, he reasoned that rather than contradicting Copernican theory, the text actually supports it. According to the Ptolemaic model, "it is absolutely impossible to stop the sun and lengthen the day," Galileo wrote.

The letter was copied and circulated, and religious authorities soon took notice. Pope Paul V convened a panel of theologians to investigate Galileo's teachings and the Copernican model in general. In 1616, the panel concluded that Copernican theory did not align with religious doctrine and instructed Galileo to "not hold, teach or defend it in any way either by speech or writing."

For a time, Galileo acquiesced to the church's demands. However, when his friend Cardinal Maffeo Barberini was elevated to become Pope Urban VIII in 1623, he had reason to hope that Copernican theory might receive a better reception at the Vatican. Following audiences with Urban VIII, Galileo came away with the impression that he could resume his explorations, provided he avoid references to religious texts and approach heliocentrism as a mathematical hypothesis.

Emboldened, Galileo penned *Dialogue Concerning the Two Chief World Systems*, in which he laid out his case in support of Copernicus's model and against Ptolemy's. Published in 1632, the dialogue featured three characters: Salviati, who argues for the heliocentric system; Simplicio, a proponent of geocentrism—and, as his name implies, somewhat simple-minded; and Sagredo, a thoughtful and initially impartial participant. Galileo's argument created a stir across Europe. Unfortunately, Urban VIII was not pleased and, in fact, thought Galileo had mocked him, seeing his own words reproduced in some of Simplicio's comments. The pope banned the book and empanelled a Vatican commission to investigate Galileo for heresy. After uncovering evidence from his earlier brush with religious authorities, including the order that he abandon Copernican theory, the commission referred the matter to the Holy Office—the Inquisition—which soon called a gravely ill Galileo to Rome to defend himself.

In several appearances before the Holy Office in 1633, Galileo repeatedly denied the charges, claiming he did not recall the 1616 order and did not support the Copernican model. Given the evidence, his testimony was problematic. Though he was not interrogated under torture—a common practice at the time—he was threatened with it. The stakes involved were high. Indeed, several decades earlier, in 1600, the astronomer Giordano Bruno had been burned at the stake for suggesting that the earth revolved around the sun, among other supposed heresies. While his reputation and fame as a scholar and a network of influential defenders probably shielded Galileo from such a fate, his life was effectively on the line during the trial. The Holy Office did not believe his denials and found him guilty of heresy. To avoid imprisonment, they ordered him to read a statement confessing to his alleged crimes and renouncing his heliocentric theories. According to legend, after reading his confession, Galileo muttered, "And yet, it moves," supposedly referring to the earth. Thereafter, he was confined to an indefinite house arrest, mostly in his villa outside Florence.

Until his death on January 8, 1642, Galileo spent his last years in studious seclusion and declining health. Avoiding astronomy, he concentrated on his early passion, physics, writing *Discourses and Mathematical Demonstrations Concerning Two New Sciences*, a treatise on geometry and motion published in 1638. It took centuries for the Vatican to clear Galileo's name. In 1822, the church removed Dialogue from its list of forbidden books. In 1992, 350 years after his death, the Vatican declared Galileo innocent of the charges. Though persecuted and silenced by the church, Galileo remained a devout Catholic throughout his life. Although his story suggests to some that faith and science must always be in opposition, he never felt such, seeing in both the human mind and the structures governing the universe the work of a divine creator.

The relationship between faith and science has not grown any less complicated since Galileo faced the Inquisition in Rome. Religious institutions no longer wield the sort of blunt temporal authority exercised by the seventeenth-century Vatican, and scientists can carry out their investigations without fear of religious tribunals. Yet faith and science are still not always at ease with one another. In the 1500s and 1600s, the dispute was over the Copernican model. In the modern era, the debate has focused on natural selection and the theory of evolution.

Evolutionary biology and astronomy are vastly different fields of scientific study. The twenty-first-century world is vastly different from the world of the seventeenth century, yet humankind continues to weigh questions regarding science and religion. More than three hundred years ago, the Vatican gave Galileo its answer. In the modern era, many still believe that science should be deferential to the articles of faith. There are also people who feel that religion is a hindrance to human progress, and use science as a tool to make the case against religious dogma. As Richard Dawkins—a renowned evolutionary biologist, avowed atheist, and author of *The God Delusion* (2006)—argues, "Once you buy into the position of faith, then suddenly you find yourself losing all of your natural skepticism and your scientific—really scientific—credibility."

Still, these are not the only perspectives. The evolutionary biologist Stephen Jay Gould contended that neither religion nor science has primacy and that in reality there is no clash between them. Rather, as distinct spheres of human study, or "magisteria," they are wholly separate disciplines that ought to have no bearing on one another. Discussing "the principled resolution of supposed 'conflict' or 'warfare' between science and religion," Gould declares, "No such conflict should exist because each subject has a legitimate magisterium, or domain of teaching authority—and these magisteria do not overlap." According to Gould, science "covers the empirical universe: what is it made of (fact) and why does it work this way (theory)." Religion, on the other hand, "extends over questions of moral meaning and value." Thus, he recommends leaving science to the scientists and religion to the religious: "We [scientists] get the age of rocks, and religion retains the rock of ages," he concludes. "We study how the heavens go, and they determine how to go to heaven."

Galileo's vision of a symbiotic relationship between science and faith, one discipline informing the other, is an influential one, and many today are uncomfortable keeping the two separated, or declaring one field subservient to the other. German physicist Albert Einstein offered an eloquent summation of this viewpoint, observing, "Science without religion is lame, and religion without science is blind." The geneticist Francis Collins further articulated the position, stating, "Gould sets up an artificial wall between the two worldviews that doesn't exist in my life. Because I do believe in God's creative power in having brought it all into being in the first place, I find that studying the natural world is an opportunity to observe the majesty, the elegance, the intricacy of God's creation."

Of course, perceiving the influence of the divine in the natural world is one thing, reconciling the divergence between science and Scripture's understanding of that natural world is quite another. As the Ptolemaic and Copernican models demonstrate, these differences can be enormous. A literal reading of the Bible suggests that the earth is roughly 6,000 years old; according to scientific estimates, the planet came into being over 4 billion years ago. Such wild discrepancies lead Collins to refer to St. Augustine, who, he says, "wrote that basically it is not possible to understand what was being described in Genesis. It was not intended as a science textbook. It was intended as a description of who God was, who we are and what our relationship is supposed to be with God." His argument is a slight twist on the one Galileo made in the 1616 letter that first drew the punitive attention of the Vatican. Scripture isn't wrong, in this view, but it needs to be interpreted correctly. According to Collins, Augustine suggests that some parts of Scripture are beyond interpretation. Collins thus concludes that while faith and science are interconnected and share common ground, Scripture is not meant to serve as an empirical guide to the inner workings of the universe.

Religion and Science

By Albert Einstein
The New York Times Magazine, November 9, 1930

Everything that the human race has done and thought is concerned with the satisfaction of deeply felt needs and the assuagement of pain. One has to keep this constantly in mind if one wishes to understand spiritual movements and their development. Feeling and longing are the motive force behind all human endeavor and human creation, in however exalted a guise the latter may present themselves to us. Now what are the feelings and needs that have led men to religious thought and belief in the widest sense of the words? A little consideration will suffice to show us that the most varying emotions preside over the birth of religious thought and experience. With primitive man it is above all fear that evokes religious notions—fear of hunger, wild beasts, sickness, death. Since at this stage of existence understanding of causal connections is usually poorly developed, the human mind creates illusory beings more or less analogous to itself on whose wills and actions these fearful happenings depend. Thus one tries to secure the favor of these beings by carrying out actions and offering sacrifices which, according to the tradition handed down from generation to generation, propitiate them or make them well disposed toward a mortal. In this sense I am speaking of a religion of fear. This, though not created, is in an important degree stabilized by the formation of a special priestly caste which sets itself up as a mediator between the people and the beings they fear, and erects a hegemony on this basis. In many cases a leader or ruler or a privileged class whose position rests on other factors combines priestly functions with its secular authority in order to make the latter more secure; or the political rulers and the priestly caste make common cause in their own interests.

The social impulses are another source of the crystallization of religion. Fathers and mothers and the leaders of larger human communities are mortal and fallible. The desire for guidance, love, and support prompts men to form the social or moral conception of God. This is the God of Providence, who protects, disposes, rewards, and punishes; the God who, according to the limits of the believer's outlook, loves and cherishes the life of the tribe or of the human race, or even or life itself; the comforter in sorrow and unsatisfied longing; he who preserves the souls of the dead. This is the social or moral conception of God.

The Jewish scriptures admirably illustrate the development from the religion of fear to moral religion, a development continued in the New Testament. The religions of all civilized peoples, especially the peoples of the Orient, are primarily moral religions. The development from a religion of fear to moral religion is a great step in peoples'

Originally printed in *The New York Times Magazine* (9 November 1930).

lives. And yet, that primitive religions are based entirely on fear and the religions of civilized peoples purely on morality is a prejudice against which we must be on our guard. The truth is that all religions are a varying blend of both types, with this differentiation: that on the higher levels of social life the religion of morality predominates.

Common to all these types is the anthropomorphic character of their conception of God. In general, only individuals of exceptional endowments, and exceptionally high-minded communities, rise to any considerable extent above this level. But there is a third stage of religious experience which belongs to all of them, even though it is rarely found in a pure form: I shall call it cosmic religious feeling. It is very difficult to elucidate this feeling to anyone who is entirely without it, especially as there is no anthropomorphic conception of God corresponding to it.

The individual feels the futility of human desires and aims and the sublimity and marvelous order which reveal themselves both in nature and in the world of thought. Individual existence impresses him as a sort of prison and he wants to experience the universe as a single significant whole. The beginnings of cosmic religious feeling already appear at an early stage of development, e.g., in many of the Psalms of David and in some of the Prophets. Buddhism, as we have learned especially from the wonderful writings of Schopenhauer, contains a much stronger element of this.

The religious geniuses of all ages have been distinguished by this kind of religious feeling, which knows no dogma and no God conceived in man's image; so that there can be no church whose central teachings are based on it. Hence it is precisely among the heretics of every age that we find men who were filled with this highest kind of religious feeling and were in many cases regarded by their contemporaries as atheists, sometimes also as saints. Looked at in this light, men like Democritus, Francis of Assisi, and Spinoza are closely akin to one another.

How can cosmic religious feeling be communicated from one person to another, if it can give rise to no definite notion of a God and no theology? In my view, it is the most important function of art and science to awaken this feeling and keep it alive in those who are receptive to it.

We thus arrive at a conception of the relation of science to religion very different from the usual one. When one views the matter historically, one is inclined to look upon science and religion as irreconcilable antagonists, and for a very obvious reason. The man who is thoroughly convinced of the universal operation of the law of causation cannot for a moment entertain the idea of a being who interferes in the course of events—provided, of course, that he takes the hypothesis of causality really seriously. He has no use for the religion of fear and equally little for social or moral religion. A God who rewards and punishes is inconceivable to him for the simple reason that a man's actions are determined by necessity, external and internal, so that in God's eyes he cannot be responsible, any more than an inanimate object is responsible for the motions it undergoes. Science has therefore been charged with undermining morality, but the charge is unjust. A man's ethical behavior should be based effectually on sympathy, education, and social ties and needs; no religious basis is necessary. Man would indeed be in a poor way if he had to be restrained by fear of punishment and hopes of reward after death.

It is therefore easy to see why the churches have always fought science and persecuted its devotees. On the other hand, I maintain that the cosmic religious feeling is the strongest and noblest motive for scientific research. Only those who realize the immense efforts and, above all, the devotion without which pioneer work in theoretical science cannot be achieved are able to grasp the strength of the emotion out of which alone such work, remote as it is from the immediate realities of life, can issue. What a deep conviction of the rationality of the universe and what a yearning to understand, were it but a feeble reflection of the mind revealed in this world, Kepler and Newton must have had to enable them to spend years of solitary labor in disentangling the principles of celestial mechanics! Those whose acquaintance with scientific research is derived chiefly from its practical results easily develop a completely false notion of the mentality of the men who, surrounded by a skeptical world, have shown the way to kindred spirits scattered wide through the world and through the centuries. Only one who has devoted his life to similar ends can have a vivid realization of what has inspired these men and given them the strength to remain true to their purpose in spite of countless failures. It is cosmic religious feeling that gives a man such strength. A contemporary has said, not unjustly, that in this materialistic age of ours the serious scientific workers are the only profoundly religious people.

> *How can cosmic religious feeling be communicated from one person to another, if it can give rise to no definite notion of a God and no theology? In my view, it is the most important function of art and science to awaken this feeling and keep it alive in those who are receptive to it.*

Science at the Crossroads

By Tenzin Gyatso, the Dalai Lama
DalaiLama.com, November 12, 2005

This article is based on a talk given by the Dalai Lama at the annual meeting of the Society for Neuroscience on November 12, 2005, in Washington DC.

The last few decades have witnessed tremendous advances in the scientific understanding of the human brain and the human body as a whole. Furthermore, with the advent of the new genetics, neuroscience's knowledge of the workings of biological organisms is now brought to the subtlest level of individual genes. This has resulted in unforeseen technological possibilities of even manipulating the very codes of life, thereby giving rise to the likelihood of creating entirely new realities for humanity as a whole. Today the question of science's interface with wider humanity is no longer a matter of academic interest alone; this question must assume a sense of urgency for all those who are concerned about the fate of human existence. I feel, therefore, that a dialogue between neuroscience and society could have profound benefits in that it may help deepen our basic understanding of what it means to be human and our responsibilities for the natural world we share with other sentient beings. I am glad to note that as part of this wider interface, there is a growing interest among some neuroscientists in engaging in deeper conversations with Buddhist contemplative disciplines.

Although my own interest in science began as the curiosity of a restless young boy growing up in Tibet, gradually the colossal importance of science and technology for understanding the modern world dawned on me. Not only have I sought to grasp specific scientific ideas but have also attempted to explore the wider implications of the new advances in human knowledge and technological power brought about through science. The specific areas of science I have explored most over the years are subatomic physics, cosmology, biology and psychology. For my limited understanding of these fields I am deeply indebted to the hours of generous time shared with me by Carl von Weizsacker and the late David Bohm both of whom I consider to be my teachers in quantum mechanics, and in the field of biology, especially neuroscience, by the late Robert Livingstone and Francisco Varela. I am also grateful to the numerous eminent scientists with whom I have had the privilege of engaging in conversations through the auspices of the Mind and Life Institute which initiated the Mind and Life conferences that began in 1987 at my residence in Dharamsala, India. These dialogues have continued over the years and in fact the latest Mind and Life dialogue concluded here in Washington just this week.

Some might wonder "What is a Buddhist monk doing taking such a deep interest in science? What relation could there be between Buddhism, an ancient Indian philosophical and spiritual tradition, and modern science? What possible benefit could there be for a scientific discipline such as neuroscience in engaging in dialogue with Buddhist contemplative tradition?"

Although Buddhist contemplative tradition and modern science have evolved from different historical, intellectual and cultural roots, I believe that at heart they share significant commonalities, especially in their basic philosophical outlook and methodology. On the philosophical level, both Buddhism and modern science share a deep suspicion of any notion of absolutes, whether conceptualized as a transcendent being, as an eternal, unchanging principle such as soul, or as a fundamental substratum of reality. Both Buddhism and science prefer to account for the evolution and emergence of the cosmos and life in terms of the complex interrelations of the natural laws of cause and effect. From the methodological perspective, both traditions emphasize the role of empiricism. For example, in the Buddhist investigative tradition, between the three recognized sources of knowledge—experience, reason and testimony—it is the evidence of the experience that takes precedence, with reason coming second and testimony last. This means that, in the Buddhist investigation of reality, at least in principle, empirical evidence should triumph over scriptural authority, no matter how deeply venerated a scripture may be. Even in the case of knowledge derived through reason or inference, its validity must derive ultimately from some observed facts of experience. Because of this methodological standpoint, I have often remarked to my Buddhist colleagues that the empirically verified insights of modern cosmology and astronomy must compel us now to modify, or in some cases reject, many aspects of traditional cosmology as found in ancient Buddhist texts.

Since the primary motive underlying the Buddhist investigation of reality is the fundamental quest for overcoming suffering and perfecting the human condition, the primary orientation of the Buddhist investigative tradition has been toward understanding the human mind and its various functions. The assumption here is that by gaining deeper insight into the human psyche, we might find ways of transforming our thoughts, emotions and their underlying propensities so that a more wholesome and fulfilling way of being can be found. It is in this context that the Buddhist tradition has devised a rich classification of mental states, as well as contemplative techniques for refining specific mental qualities. So a genuine exchange between the cumulative knowledge and experience of Buddhism and modern science on a wide-ranging issues pertaining to the human mind, from cognition and emotion to understanding the capacity for transformation inherent in the human brain, can be deeply interesting and potentially beneficial as well. In my own experience, I have felt deeply enriched by engaging in conversations with neuroscientists and psychologists on such questions as the nature and role of positive and negative emotions, attention, imagery, as well the plasticity of the brain. The compelling evidence from neuroscience and medical science of the crucial role of simple physical touch for even the physical enlargement of an infant's brain during the first few weeks powerfully brings home the intimate connection between compassion and human happiness.

Buddhism has long argued for the tremendous potential for transformation that exists naturally in the human mind. To this end, the tradition has developed a wide range of contemplative techniques, or meditation practices, aimed specifically at two principal objectives—the cultivation of a compassionate heart and the cultivation of deep insights into

On the philosophical level, both Buddhism and modern science share a deep suspicion of any notion of absolutes, whether conceptualized as a transcendent being, as an eternal, unchanging principle such as soul, or as a fundamental substratum of reality.

the nature of reality, which are referred to as the union of compassion and wisdom. At the heart of these meditation practices lie two key techniques, the refinement of attention and its sustained application on the one hand, and the regulation and transformation of emotions on the other. In both of these cases, I feel, there might be great potential for collaborative research between the Buddhist contemplative tradition and neuroscience. For example, modern neuroscience has developed a rich understanding of the brain mechanisms that are associated with both attention and emotion. Buddhist contemplative tradition, given its long history of interest in the practice of mental training, offers on the other hand practical techniques for refining attention and regulating and transforming emotion. The meeting of modern neuroscience and Buddhist contemplative discipline, therefore, could lead to the possibility of studying the impact of intentional mental activity on the brain circuits that have been identified as critical for specific mental processes. In the least such an interdisciplinary encounter could help raise critical questions in many key areas. For example, do individuals have a fixed capacity to regulate their emotions and attention or, as Buddhist tradition argues, their capacity for regulating these processes are greatly amenable to change suggesting similar degree of amenability of the behavioral and brain systems associated with these functions? One area where Buddhist contemplative tradition may have important contributions to make is the practical techniques it has developed for training in compassion. With regard to mental training both in attention and emotional regulation it also becomes crucial to raise the question of whether any specific techniques have time-sensitivity in terms of their effectiveness, so that new methods can be tailored to suit the needs of age, health, and other variable factors.

A note of caution is called for, however. It is inevitable that when two radically different investigative traditions like Buddhism and neuroscience are brought together in an interdisciplinary dialogue, this will involve problems that are normally attendant to exchanges across boundaries of cultures and disciplines. For example, when we speak of the "science of meditation," we need to be sensitive to exactly what is meant by such a statement. On the part of scientists, I feel, it is important to be sensitive to the different connotations of an important term such as meditation in their traditional context. For example, in its traditional context, the term for meditation is bhavana (in Sanskrit) or gom (in Tibetan). The Sanskrit term connotes the idea of cultivation, such as cultivating a particular habit or a way of being, while the Tibetan term gom has the connotation of cultivating familiarity. So, briefly stated, meditation in the traditional Buddhist context refers to a deliberate mental activity that involves cultivating familiarity, be it with a chosen object, a fact, a theme, habit, an outlook, or a way of being. Broadly speaking, there are two categories of meditation practice—one focusing on stilling the mind and the other on the cognitive processes of understanding. The two are referred to as (i) stabilizing meditation and (ii) discursive meditation. In both cases, the meditation can take many different forms. For example, it may take the form of taking something as object of one's cognition, such as meditating on one's transient nature. Or it may take the form of cultivating a specific mental state, such as compassion by developing a heartfelt, altruistic yearning to alleviate others' suffering. Or it could take the form of imagination, exploring the human potential for generating mental imagery, which may be used in various ways to cultivate mental well-being. So it is critical to be aware of what specific forms of meditation one might be investigating when engaged in collaborative research so that the complexity of meditative practices being studied is matched by the sophistication of the scientific research.

Another area where a critical perspective is required on the part of the scientists is the ability to distinguish between the empirical aspects of Buddhist thought and contemplative practice on the one hand and the philosophical and metaphysical assumptions associated with these meditative practices. In other words, just as we must distinguish within the scientific approach between theoretical suppositions, empirical observations based on experiments, and subsequent interpretations, in the same manner it is critical to distinguish theoretical suppositions, experientially verifiable features of mental states, and subsequent philosophical interpretations in Buddhism. This way, both parties in the dialogue can find the common ground of empirical observable facts of the human mind, while not falling into the temptation of reducing the framework of one discipline into that of the other. Although the philosophical presuppositions and the subsequent conceptual interpretations may differ between these two investigative traditions, insofar as empirical facts are concerned, facts must remain facts, no matter how one may choose to describe them. Whatever the truth about the final nature of consciousness—whether or not it is ultimately reducible to physical processes—I believe there can be shared understanding of the experiential facts of the various aspects of our perceptions, thoughts and emotions.

With these precautionary considerations, I believe, a close cooperation between these two investigative traditions can truly contribute toward expanding the human understanding of the complex world of inner subjective experience that we call the mind. Already the benefits of such collaborations are beginning to be demonstrated. According to preliminary reports, the effects of mental training, such as simple mindfulness practice on a regular basis or the deliberate cultivation of compassion as developed in Buddhism, in bringing about observable changes in the human brain correlated to positive mental states can be measured. Recent discoveries in neuroscience have demonstrated the innate plasticity of the brain, both in terms of synaptic connections and birth of new neurons, as a result of exposure to external stimuli, such as voluntary physical exercise and an enriched environment. The Buddhist contemplative tradition may help to expand this field of scientific inquiry by proposing types of mental training that may also pertain to neuroplasticity. If it turns out, as the Buddhist tradition implies, that mental practice can effect observable synaptic and neural changes in the brain, this could have far-reaching implications. The repercussions of such research will not be confined simply to expanding our knowledge of the human mind; but, perhaps more importantly, they could have great significance for our understanding of education and mental health. Similarly, if, as the Buddhist tradition claims, the deliberate cultivation of compassion can lead to a radical shift in the individual's outlook, leading to greater empathy toward others, this could have far-reaching implications for society at large.

Finally, I believe that the collaboration between neuroscience and the Buddhist contemplative tradition may shed fresh light on the vitally important question of the interface of ethics and neuroscience. Regardless of whatever conception one might have of the relationship between ethics and science, in actual practice, science has evolved primarily as an empirical discipline with a morally neutral, value-free stance. It has come to be perceived essentially as a mode of inquiry that gives detailed knowledge of the empirical world and the underlying laws of nature. Purely from the scientific point of view, the creation of nuclear weapons is a truly amazing achievement. However, since this creation has the potential to inflict so much suffering through unimaginable death and destruction, we regard it as destructive. It is the ethical evaluation that must determine what is positive and what is negative. Until recently, this approach of segregating ethics and science, with the understanding that the human capacity for moral thinking evolves alongside human knowledge, seems to have succeeded.

Today, I believe that humanity is at a critical crossroad. The radical advances that took place in neuroscience and particularly in genetics towards the end of the twentieth century have led to a new era in human history. Our knowledge of the human brain and body at the cellular and genetic level, with the consequent technological possibilities offered for genetic manipulation, has reached such a stage that the ethical challenges of these scientific advances are enormous. It is all too evident that our moral thinking simply has not been able to keep pace with such rapid progress in our acquisition of knowledge and power. Yet the ramifications of these new findings and their applications are so far-reaching that they relate to the very conception of human nature and the preservation of the human species. So it is no longer adequate to adopt the view that our responsibility as a society is to simply further scientific knowledge and enhance technological power and that the choice of what to do with this knowledge and power should be left in the hands of the individual. We must find a way of bringing fundamental humanitarian and ethical considerations to bear upon the direction of scientific development, especially in the life sciences. By invoking fundamental ethical principles, I am not advocating a fusion of religious ethics and scientific inquiry. Rather, I am speaking of what I call "secular ethics" that embrace the key ethical principles, such as compassion, tolerance, a sense of caring, consideration of others, and the responsible use of knowledge and power—principles that transcend the barriers between religious believers and non-believers, and followers of this religion or that religion. I personally like to imagine all human activities, including science, as individual fingers of a palm. So long as each of these fingers is connected with the palm of basic human empathy and altruism, they will continue to serve the well-being of humanity. We are living in truly one world. Modern economy, electronic media, international tourism, as well as the environmental problems, all remind us on a daily basis how deeply interconnected the world has become today. Scientific communities play a vitally important role in this interconnected world. For whatever historical reasons, today the scientists enjoy great respect and trust within society, much more so than my own discipline of philosophy and religion. I appeal to scientists to bring into their professional work the dictates of the fundamental ethical principles we all share as human beings.

White Lies of Dover

By Eugene W. Harper, Jr.
Commonweal, October 10, 2008

For what seemed like a generation, the late Carl Sagan was the voice of science on public television. With an exuberant confidence in the empirical method, he showed viewers of the edifying PBS series *Cosmos* how the procedures of science had successfully unraveled many mysteries of the universe.

Sagan never curtailed his understandable enthusiasm for natural science—the discipline of investigating empirically measurable phenomena in order to formulate testable hypotheses that explain and predict how the material universe works. But his enthusiasm also allowed him to convey, as though it were science, a point of view that strayed silently beyond science and into the realm of philosophy. Sagan's *Cosmos* spread the following error: Since science investigates only matter, only matter is real. That is not a scientific proposition, because it is not limited to measurable phenomena and cannot be verified or falsified empirically. The same unspoken conflation of natural science and philosophical materialism continues to be the source of much confusion in one of today's hot-button legal and educational controversies—the teaching of evolution in public schools.

The theory of evolution does not purport to explain the origins of life, or creation, or continuing existence, or to answer the primordial metaphysical question "Why is there something rather than nothing?" The theory is an enduring professional consensus about how living nature developed into a variety of species over time. It is considered scientifically dispositive because it produces empirically verifiable hypotheses. Darwin introduced a new paradigm for the science of biology. According to this paradigm, the development of species can be explained as the result of random mutation and natural selection.

But today Darwin is often in the news for reasons that have little to do with science. In 2005, for instance, there was a media frenzy surrounding a court case (Kitzmiller v. Dover Area School District) in Dover, Pennsylvania, about a school board's decision to require teachers to read a one-minute statement to students at the beginning of their ninth-grade biology course. The statement advised students that Intelligent Design (ID) was an alternative theory to evolution and referred them to a book about ID. The board's decision was challenged in court, and the case itself produced the correct result: ID does not qualify as an alternative scientific theory, and should not be presented as such in public schools. News reports, however, did little to explain why ID isn't a proper scientific theory. Instead, they embraced a "town divided" theme. The Dover judge, John E. Jones III, was even quoted as saying "it was like a civil war." On the PBS program Nova, a distinguished academic announced that one side in the debate about ID "makes people stupid," while a local observer declared, "In the beginning, God created. . . . To me, that's all I need to know." Both the court's lengthy opinion and media accounts of the case obscured several important points about this ongoing controversy.

First, the conflict between science and religion is a false one. It results from identifying the Judeo-Christian tradition with the view that the creation story in Genesis is to be interpreted literally. Thus Nova described the dispute in Dover as a "rift between science and Scripture [that] nearly destroyed the community." A representative of the National Center for Science Education told viewers of the program that the case was about a movement to "re-Christianize American society." Rarely mentioned are the many Christian criticisms of biblical literalism. St. Augustine abandoned literalism about seventeen centuries ago, when he developed a remarkably sophisticated theory of biblical interpretation to reconcile the obvious differences between our empirical knowledge of nature and the Genesis account of creation. Today, every serious Christian thinker cedes to science its proper jurisdiction over the investigation of the natural world. There is no theological argument against using scientific methods to develop evolutionary theory in order to explain how the material universe works, wherever that effort may lead.

> *The theory of evolution does not purport to explain the origins of life, or creation, or continuing existence, or to answer the primordial metaphysical question "Why is there something rather than nothing?" The theory is an enduring professional consensus about how living nature developed into a variety of species over time.*

Some secularists insist on a conflict between science and religion because they hope it will discredit all nonmaterialist viewpoints, which they hold in low regard. By associating those viewpoints with the Religious Right or with biblical literalism, they score an easy, empty point. The real issue is the relationship between science and metaphysics, and their different methods. Here the only conflicts are between different metaphysical outlooks—not between science and religion. Religion, despite its metaphysics, can accommodate science's materialist method; and science, despite its materialist method, can accommodate religion's nonmaterialist metaphysics.

Second, although religion addresses metaphysical questions, not every metaphysical position is religious. By carelessly equating a metaphysical position with religion, our public discourse assumes a conflict between one kind of philosophy and the First Amendment's establishment clause. That clause states that "Congress shall make no law respecting an establishment of religion." Since 1947, those ten words have given rise to thousands of pages of judicial and academic interpretation.

Recently, Chicago legal historian Philip Hamburger convincingly argued that by forbidding the new U.S. government to legislate either for any national, or against any state, establishment of religion, the establishment clause never mandated the separation of church and state. But whatever the establishment clause permits or prohibits, it was clearly not intended to keep any philosophical viewpoint out of schools or other public venues. Once that point is clear, it is hard to credit Nora's claim that "the future of science education, the separation of church and state, and the very nature of scientific inquiry were all on trial" in Dover.

It was also a mistake to equate the motivation of ID proponents with the "theory" of ID itself. Nova told viewers that the climax of the trial would be the judge's ruling on a question: "When they introduced intelligent design into the classroom, were members of the Dover School Board motivated by religion?" If so, that would amount to a violation of part of the First Amendment to the Constitution, the establishment clause, which mandates the separation of church and state.

The false equation of individual motivation with legal purpose or effect leads to a conclusion everyone would reject: that lawmakers motivated by, say, the Ten Commandments or the Sermon on the Mount could not make valid laws penalizing murder, theft, or fraud, or authorizing antipoverty programs. In Dover, the real problem—apart from the fact that ID is not a properly formed scientific theory—was that proponents of ID misled everybody about their motivation, so discrediting themselves and angering the judge, who ruled against them.

A common confusion in public discourse is to mischaracterize a dispute over academic norms as a clash over the First Amendment. This transforms a dispute that should be resolved by voters or their representatives on school boards and in legislatures—prudently, and with the advice of educators—into an issue to be decided by a judge. Voters in Dover did finally resolve the matter, as they might have done without any lawsuit. They elected a new school board controlled by those who supported teaching evolution in science class without reference to ID. Since ID has not yet proposed—and may never propose—any testable hypotheses, the voters were indisputably correct, for reasons that have nothing to do with the First Amendment. But even if the normal political process had failed to solve the problem, the appropriate judicial remedy would be a challenge based on statutory or administrative academic norms, not a challenge based on church-state constitutional norms, which can ignite sectarian "civil war."

In France and Germany, the subject of philosophy is part of the secondary-school curriculum. It is taught as a subject wholly distinct from religion or theology. In contrast to religious faith, philosophy is reason's construction of a theory about fundamental aspects of our experience (so metaphysics is a theory of the real, epistemology a theory of knowledge, and ethics a theory of right action). Discussions of philosophical questions have been largely absent from U.S. public schools, whose curriculum was shaped by the disciples of the pragmatist John Dewey. But American pragmatism is itself a philosophical theory about fundamental aspects of our experience. Its characteristic rejection of metaphysics, like the hard materialism of many scientists, is part of an ongoing discussion within philosophy about what counts as real. High school students should be introduced to this discussion by teachers who know something about its complexity. Philosophical theories should not be mere footnotes, or suppressed axioms, of a literature, civics, or biology curriculum.

There is no good reason that a teleological theory of the cosmos, like the one awkwardly advanced by proponents of ID, should not be addressed in our public high schools—not in a biology class but in a philosophy course governed by sound academic norms. Just as educators need to avoid crossing over from religion into empirical science, they also need to avoid crossing over from empirical science into speculative metaphysics. For science to be confused with philosophy, or for either to be branded as religion, is to violate what Dominic Balestra, Fordham University philosopher of science, has called "epistemic justice"—which requires us to give each field of inquiry its proper respect and autonomy. The difference of scope and method between natural science and metaphysics is something public schools (and public television) should help our students understand. For now, they are mainly adding to the confusion.

Eugene W. Harper Jr. is an adjunct fellow of the Center for Educational Innovation-Public Education Association, and a partner of Squire, Sanders & Dempsey L.L.P. in New York. The views expressed here are his own.

God vs. Science

By Dean Nelson
The Saturday Evening Post, September 2011

How an acclaimed physicist is struggling to reconcile one of the great philosophical arguments of the modern age.

John Polkinghorne remembers the day when some of his colleagues thought he had lost his mind. He was already famous as a physicist at Cambridge University for his work in explaining the existence of quarks and gluons, the world's smallest known particles. He had won heaps of awards in his 27 years there, including membership in Britain's Royal Society, one of the highest honors that can be bestowed on a scientist.

It was the end of the academic year, and he had invited some colleagues to his office for a meeting. At the conclusion, they gathered their papers, ready to leave. "Before you go," Polkinghorne said, "I have something to tell you."

The audience settled back into their chairs. "I am leaving the university to enter the Anglican priesthood. I will be enrolling in seminary next year." Stunned silence filled the room for several seconds until one of his colleagues, an atheist, finally uttered what was probably on everyone's mind: "You don't know what you're doing."

A few others were supportive of his personal choice, but there was a muttered consensus that this beacon of the scientific world had just committed intellectual suicide.

Can religion and science co-exist? Many would say no. Science, after all, deals with what can be measured, tested, and verified. Religion deals with things that can, by definition, only be taken on faith. Today, John Polkinghorne inhabits both worlds, but he understands why this is confusing to some.

"When you say that you're a scientist and a Christian, people sometimes give you a funny look, as if you'd said, 'I'm a vegetarian butcher.' Many people out there think science and religion are actually at war with each other, but I believe that science and religion are friends, not foes."

Science and religion are not mutually exclusive, Polkinghorne argues. In fact, both are necessary to our understanding of the world. "Science asks how things happen. But there are questions of meaning and value and purpose which science does not address. Religion asks why. And it is my belief that we can and should ask both questions about the same event."

As a for-instance, Polkinghorne points to the homey phenomenon of a tea kettle boiling merrily on the stove.

"Science tells us that burning gas heats the water and makes the kettle boil," he says.

But science doesn't explain the "why" question. "The kettle is boiling because I want to make a cup of tea; would you like some?"

"I don't have to choose between the answers to those questions," declares Polkinghorne. "In fact, in order to understand the mysterious event of the boiling kettle, I need both those kinds of answers to tell me what's going on. So I need the insights of science and the insights of religion if I'm to understand the rich and many-layered world in which we live."

Seeing the world from both the perspective of science and the perspective of religion is something Polkinghorne describes as seeing the world with "two eyes instead of one." He explains: "Seeing the world with two eyes—having binocular vision—enables me to understand more than I could with either eye on its own."

Polkinghorne was just 47 when he left Cambridge to become a priest in the Anglican Church. The year was 1979. The reason he left his physics post was multifaceted. He had been part of a neighborhood Bible study and wanted to participate more in the sacraments at his church. Plus, he was ready to move on. "I had done my bit for physics," he asserts, "and, unlike some other things in life, one doesn't necessarily get better at physics the older one gets."

After being ordained, he first served in the village of Blean, just up the hill from Canterbury Cathedral. At first parishioners were leery that this towering intellect would be difficult to understand. But Polkinghorne soon won them over with clarity and reason (that metaphor about the boiling teapot is recalled by one church member), and so his presence was welcomed into the community. In 1986, he returned to Cambridge, first as a chaplain to one of the colleges and eventually as president of Queens' College, a position he held until he retired in 1996.

Over the years he has preached his unique "binocular vision" theory to explain how a person committed to scientific inquiry could also be committed to the teachings of the Bible. He's written many books on the harmony of religion and science, served on boards concerned with ethical standards for medical research, and received numerous honors. For his contributions, Polkinghorne was knighted by The Queen. (As a priest, however, he cannot be addressed as "Sir Polkinghorne.") He's also a highly regarded public speaker, putting into words a philosophy that is so moderate and reasonable that it was bound to make enemies on both ends of the religious spectrum.

Religious fundamentalists—those who believe in a six-day creation, a literal Adam and Eve, and an earth that is 6,000 years old—tend to repudiate Polkinghorne's acceptance of evolution, the Big Bang, and a universe that is billions of years old. Bill Hoesch, curator of the Creation and Earth History Museum in Santee, California, derides Polkinghorne's beliefs as "idol worship."

Hoesch doesn't see how scientific theory can enter the picture when the subject is the miracle of creation. "Is [Polkinghorne] just wrong? Yeah. He's been deluded," says Hoesch. (Polkinghorne actually toured Hoesch's museum last November. While there, he stopped at a poster that claimed there was no suggestion of death in the Bible until the sin of Adam and Eve. "It may not be in the Bible, but the evidence is everywhere else," Polkinghorne said, shaking his head.)

On the other extreme, atheists don't exactly cotton to his ideas either. "In the very difficult context of theoretical mathematical physics, John made a real contribution," allows Steven Weinberg, a Nobel Prize–winning physicist from the University of Texas who is also Polkinghorne's friend and debating partner. "As for his religious interests, I'm sure he means well, but I don't find his search for common ground a good thing. There is a relationship between science and faith, I suppose, but science tends to weaken faith.

> *When you say that you're a scientist and a Christian, people sometimes give you a funny look, as if you'd said, 'I'm a vegetarian butcher.'*

"I don't want to see John go away," Weinberg adds, laughing. "Just his beliefs."

Religion doesn't have all the answers, Polkinghorne agrees. He points out that magical Biblical explanations for lightning and plague were long ago debunked by science—and that the problems were solved with lightning rods and rat poison. "That's one of the ways science has been helpful to religion," notes Polkinghorne. "Religious explanations make mistakes, and science helps us see that some things are a natural phenomenon. That's helpful to religion. Truth is very beneficial to both sides and helps both see more clearly. It helps and corrects some mistakes. But that doesn't mean all religious belief is a mistake."

And therein lies the key to Polkinghorne's uniqueness: He addresses challenges—even rude ones—from both sides with such grace that it's nearly impossible to be angry with the man, whatever your point of view. "There is no one else in the world like him," said Darrel Falk, biologist, president of the BioLogos Foundation, and author of the book *Coming to Peace with Science*. "He is the best representative of the dialogue between faith and science because he has struggled with—and achieved so much in—both fields. He's the most respected voice out there."

As to the question of which has the clearer view of reality—faith or science?—Polkinghorne answers that it's a false question. "You have to be two-eyed about it. If we had only one eye, then we could say it's religion, because it relates to the deepest value of being human. Science doesn't plumb the depths that religion does. Atheists aren't stupid—they just explain less."

Polkinghorne thinks atheists fail to consider the possibility that there might be more to life than what we can see and test and verify—that life might have transcendent and ultimate meaning. In addition, Polkinghorne argues, atheists have faiths of their own—beliefs that aren't visible, testable, or verifiable any more than religion is, yet they inform one's point of view in a manner similar to religious faith.

Ultimately, people of faith should not be afraid of science because both pursue truth. "Because people of faith worship the God of Truth, they should welcome truth from whatever source it comes," Polkinghorne says. "Not all truth comes from science, but some does. It grieves me when I see Christian people turning their backs on science in a willful way, not taking seriously the insights it has to offer. All truth interacts with each other, and all truth is helpful."

Likewise, people of science do not need to be afraid of faith. "Science doesn't tell you everything. Those who think it does take a very diminished and arid form or view of life."

For Polkinghorne, science made his faith stronger, and that faith made him a better scientist. Both approaches fulfill one of his favorite verses in scripture, I Thessalonians 5:21, which the esteemed physicist paraphrases: Test everything. Hold fast to what is true.

Einstein's Religious Awakening

By William Berkson
Reform Judaism, December 1, 2010

Albert Einstein's pronouncements on religion led some to view him as devoutly religious, while others declared him an atheist. What did Einstein really believe?

Young Albert received his first exposure to religion in a local Munich Catholic elementary school. It seemed an appropriate choice to his proudly secular parents, Hermann and Pauline, who had rejected the Jewish rituals of their ancestors as outdated superstitions—that is, until their son seemed rather too influenced by Catholic religious instruction.

A distant relative was then hired to tutor Albert in Judaism—again, to a far stronger effect than anticipated. He became fervently religious and started keeping kosher.

This stage ended abruptly at age 12, when a poor Jewish medical student, Max Talmud (later Dr. Max Talmey), whom his parents hosted for weekly dinners, gave popular science books to the boy which introduced him to the Positivist critique of religion (the notion that the only authentic, "positive" knowledge is that which can be verified by observation and experiment). The books characterized Judaism and Christianity as belief systems operating largely on fear of God's punishment. Young Einstein suddenly saw a punishing God as a dishonest trick played on children to scare them into obedience. He also came to believe that the miracles in the Bible conflicted with scientific knowledge and therefore could not be true. It was, he later wrote, a "shattering experience," which led him to distrust all religious authority, as symbolized by his refusing to have a bar mitzvah. Instead, he turned to scientific inquiry "to free myself from the chains of the 'merely-personal,' from an existence which is dominated by wishes, hopes, and primitive feelings. Out yonder there was this huge world, which exists independently of human beings and stands before us like a great, eternal riddle. . . . The contemplation of this world beckoned like a liberation, and I soon noticed that many a man whom I had learned to esteem and to admire had found inner freedom and security in devoted occupation with it."

One such man he grew to admire was the 17th-century Dutch Jewish philosopher Baruch Spinoza. A man of the Age of Reason, Spinoza asserted that everything of importance could be proven, including truths concerning the existence of God (who, he believed, was identical to Nature), human psychology, and ethics. Spinoza openly rejected the divinity and literal truth of the Bible. While in his time Spinoza was regarded by most Christians and Jews as an "infamous atheist," centuries later the romantic poet Novalis called him a "God intoxicated man." Einstein identified so strongly with Spinoza, he wrote what may be the only poem in praise of Spinoza—"To Spinoza's Ethic." The first verse reads: How I love that noble man /More than I can say with words. /Though I'm afraid he'll have to stay all alone /Him with his shining halo.

Einstein's own views caused storms of protest reminiscent of those surrounding his hero: Was the scientist a religious believer or a confirmed atheist? Einstein endeavored to find a congenial point between the polar opposites of Positivism and traditional religion. Whereas Spinoza's spirituality was grounded in what was knowable, Einstein's was inspired by the mystery and wonder of what he did not know—the reality beyond human understanding. As he wrote at the age of 50 in his "credo" Mein Weltbilt, "My World View" (1930):

> The most beautiful experience we can have is the mysterious. It is the fundamental emotion which stands at the cradle of true art and true science. Whoever does not know it and can no longer wonder, no longer marvel, is as good as dead, and his eyes are dimmed. . . . A knowledge of the existence of something we cannot penetrate, our perceptions of the profoundest reason and the most radiant beauty, which only in their most primitive forms are accessible to our minds—it is this knowledge and this emotion that constitute true religiosity; in this sense, and this alone, I am a deeply religious man (Ideas and Opinions).

In a sense, Einstein's approach to God reflected the classic talmudic notion of yirat shamayim, "awe of heaven." While most of us may feel awe when gazing at a grand vista, or a star-filled sky on a clear dark night, Einstein's awe extended beyond what he could see to the awesome power behind it. While traditional Jews studied the books of the Torah, Einstein studied the book of nature, sustained by the experience of "cosmic religious feeling" emanating from the natural world.

In a sense, Einstein's approach to God reflected the classic talmudic notion of yirat shamayim, "awe of heaven." While most of us may feel awe when gazing at a grand vista, or a star-filled sky on a clear dark night, Einstein's awe extended beyond what he could see to the awesome power behind it.

Einstein believed that a religious outlook was essential to living a good life: "The man who regards his own life and that of his fellow creatures as meaningless is not merely unhappy, but hardly fit for life" (Ideas and Opinions). Although he rejected the notion of "a God who rewards and punishes his creatures or has a will of the kind that we experience in ourselves," he stated that belief in a personal God is "preferable to the lack of any transcendental outlook on life."

Still, some religious leaders dismissed Einstein as an atheist. How, they asked, does his notion of "cosmic religious feeling" translate to moral action, to the observance of ethical commandments? "Who would lay his life down for the Milky Way?" chided the American Catholic leader Fulton J. Sheen (later to become bishop and one of the first popular television personalities). Sheen quipped that the "s" should be removed from Einstein's "cosmical religion" (Einstein and Religion by Max Jammer).

Einstein did eventually change his position on the relationship between religion and ethics. In 1930, influenced by both Positivistic thinking on the separation of ethics and religion and academic Western philosophy, he argued that a person with cosmic religious feeling "has no use for the religion of fear and equally little for social or moral religion. . . . A man's ethical behavior should be based effectually on sympathy, education, and social ties and needs; no religious basis is necessary." In a similar vein, Einstein declared, "There is nothing divine about morality; it is a purely human affair." But nine years later, Einstein rejected the Positivist conception of ethics:

> "Scientific method can teach us nothing beyond how facts are related to and conditioned by each other. . . . One can have the clearest and most complete knowledge of what is and yet not be able to deduce from that what should be the goal of our human aspirations. . . . Intelligence makes clear to us the interrelation of means and ends. But mere thinking cannot give us a sense of ultimate and fundamental ends. [This is] precisely the most important function which religion has to perform in the social life of man. . . . The highest principles . . . are given to us in the Jewish-Christian religious tradition" (Ideas and Opinions).

Einstein also came to regard religious values as a bulwark holding back humanity from a descent into barbarism. Most likely, the ascent of Nazism influenced his change of heart—just as the rising tide of antisemitism in Germany and in the Arab world led him to fervently support the creation of a Jewish state in Palestine.

A hero to the Jewish people because of his celebrity status as a scientist, Einstein was offered many honors, including the presidency of Hebrew University, Brandeis University, and even (in 1952) the State of Israel. He declined all. In a letter expressing his regrets for not accepting Israel's presidency, Einstein described himself as being "unsuited to fulfill the duties of that high office." He concluded with the affirmation: "My relationship to the Jewish people has become my strongest human bond, ever since I became fully aware of our precarious situation in the world."

Later in Einstein's life, his scientific explorations reflected his religious thinking, particularly in his quest for a Unified Field Theory that would encompass matter, gravity (which his general theory of relativity covers), and electromagnetism. This pursuit, explained Jewish philosopher and historian of science Emil Meyerson, was similar to the sense of wonder a scientist experiences in discovering underlying unity in nature: that the same atoms underlie living and inanimate matter, and that living creatures which appear very different share the same basic DNA (even if it is structured differently).

Just as the kabbalists believe that "all is one" and the Shema prayer affirms that a fundamental force unites all things (Hear, O Israel! The Lord is our God, the Lord is One, Deuteronomy 6:7), Einstein, to his dying day, sought to discover a unifying principle of the universe.

Einstein was under no illusion that he had come close to a solution, but his awe of nature and its order, as well as his endeavors to understand its great mysteries, never waned.

William Berkson is director of the Jewish Institute for Youth and Family; author of Fields of Force: The Development of a World View from Faraday to Einstein *(Routledge 1974) as well as* Pirkei Avot: Timeless Wisdom for Modern Life *(Jewish Publication Society, 2010); and a member of Temple Rodef Shalom in Falls Church, Virginia.*

2

Is Your Brain
Hardwired for Religion?

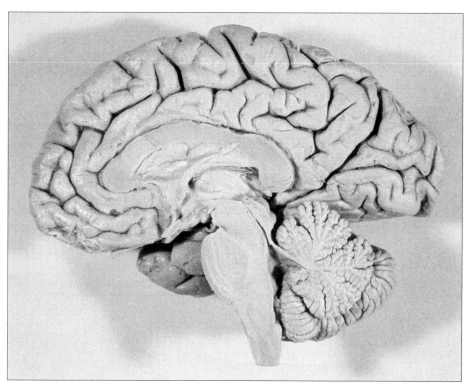

Neurotheology explores religious experience and behavior through the study of the brain. It examines how the brain can change in response to religious belief and prayer, meditation, and long-held religious devotion, as well as how religiosity affects health, aging, and cognitive functions.

"It's Just All One": Neurotheology, Religion, and the Brain

By Paul McCaffrey

The world is home to a great diversity of religious faiths. Hinduism, Buddhism, Christianity, Islam, Judaism, and other denominations each have their own unique belief system and religious practices. Each has its own views of the divine, the material world, and humanity's relationship to both. Furthermore, within each faith, there are a number of branches with their own individualized customs and nuanced take on religious doctrine. Modern Judaism, for example, is composed of Orthodox, Reformed, and Conservative varieties; Islam has Sunni, Shia, and other sects; Christianity includes variants of Catholicism and Protestantism.

Despite their assortment of rituals and traditions, each religion seeks to explain humankind's place in the world, and offers its adherents a community and a venue where they can express their spiritual beliefs. Religious explanations regarding God and humankind are often wildly divergent. Motivated by differing conceptions of God, creation, and the afterlife, these faiths would seem to offer a singular religious experience, the sensation of a Muslim fasting during Ramadan bearing little resemblance to a Catholic receiving Holy Communion or a Buddhist engaging in a ritual incantation. Yet researchers in neurotheology, an emerging field of neuroscience, are finding that the physiological nature of spirituality is surprisingly uniform from one faith to another.

Neurotheology explores the relationship between faith and the brain. Using magnetic resonance imaging (MRI) and other technology, neurotheologists observe how prayer, meditation, and other religious activities stimulate certain areas of the brain, and how it impacts brain chemistry and structure over time. Based on his brain-scan studies of Buddhist monks, Sikhs, Catholic nuns, and Pentecostal Christians in the midst of their devotions, Andrew B. Newberg, a neuroscientist and author of *Principles of Neurotheology* (2010), observes, "When we think of religious and spiritual beliefs and practices, we see a tremendous similarity across practices and across traditions." As it relates to the brain and religious experience, he remarks, "There is no Christian, there is no Jewish, there is no Muslim, it's just all one."

Newberg identifies three particular types of spiritual sensation and associates them with three specific areas of the brain—the frontal lobe, the parietal lobe, and the limbic system. First, there is the prolonged focus that occurs during acts of prayer and meditation. Such experiences stimulate the frontal lobe, a region linked with concentration. Meanwhile, scientists have observed that the parietal lobe is noticeably inactive during prayer. The parietal lobe "is an area that normally takes our sensory information, tries to create for us a sense of ourselves and orient that self in the world," Newberg comments. Our notions of where we are in terms of time and place, for example, are related to activity in the parietal lobe. "When people lose their sense of self, feel a sense of oneness, a blurring of the boundary between self and other," Newberg remarks, "we have found decreases in activity in that area." As the parietal region goes dark, believers often enjoy a feeling of connection with the larger world and with a higher power. Finally, Newberg has found that religious experiences affect the brain's limbic system, which is connected to such emotions as exultation and joy.

The three religious moods described above—intense focus, a sense of "oneness," and elation—are common experiences among devout adherents of religion. But there are other forms of spiritual feeling that are more unusual. According to studies, about one in three people during the course of their lives undergo a mystical experience. Whether a holy vision or religious trance, a mystical experience is of a different order of magnitude than the more run-of-the-mill spiritual sensations. Rather than a feeling of focus or "oneness," these phenomena resemble vivid hallucinations or violent seizures. Religious history and scripture includes many examples of such occurrences. In the Judeo-Christian tradition, there is Moses's encounter with the burning bush or St. Paul's sudden conversion on the road to Damascus. In more recent times, there is the example of Ellen White, one of the founders of what became the Seventh Day Adventist Church, a Christian movement that emerged in the nineteenth century. After suffering a head injury as a child, White started having regular mystical visions. Recently researchers have hypothesized that her visions, whether divinely inspired or not, may have been influenced by a condition called temporal lobe epilepsy (TLE), a malady known for causing recurrent seizures. These seizures are often accompanied by heightened mental states featuring vivid emotions and altered sensory experiences, even hallucinations. Throughout history, epileptic seizures have been associated with both great works of art and with mystical experiences. Indeed, a significant percentage of people with TLE report religious visions.

Individuals with TLE are more prone to religious sensations, leading scientists to speculate that stimulating the temporal lobes—regions of the brain affecting memory, the auditory senses, and speech—could contribute to mystical states. Dr. Michael Persinger, a neuroscientist at Laurentian University in Canada, tested this theory, equipping subjects with a "God helmet" that applies a weak magnetic field to the temporal lobes. According to Persinger's team, about four out of five participants responded to the magnetic field, with a number of them reporting the feeling of a "sensed presence." Although Persinger's findings have not been replicated in similar studies, and the scientific community has not fully embraced his results, his work points to a correlation between religious experiences and the temporal lobes.

Scientists have also studied the effects of religion on the brain over the long term. Studies have shown that religion can positively influence how the brain functions, and reduce anxiety and depression. They have also found that it is possible to "train" the brain. The neuroscientist Richard Davidson of the University of Wisconsin scanned the brains of Buddhist monks, finding that their years of intense meditation had effectively disciplined their minds, giving them increased focus and a more developed sense of compassion. Davidson wondered if such results could be reproduced among people who hadn't put in the years of religious devotion. What he discovered was that regular meditation, even over as small an interval as two weeks' time, can bring about noticeable changes in brain function. Similar studies offer comparable results. One examination conducted at a technology firm required employees to meditate daily for several minutes over a series of weeks. According to Davidson, "Just two months' practice among rank amateurs led to a systematic change in both the brain as well as the immune system in more positive directions." Researchers attribute this brain training to a concept called neuroplasticity. The brain, it turns out, is surprisingly malleable. "You can sculpt your brain just as you'd sculpt your muscles if you went to the gym," Davidson observes. "Our brains are continuously being sculpted, whether you like it or not, wittingly or unwittingly."

When Davidson uses the term "sculpt," he is speaking literally. Religion does more than train your brain and alter its functioning. Over time, religion—and the absence of it—has the potential to change the underlying structure of the brain. Of course, spiritual activity isn't the only sort that can lead to such renovations. For example, an analysis of the brains of British taxi drivers conducted by University College London revealed that the rear section of a cabby's hippocampus tended to be larger than that of a non-cabby. The hippocampus is a component of the limbic system and tied to navigation and locational awareness as well as emotion, memory, and organization. The longer a taxi driver's tenure on the job, the analysis indicated, the larger that area of the hippocampus.

In a study carried out at Massachusetts General Hospital, neuroscientist Sarah Lazar used MRI to examine the brains of meditators relative to a control group. According to her data, the thickness of the cortex—the outer layer of various parts of the brain—was greater among the meditators. This included the thickness of the prefrontal cortex, a region of the frontal lobe.

Like driving a cab, religion also affects the hippocampus. In 2011, neurologist Amy Owen and other scientists at Duke University revealed that certain intense religious experiences—being "born again," for example—are correlated with shrinkage, or atrophy, in the hippocampus. Owen and her colleagues employed MRI to analyze the brains of subjects over the age of 58. According to their findings, those who reported having had a transcendent mystical experience during their lives suffered from greater rates of atrophy. On the whole, the data indicated that Catholics and born-again Protestants had more hippocampal shrinkage than did regular Protestants. Atheists and those who did not identify with a faith community were not immune from atrophy either, but had levels similar to the Catholics and born-again Protestants.

The Duke team could only speculate as to the precise cause of the hippocampal shrinkage. Because earlier scholarship indicates that stress hormones can reduce the size of the hippocampus, it has been theorized that faith-related stress could have something to do with hippocampal atrophy. Religious devotion has been demonstrated to have a generally beneficial influence on physiology and health outcomes. But prayer-inspired concentration and the feelings of joy and "oneness" identified by Newberg are not the only faith-based emotions. Doubt may creep in from time to time, or be regularly present. Additionally, feelings of guilt and shame can occur. Though nonbelievers may avoid these drawbacks of religious faith, they may also lack the benefits of regular spiritual practice, and an absence of faith may have its own attendant stresses. The Duke researchers' theories serve as a reminder that religious faith might affect the brain in both positive and negative ways. Believers may have much to gain from it, but they may also have to give something in return.

Reducing religious feelings and practices and their long-term effects to their physiological components is a clinical exercise that does not fully express the impact a transcendent spiritual moment can have on a person. Being born again in a Christian context, or of achieving a stage of enlightenment in Buddhism, are not experiences that can be understood by brain analysis alone. Neurotheologists have yet to offer any insight into some of the larger questions pertaining to spirituality and humankind. "[Neuroscientists] may trace a sense of transcendence to this bulge in our gray matter," writes Sharon Begley in *Newsweek*. "And they may trace a feeling of the divine to that one. But it is likely that they will never resolve the greatest question of all—namely, whether our brain wiring creates God, or whether God created our brain wiring. Which you believe is, in the end, a matter of faith."

The Biology of Belief

By Jeffrey Kluger
Time, February 12, 2009

Most folks probably couldn't locate their parietal lobe with a map and a compass. For the record, it's at the top of your head—aft of the frontal lobe, fore of the occipital lobe, north of the temporal lobe. What makes the parietal lobe special is not where it lives but what it does—particularly concerning matters of faith.

If you've ever prayed so hard that you've lost all sense of a larger world outside yourself, that's your parietal lobe at work. If you've ever meditated so deeply that you'd swear the very boundaries of your body had dissolved, that's your parietal too. There are other regions responsible for making your brain the spiritual amusement park it can be: your thalamus plays a role, as do your frontal lobes. But it's your parietal lobe—a central mass of tissue that processes sensory input—that may have the most transporting effect.

Needy creatures that we are, we put the brain's spiritual centers to use all the time. We pray for peace; we meditate for serenity; we chant for wealth. We travel to Lourdes in search of a miracle; we go to Mecca to show our devotion; we eat hallucinogenic mushrooms to attain transcendent vision and gather in church basements to achieve its sober opposite. But there is nothing we pray—or chant or meditate—for more than health.

Health, by definition, is the sine qua non of everything else. If you're dead, serenity is academic. So we convince ourselves that while our medicine is strong and our doctors are wise, our prayers may heal us too.

Here's what's surprising: a growing body of scientific evidence suggests that faith may indeed bring us health. People who attend religious services do have a lower risk of dying in any one year than people who don't attend. People who believe in a loving God fare better after a diagnosis of illness than people who believe in a punitive God. No less a killer than AIDS will back off at least a bit when it's hit with a double-barreled blast of belief. "Even accounting for medications," says Dr. Gail Ironson, a professor of psychiatry and psychology at the University of Miami who studies HIV and religious belief, "spirituality predicts for better disease control."

It's hard not to be impressed by findings like that, but a skeptic will say there's nothing remarkable—much less spiritual—about them. You live longer if you go to church because you're there for the cholesterol-screening drive and the visiting-nurse service. Your viral load goes down when you include spirituality in your fight against HIV because your levels of cortisol—a stress hormone—go down first. "Science doesn't deal in supernatural explanations," says Richard Sloan, professor of behavioral medicine at Columbia University Medical Center and author of *Blind Faith: The Unholy Alliance of Religion and Medicine*. "Religion and science address different concerns."

That's undeniably true—up to a point. But it's also true that our brains and bodies contain an awful lot of spiritual wiring. Even if there's a scientific explanation for every strand of it, that doesn't mean we can't put it to powerful use. And if one of those uses can make us well, shouldn't we take advantage of it? "A large body of science shows a positive impact of religion on health," says Dr. Andrew Newberg, a professor of radiology, psychology and religious studies at the University of Pennsylvania and co-founder of Penn's Center for Spirituality and the Mind. "The way the brain works is so compatible with religion and spirituality that we're going to be enmeshed in both for a long time."

It's All in Your Head

"Enmeshed in the brain" is as good a way as any to describe Newberg's work of the past 15 years. The author of four books, including the soon-to-be-released *How God Changes Your Brain*, he has looked more closely than most at how our spiritual data-processing center works, conducting various types of brain scans on more than 100 people, all of them in different kinds of worshipful or contemplative states. Over time, Newberg and his team have come to recognize just which parts of the brain light up during just which experiences.

When people engage in prayer, it's the frontal lobes that take the lead, since they govern focus and concentration. During very deep prayer, the parietal lobe powers down, which is what allows us to experience that sense of having loosed our earthly moorings. The frontal lobes go quieter when worshippers are involved in the singular activity of speaking in tongues—which jibes nicely with the speakers' subjective experience that they are not in control of what they're saying.

Pray and meditate enough and some changes in the brain become permanent. Long-term meditators—those with 15 years of practice or more—appear to have thicker frontal lobes than nonmeditators. People who describe themselves as highly spiritual tend to exhibit an asymmetry in the thalamus—a feature that other people can develop after just eight weeks of training in meditation skills. "It may be that some people have fundamental asymmetry [in the thalamus] to begin with," Newberg says, "and that leads them down this path, which changes the brain further."

No matter what explains the shape of the brain, it can pay dividends. Better-functioning frontal lobes help boost memory. In one study, Newberg scanned the brains of people who complained of poor recall before they underwent meditation training, then scanned them again after. As the lobes bulked up, memory improved.

Faith and health overlap in other ways too. Take fasting. One of the staples of both traditional wellness protocols and traditional religious rituals is the cleansing fast, which is said to purge toxins in the first case and purge sins or serve other pious ends in the second. There are secular water fasts, tea fasts and grapefruit fasts, to say nothing of the lemon, maple-syrup and cayenne-pepper fast. Jews fast on Yom Kippur; Muslims observe Ramadan; Catholics have Lent; Hindus give up food on

18 major holidays. Done right, these fasts may lead to a state of clarity and even euphoria. This, in turn, can give practitioners the blissful sense that whether the goal of the food restriction is health or spiritual insight, it's being achieved. Maybe it is, but there's also chemical legerdemain at work.

The brain is a very energy-intensive organ, one that requires a lot of calories to keep running. When food intake is cut, the liver steps into the breach, producing glucose and sending it throughout the body—always making sure the brain gets a particularly generous helping. The liver's reserve lasts only about 24 hours, after which, cells begin breaking down the body's fats and proteins—essentially living off the land. As this happens, the composition of the blood—including hormones, neurotransmitters and metabolic by-products—changes. Throw this much loopy chemistry at a sensitive machine like the brain and it's likely to go on the blink. "There are very real changes that occur in the body very rapidly that might explain the clarity during fasting," says Dr. Catherine Gordon, an endocrinologist at Children's Hospital in Boston. "The brain is in a different state even during a short-term fast." Biologically, that's not good, but the light-headed sense of peace, albeit brief, that comes with it reinforces the fast and rewards you for engaging in it all the same.

How Powerful Is Prayer?

For most believers, the element of religious life that intersects most naturally with health is prayer. Very serious theologians believe in the power of so-called intercessory prayer to heal the sick, and some very serious scientists have looked at it too, with more than 6,000 published studies on the topic just since 2000. Some of them have been funded by groups like the John Templeton Foundation—part of whose mission is to search for overlaps of religion and science—but others have come from more dispassionate investigators.

As long ago as 1872, Francis Galton, the man behind eugenics and fingerprinting, reckoned that monarchs should live longer than the rest of us, since millions of people pray for the health of their King or Queen every day. His research showed just the opposite—no surprise, perhaps, given the rich diet and extensive leisure that royal families enjoy. An oft discussed 1988 study by cardiologist Randolph Byrd of San Francisco General Hospital found that heart patients who were prayed for fared better than those who were not. But a larger study in 2005 by cardiologist Herbert Benson at Harvard University challenged that finding, reporting that complications occurred in 52% of heart-bypass patients who received intercessory prayer and 51% of those who didn't. Sloan says even attempting to find a scientific basis for a link between prayer and healing is a "fool's errand"—and for the most basic methodological reason. "It's impossible to know how much prayer is received," he says, "and since you don't know that, you can't determine dose."

Such exactitude does not dissuade believers—not surprising, given the centrality of prayer to faith. But there is one thing on which both camps agree: when you're setting up your study, it matters a great deal whether subjects know they're being prayed for. Give them even a hint as to whether they're in the prayer group or a control group and the famed placebo effect can blow your data to bits.

First described in the medical literature in the 1780s, the placebo effect can work all manner of curative magic against all manner of ills. Give a patient a sugar pill but call it an analgesic, and pain may actually go away. Parkinson's disease patients who underwent a sham surgery that they were told would boost the low dopamine levels responsible for their symptoms actually experienced a dopamine bump. Newberg describes a cancer patient whose tumors shrank when he was given an experimental

> *"The brain appears to be able to target the placebo effect in a variety of ways," says Newberg. There's no science proving that the intercessions of others will make you well. But it surely does no harm—and probably helps—to know that people are praying for you.*

drug, grew back when he learned that the drug was ineffective in other patients and shrank again when his doctor administered sterile water but said it was a more powerful version of the medication. The U.S. Food and Drug Administration ultimately declared the drug ineffective, and the patient died. All that may be necessary for the placebo effect to kick in is for one part of the brain to take in data from the world and hand that information off to another part that controls a particular bodily function. "The brain appears to be able to target the placebo effect in a variety of ways," says Newberg. There's no science proving that the intercessions of others will make you well. But it surely does no harm—and probably helps—to know that people are praying for you.

Faith and Longevity

If belief in a pill can be so powerful, belief in God and the teachings of religion—which touch devout people at a far more profound level than mere pharmacology—ought to be even more so. One way to test this is simply to study the health of regular churchgoers. Social demographer Robert Hummer of the University of Texas has been following a population of subjects since 1992, and his results are hard to argue with. Those who never attend religious services have twice the risk of dying over the next eight years as people who attend once a week. People who fall somewhere between no churchgoing and weekly churchgoing also fall somewhere between in terms of mortality.

A similar analysis by Daniel Hall, an Episcopal priest and a surgeon at the University of Pittsburgh Medical Center, found that church attendance accounts for two to three additional years of life. To be sure, he also found that exercise accounts for three to five extra years and statin therapy for 2.5 to 3.5. Still, joining a flock and living longer do appear to be linked.

Investigators haven't teased out all the variables at work in this phenomenon, but Hummer, for one, says some of the factors are no surprise: "People embedded in religious communities are more likely to rely on one another for friendship, support, rides to doctor's appointments."

But even hard scientists concede that those things aren't the whole story and that there's a constellation of other variables that are far harder to measure. "Religious belief is not just a mind question but involves the commitment of one's body as well," says Ted Kaptchuk, a professor of medicine at Harvard Medical School. "The sensory organs, tastes, smells, sounds, music, the architecture of religious buildings [are involved]." Just as the very act of coming into a hospital exposes a patient to sights and smells that are thought to prime the brain and body for healing, so may the act of walking into a house of worship.

Neal Krause, a sociologist and public-health expert at the University of Michigan, has tried to quantify some of those more amorphous variables in a longitudinal study of 1,500 people that he has been conducting since 1997. He has focused particularly on how regular churchgoers weather economic downturns as well as the stresses and health woes that go along with them. Not surprisingly, he has found that parishioners benefit when they receive social support from their church. But he has also found that those people who give help fare even better than those who receive it—a pillar of religious belief if ever there was one. He has also found that people who maintain a sense of gratitude for what's going right in their lives have a reduced incidence of depression, which is itself a predictor of health. And in another study he conducted that was just accepted for publication, he found that people who believe their lives have meaning live longer than people who don't. "That's one of the purported reasons for religion," Krause says. "The sign on the door says, 'Come in here and you'll find meaning.'"

African-American churches have been especially good at maximizing the connection between faith and health. Earlier in American history, churches were the only institutions American blacks had the freedom to establish and run themselves, and they thus became deeply embedded in the culture. "The black church is a different institution than the synagogue or mosque or even the white church," says Ken Resnicow, a professor of health and behavior education at the University of Michigan School of Public Health. "It is the center of spiritual, community and political life."

Given the generally higher incidence of obesity, hypertension and other lifestyle ills among African Americans, the church is in a powerful position to do a lot of good. In the 1990s, Marci Campbell, a professor of nutrition at the University of North Carolina, helped launch a four-year trial called North Carolina Black Churches United for Better Health. The project signed up 50 churches with a goal of helping the 2,500 parishioners eat better, exercise more and generally improve their fitness. The measures taken included having pastors preach health in their sermons and getting churches to serve healthier foods at community events.

The program was so successful that it has been renamed the Body and Soul project and rolled out nationally—complete with literature, DVDs and cookbooks—in collaboration with the National Cancer Institute and the American Cancer Society. To skeptics who conclude that the churches have played a secondary role in the success of the programs—as a mere venue for secular health counseling—Campbell points out that in her studies, the most effective pitches came not from the nutritionists but from the pulpit. "The body is a temple, and the connection was made between the physical body and religious and spiritual well-being," she says.

Joining Hands

Many scientists and theologians who study these matters advocate a system in which both pastoral and medical care are offered as parts of a whole. If a woman given a diagnosis of breast cancer is already offered the services of an oncologist, a psychologist and a reconstructive surgeon, why shouldn't her doctor discuss her religious needs with her and include a pastor in the mix if that would help?

While churches are growing increasingly willing to accept the assistance of health-care experts, doctors and hospitals have been slower to seek out the help of spiritual counselors. The fear has long been that patients aren't interested in asking such spiritually intimate questions of their doctors, and the doctors, for their part, would be uncomfortable answering them. But this turns out not to be true. When psychologist Jean Kristeller of Indiana State University conducted a survey of oncologists, she found that a large proportion of them did feel it was appropriate to talk about spiritual issues with patients and to offer a referral if they weren't equipped to address the questions themselves. They didn't do so simply because they didn't know how to raise the topic and feared that their patients would take offense, in any event. When patients were asked, they insisted that they'd welcome such a conversation but that their doctors had never initiated one. What both groups needed was someone to break the ice.

Kristeller, who had participated in earlier work exploring how physicians could help their patients quit smoking, recalled a short—five- to seven-minute—conversation that the leader of a study had devised to help doctors address the problem. The recommended dialogue conformed to what's known as patient-centered care—a clinical way of saying doctors should ask questions then clam up and listen to the answers. In the case of smoking, they were advised merely to make their concern known to patients, then ask them if they'd ever tried to quit before. Depending on how that first question was received, they could ask when those earlier attempts had been made, whether the patients would be interested in trying again and, most important, if it was all right to follow up on the conversation in the future. "The more patient-centered the conversations were, the more impact they had," Kristeller says.

The success of that approach led her to develop a similar guide for doctors who want to discuss religious questions with cancer patients. The approach has not yet been tested in any large-scale studies, but in the smaller surveys Kristeller has conducted, it has been a roaring success: up to 90% of the patients whose doctors approached them in this way were not offended by the overture, and 75% said it was very helpful. Within as little as three weeks, the people in that group reported reduced feelings of depression, an improved quality of life and a greater sense that their doctors cared about them.

Even doctors who aren't familiar with Kristeller's script are finding it easier to combine spiritual care and medical care. HealthCare Chaplaincy is an organization of Christian, Jewish, Muslim and Zen Buddhist board-certified chaplains affiliated with more than a dozen hospitals and clinics in the New York City area. The group routinely provides pastoral care to patients as part of the total package of treatment. The chaplains, like doctors, have a caseload of patients they visit on their rounds, taking what amounts to a spiritual history and either offering counseling on their own or referring patients to others. The Rev. Walter Smith, president and CEO of the chaplaincy and an end-of-life specialist, sees what his group offers as a health-care product—one that is not limited to believers.

What patients need, he says, is a "person who can make a competent assessment and engage a patient's spiritual person in the service of health. When people say, 'I'm not sure you can help because I'm not very religious,' the chaplains say, 'That's not a problem. Can I sit down and engage you in conversation?'"

Patients who say yes often find themselves exploring what they consider secular questions that touch on such primal matters of life and death, they might as well be spiritual ones. The chaplains can also refer patients to other care providers, such as social workers, psychologists and guided-imagery specialists. The point of all this isn't so much what the modality is; it's that the patient has a chance to find one that works. "People say you tell the truth to your doctor, your priest and your funeral director," says Smith, "because these people matter at the end." It's that truth—or at least a path to it—that chaplains seek to provide.

Smith's group is slowly going national, and even the most literal-minded scientists welcome the development. Says Sloan, the author of *Blind Faith*: "I think that a chaplain's job is to explore the patient's values and help the patient come to some decision. I think that's absolutely right."

Sloan's view is catching on. Few people think of religion as an alternative to medicine. The frontline tools of an emergency room will always be splints and sutures, not prayers—and well-applied medicine along with smart prevention will always be the best ways to stay well. Still, if the U.S.'s expanding health-care emergency has taught us anything, it's that we can't afford to be choosy about where we look for answers. Doctors, patients and pastors battling disease already know that help comes in a whole lot of forms. It's the result, not the source, that counts the most.

With reporting by Alice Park and Bryan Walsh.

Divided Minds, Specious Souls

By David Weisman
Seed Magazine, September 1, 2010

The experience of a unified mind and the possibility of an everlasting soul are connected. And there is scant evidence to support the existence of either.

There is a common idea: because the mind seems unified, it really is. Many go only a bit further and call that unified mind a "soul." This step, from self to soul, is an ancient assumption which now forms a bedrock in many religions: a basis for life after death, for religious morality, and a little god within us, a support for a bigger God outside us.

For the believers in the soul, let's call them soulists, the soul assumption appears to be only the smallest of steps from the existence of a unified mind. Yet the soul is a claim for which there isn't any evidence. Today, there isn't even evidence for that place soulists step off from, the unified mind. Neurology and neuroscience, working unseen over the past century, have eroded these ideas, the soul and the unified mind, down to nothing. Experiences certainly do *feel* unified, but to accept these feelings as reality is a mistake. Often, the way things feel has nothing to do with how they are.

There are historical parallels. An 18th-century scientist believed a substance called "caloric" made hot materials hot and flowed into colder materials to make them warmer. It seemed to be true, but subsequent investigation showed mechanical vibration equates to heat. Science is littered with similarly discredited theories; the soul is one of them.

The evidence supports another view: Our brains create an illusion of unity and control where there really isn't any. Within the wide range of works arranged along the axis of soulism, from *Life After Death: The Evidence*, by Dinesh D'Souza, to *Absence of Mind*, by Marilynne Robinson, it is clear there is very little understanding of the brain. In fact, to advance their ideas, these authors have to be almost completely unaware of neurology and neuroscience. For example, Robinson tells us, "Our religious traditions give us as the name of God two deeply mysterious words, one deeply mysterious utterance: I AM." The translation might be, "indoctrination tells us we have a soul, it feels like we are a unified little god in control of our bodies, so we are."

In explaining why science suggests that the unified mind is illusory, there are thousands of supporting cases and experiments to choose from, but let's take one case from the Emergency Room.

After eating dinner with her husband, Mrs. Blanford collapsed. She could not move the left side of her body. I met Mrs. Blanford soon afterwards: Her speech was normal, but she couldn't see objects to her left, and she couldn't move or feel the left side of her face, or her left arm or leg. Mrs. Blanford was suffering a stroke.

An interesting thing happened when I brought her left arm up across her face so she could see it. I asked, as I always ask such patients, "Whose arm is this?"

"That is your arm."

"Then why am I wearing your ring?" I pointed to her wedding band.

"That wedding band belongs on the arm of Mrs. Blanford."

"So whose arm is this?"

"That is your arm."

Patients like Mrs. Blanford sometimes accuse me of stealing their rings or watches. Even if we demonstrate that their arm is attached to their body, they are never convinced the arm actually belongs to them. At most, one is able to render them briefly confused, and then the condition reestablishes itself. The condition is called "neglect." There is nothing extraordinary here. Mrs. Blanford's case is not rare. There are countless cases of left-side neglect due to right-brain strokes.

> *I wish there were a term in the English language that honestly captures the idea that all we experience is due to brain function. "Materialism" comes close, but is laden with excess metaphysical baggage. The philosopher John Searle coined "biological naturalism" as a mind-body theory within philosophy, and that comes very close. "Asoulism" is more modest: a simple disbelief in the existence of souls based on evidence.*

How can we explain this? Given that we find neglect soon after right-brain damage, we are best served by adopting a neurological point of view. To do so, we need to understand a bit about how the brain works. In general, and in the broadest strokes, the brain is divided into two hemispheres. The left hemisphere processes speech and the motor and sensory information for the right side of the world. The right hemisphere processes nonverbal information and representations from the left side. This particular stroke rendered Mrs. Blanford's right hemisphere dysfunctional, unable to process anything from the left side of her world. It is not the left hemisphere's job to recognize the left arm, and the left hemisphere can't immediately step in to do that task. To the left brain, the left side of the body essentially does not exist. The right brain has failed, not only to process arm information, but failed to let the left hemisphere know it failed.

For Mrs. Blanford, it isn't only that her left brain can't do the right brain's task. The left hemisphere also can't recognize that there is missing data, or that there is something wrong with the data it receives. It has to use the data it has, so the left hemisphere comes up with confabulations, creating verbal fabrications to explain away missing information. In this case the confabulation becomes, "That is your arm, not mine." Although easy to falsify, the idea is internally consistent, makes some sense of the scrambled internal data, and feels correct. The injured brain creates a confabulation to maintain a unity of self and a feeling of control. We find a brain convincing itself of something that feels right, but isn't.

A neglect case only makes sense if you consider each hemisphere as its own separate entity. We see that when a stroke damages the right brain just so, the mind follows as a result. It is expected, to be compared with the unplugging of a mouse resulting in a frozen cursor.

Now consider yourself. Consider your own left arm. It feels perfect, under your control, a part of you, exactly where it should be. But this unified perception relies on neuronal machinery humming in the background, far beneath conscious awareness. Your sense of unity, only perceptible to you, is a sheen on the surface, not a deeper layer of reality.

Where does this leave the soul? Does the soul make any sense in the face of a brain and mind so easily fractured by ischemia? A soul is immaterial, eternal, a little god, impervious to injury, able to survive our deaths. Yet here we see one injured, tethered so close to the injured brain that there is no string. We see a hole, and through it we get a glimpse into the brain's inner workings. One part is damaged; another part falsely thinks it is whole. How does the idea of a unified soul make any sense in the face of this data?

I wish there were a term in the English language that honestly captures the idea that all we experience is due to brain function. "Materialism" comes close, but is laden with excess metaphysical baggage. The philosopher John Searle coined "biological naturalism" as a mind-body theory within philosophy, and that comes very close. "Asoulism" is more modest: a simple disbelief in the existence of souls based on evidence.

The soul is an ancient hypothesis, older than caloric and just as specious, left unsupported by the collected works of neurology and neuroscience. This leaves a distinct absence of soul, by whatever name. Importantly, this absence does *not* arise because of cultural biases and inertias, or because of overarching dogmas and hidden agendas and wishful thinking. It leaves an absence because the available data supports it and tends to falsify everything else.

Almost one hour after symptom onset and less than 50 minutes from the time she came to the ER, we treated Mrs. Blanford's stroke with tissue plasminogen activator. We also enrolled her into an acute stroke treatment trial, thus ensuring that medical science took another tiny step forward. Perhaps because of our treatments, or her personal biology, Mrs. Blanford defied the typical course for a large right brain stroke. She recovered nearly all her function and walked out of our hospital about a week later, seeming nearly whole. She felt unified with her body and her mind, even though some of us believe otherwise, that reconnection isn't unification, and that the way things seem isn't always how they are.

How I Learned To Stop Worrying and Love the Brain

By David A. Hogue
Religious Education, May 2011

Twenty-five years ago I was taking a required class in neuropsychology. We had been introduced to the amazing structure and functions of the brain. During the very last class session, exams completed, we students were relaxed, and by then had enough basic information to ask interesting questions. "Are feelings and thoughts really different from each other?" "What happens when emotions interfere with reason?" "What happens in the brain when we fall in love?" The professor graciously fielded these questions, offered answers when he could, and acknowledged the limits of science.

Finally, I ventured a question about religion. "What happens to the brain during a religious experience?" There was a pause while the professor considered his response, and one student sitting immediately behind me muttered under his breath, "That one's easy. The brain shuts down."

The comment was irreverent, if not funny. His implication was clear: religion requires the short-circuiting of rational thought, and intelligent people do not engage in that sort of thing. The professor, who later admitted to me that his mother had wanted him to be a rabbi, did not hear the comment, and proceeded to talk excitedly about some then very recent research designed to answer just that question.

In the years since I first asked that question, a cascade of discoveries from the neurosciences has touched on virtually every facet of human life, including religion. We have learned, for instance, that in certain religious experiences particular brain structures do indeed shut down—or more precisely, input to and output from those structures decreases while it increases in others. Experiences such as the loosening of boundaries around the self, loss of spatial orientation, and deeply felt connections with others and with God, can be described in part by neurological processes.

In hindsight, that course prompted a kind of conversion experience for me. In some deep way, the psychology and theology I had been studying for years found an embodied ground, what former colleague and pastoral theologian Jim Ashbrook called an "anchoring metaphor." This research trajectory has shaped not only my work, but my understandings of people (including myself), relationships, and spirituality. Four clusters of thought have particularly influenced me: embodiment, memory and imagination, a theory of change, and the social nature of brains and bodies.

From *Religious Education* 106.3 (May/June 2011): 257–61. Copyright © 2011 by Taylor & Francis Ltd. Reprinted with permission. All rights reserved. http://www.informaworld.com.

Embodiment

The religious and cultural traditions in which I grew up valued thinking and moral reasoning over emotion and the body. The body was not merely neglected—it was distrusted. The psychotherapeutic systems of the day claimed to privilege feelings, but the most common treatment was a "talking cure." Words still won out over bodily experience.

> *Stories have become more important to me. We know that human beings are storytellers; we are learning that telling stories also grows out of our neurobiology.*

Today the brain sciences are underscoring the rootedness of human experience in flesh-and-blood bodies, and the utter dependence of our conscious experience on the intricate workings of living brains and acting, feeling bodies. The mind–body dualisms of the past are crumbling; we are unitary beings—soul, mind, and body. We are learning that thinking without feeling is often misguided at best and destructive at worst.

The religious practices of my Protestant upbringing valued speaking and reading over doing and feeling. Word inevitably won out over Sacrament. The neurosciences have awakened in me a deep appreciation of our need to ritualize, to act and perform in ways that both shape and express our deepest religious and social commitments. Rather than using words to crowd out or contain the ineffable, the unspoken (or unspeakable) is gaining a rightful place alongside the spoken. Gesture, posture, and movement have become meaningful, as has the power of the symbolic—cross, Table, and Font. Instead of distrusting "empty rituals," an unfortunate legacy of the Reformation, I am increasingly convinced of the religious power of experiences beyond our words.

Stories and Memory

One of my early forays into the neurosciences was a desire to understand more fully how we remember, since stories and memories are the very "stuff" of education and pastoral care. I had generally thought of memories as packets of facts, or YouTube videos, locked away in "file cabinets" in the brain, awaiting recall as needed. All we had to do was locate the right file and open it. Some memories are more difficult to recall, of course, but remembering required unlocking files. I learned, instead, that the brain records ("encodes") memories by distributing pieces all over the brain (e.g., images in the visual cortex, sounds in the auditory cortex) and "re-collecting" those pieces every time we recall them. And memories can change any time we recall them. Memories (my own and others') now seem much more dynamic and fluid, influenced by how we feel while we are remembering as well as by what we were experiencing when recording the memory.

Stories have become more important to me. We know that human beings are storytellers; we are learning that telling stories also grows out of our neurobiology. Our brains automatically construct narratives to make sense of our experiences, even when we do not have all the "facts." Some scientists even argue that our auto-biographical stories are complete fiction, fooling us into thinking we are making rational choices, when we are merely explaining our actions to ourselves after the fact.

I am much less skeptical than those scientists about human agency and responsibility. We do make choices, and we are accountable. Nevertheless, I listen more carefully to the sub-texts of stories, including my own, and ponder how some small shift might change those stories. I believe that in some ways we can change the past.

Theory of Change

As a teacher and pastoral counselor I now think in very different ways about how people learn and how they heal. Two specific mechanisms of change have particularly intrigued me. Since stories are constructed by a brain that does what it can to make sense of the world, these stories can also change. Increasingly I am listening for the pieces of stories that do not quite fit together, where some missing information might change the story's meaning, or where rearranging the details might provide for a more liberating story. I have a new appreciation for the ways we can deceive ourselves, but also our capacity to re-imagine both past and future.

My first readings about *neuroplasticity*, or cortical remapping, deepened my understanding of the ways we change. Scientists have confirmed the capacity of the brain to rewire itself in the face of new experiences or practices. Following injury or disease, the brain is sometimes even able to restore lost functions by recruiting neural networks previously used for other functions. This discovery convinces me that our religious practices, our spiritual disciplines, shape us more deeply than I would have previously thought, and helps me understand why they are called disciplines. Healing of the soul and mind have become embodied processes, underscoring my Christian conviction that our bodies are indeed the temples of the Holy Spirit.

Social Brains

Last but not least, the neurosciences have convinced me of the deeply embodied reality of love. Significant recent research is exploring how human brains relate to each other—how we empathize, understand each other's intentions, how we connect. Further studies are illuminating how our brains shape and are shaped by our relationships. The growing consensus is that our needs for connection with others permeate every fiber of our being, particularly those fibers in our brains. Such growing evidence has convinced me that we are made by and for relationships at the core of our biology.

For years I have invested much time and effort in attempts to teach students to empathize, and I will continue to do so. But recognizing that our brains are built to empathize has shifted how I think about that task. Empathy is not an "add-on," something we have to force ourselves to do, or teach to each other; we are instead building on the brain's inherent relatedness, clearing away obstacles and creating spaces for our brains to do their natural work. Religious education and pastoral care are practices of physical liberation.

Conclusion

Little did I know in that neuropsychology class so long ago that I was embarking on a journey that would shape my psychological and theological understandings so profoundly. I could not have imagined that I would gain such an appreciation for creation, and that my own embodiedness would link me in intimate ways to others, to the world, and to God.

My theological commitments now value and honor the body and the physical world of which it is a part—a marked contrast to the body-neglecting (or denying) theologies of my youth. Participating in liturgies of the church has become more personally meaningful, and my scholarship on the borders of theology and science provides new discoveries and insights nearly every week. My classmate of years ago might be surprised to learn that religious experiences do much more than shut down our brains; for many of us, our faith is invigorated and renewed by understanding the workings of the mind and brain.

David A. Hogue is Professor of Pastoral Theology and Counseling at Garrett-Evangelical Theological Seminary in Evanston, Illinois.

Does Analytic Thinking Erode Religious Belief?

By Andrew Aghapour
Religious Dispatches Magazine, May 29, 2012

I have some secrets for you; feel free to tell everyone. Psychopaths have distinct types of brains, and so do left-handed people. Bar Mitzvahs aid myelination, the conversion of gray-matter neurons into white-matter neurons. Bragging makes us feel really good, which is why Facebook is better than sex. If that concerns you, don't worry, because the pharmaceutical industry is going to save marriage. Shakespeare tickles the visual association cortex. Dopamine makes us do bad things, but meditation makes your brain quicker. Bloody Mary (the apparition, not the drink) is probably a facial recognition error. Babies are a little bit racist.

Like the zombies that populate our screens, Americans have an immense appetite for brains. Most of the above stories come from just the past month, and they are only a small sample of neuroscience's prominent circulation in the news cycle. Neuroscience can tell us who we are, how we can improve ourselves, and why other people act in the strange ways that they do. In an increasingly complex world, brains seem to somehow point back to the one thing that all humans have in common.

Perhaps because of the high demand for news about the brain, media coverage of neuroscience is notoriously sketchy. In a recent article in the journal *Neuron*, the authors lament the ways that popular neuroscience is used to artificially "underline differences between categories of people in ways that [are] symbolically layered and socially loaded." In other words, research about the brain is often stretched and extended to support existing stereotypes about race, sex, class, and religion. Neuroscience is new enough, and our desire for brain facts is strong enough, that dubious claims about brain types circulate widely.

A Trio of Wacky Experiments

Take, for example, the latest Neuroscience-of-Religion news item to make the rounds, this one claiming that critical thinking undermines religious belief. Based on two studies from *The Journal of Experimental Psychologies and Science*, it has been picked up by *The Atlantic*, The Huffington Post, and (unsurprisingly) Richard-Dawkins.net.

In the *Scientific American* article that activated the echo chamber, Daisy Grewal claims that we possess two different ways of thinking: *intuitive* thinking, which relies on shortcuts, rules of thumb, and commonsense ideas; and *analytic* thinking, which questions our rapid-fire intuitions, but is much slower and more energy intensive. According to some "clever techniques," Grewal states, psychologists have examined whether analytic thinking "leads people away from believing in God and religion." Presumably belief in God here represents intuitive thinking, and sober scientific analysis represents the energy-intensive act of systematically questioning one's beliefs.

Three clever experiments allegedly indicate that critical thinking undermines religious belief, though the experiments range from dubious to just plain wacky. Experiment one had participants view images of artwork that were either "neutral" (e.g., the Discobulus of Myron) or associated with reflective thinking (e.g., "The Thinker"). Participants then filled out a survey about their religiosity, and those who viewed "reflective" artwork reported weaker religious beliefs.

Experiment two was a bit more subtle:

> *Problem One is the assumption that religious and non-religious belief can fit neatly into two cognitive boxes, where "intuitive thinking" is religious and "analytic thinking" is rational and secular. Even if there are two distinctive cognitive operations, it isn't clear that the rich and diverse mental lives of religious and nonreligious people will align with these two thought styles.*

Participants received sets of five randomly arranged words (e.g., "high winds the flies plane") and were asked to drop one word and rearrange the others in order to create a more meaningful sentence (e.g., "the plane flies high"). Some of their participants were given scrambled sentences containing words associated with analytic thinking (e.g., "analyze," "reason") and other participants were given sentences that featured neutral words (e.g., "hammer," "shoes"). After unscrambling the sentences, participants filled out a survey about their religious beliefs. In both studies, this subtle reminder of analytic thinking caused participants to express less belief in God and religion. The researchers found no relationship between participants' prior religious beliefs and their performance in the study. Analytic thinking reduced religious belief regardless of how religious people were to begin with.

In a third experiment, psychologists had participants fill out a survey measuring their religious beliefs that was printed in either an easy- or difficult-to-read font, since previous research has indicated that difficult fonts promote analytic thinking. Participants who filled out the difficult-to-read expressed less belief than those who filled out the same survey in an easy-to-read font.

Grewal's claim is that the act of analytic thinking corrodes religious belief, such that sentence-scrambling or even being *reminded* of reflection leads people to become less religious. Yet there are two fundamental problems with this scientific story, and they will take us from St. Thomas Aquinas to Canadian undergraduates.

St. Thomas Aquinas, Atheist

Problem One is the assumption that religious and nonreligious belief can fit neatly into two cognitive boxes, where "intuitive thinking" is religious and "analytic thinking" is rational and secular. Even if there are two distinctive cognitive operations, it isn't clear that the rich and diverse mental lives of religious and nonreligious people will align with these two thought styles. "Intuitive thinking," characterized by mental shortcuts and rules of thumb, is a fundamental part of human cognitive life, no matter what one's religious beliefs. Every day the world around us changes: the appearances of those around us alter slightly; the path to work loses and gains landmarks; the market features a new array of foods and shifting prices. "Intuitive thinking" involves collapsing these minor differences into stable wholes so that we don't, say, lose sight of our car when it is covered in pollen.

Similarly, "analytic thinking" is a powerful cognitive tool that can be applied in a variety of contexts, from questioning our assumptions about a political candidate to analyzing a text, television show, or conversation. These generalized styles of thinking can equally apply to religious belief or nonbelief. Religious believers and nonbelievers alike fall into fast and frugal "rules of thumb" about the world, and both engage in analytic thought about texts, ideas, relationships, and objects. To see past Grewal's artificial division between "intuition/religion" and "analysis/nonbelief" we need only look to Christian theology, which involves deeply analytic and critical modes of thinking, but which is more or less associated with religious thinkers. If Grewal's binary were accurate, in other words, St. Thomas Aquinas should have been an atheist!

Problem Two is serious methodological flaws in the experiments that Grewal cites: they are based on surveys, where isolated groups of people are asked to self-report on their religious beliefs. People are notoriously difficult to pin down on issues of belief—for many, religiosity is a private and shifting dimension of identity, so much so that the answers to questions about religion are likely to be influenced by the setting and the questioner at hand.

If these "clever" experiments do tell a common story, it isn't about critical thinking and belief, but about the population that was surveyed. According to the *Science* article that Grewal cites, these experiments were primarily based on surveys of Canadian undergraduates, a population that we would expect to be somewhat malleable on the subject of religion. We should not be surprised, then, that undergraduates faced with "The Thinker" or a puzzle loaded with the words "analyze" and "reason" would self-report less religiosity; it would be much the same as someone downplaying religious belief in conversation with an agnostic scientist.

To take heed of the recent call to be careful with how we inflate and extend neuroscientific findings, we should all try to be a bit more like St. Thomas Aquinas and use "analytic" thinking to parse claims like Grewal's about religion. Where our intuitive impulse might be to align critical thought with science and uncritical intuition with religion, the picture is actually much more complicated and interesting. Although it won't make many front pages, there is still a fascinating headline to be found here: "Canadian Undergraduates, Prompted with Analytic Exercises, Are Influenced to Self-Report Less Religiosity."

Science and Religion: Reality's Toolkit

By Jessica Hahne
Yale Scientific, May 10, 2012

Science and religion are often regarded as opposites; even today, many people may believe that they must compromise one to accept the other. Dr. Nihal de Lanerolle, a neurobiologist at the Yale School of Medicine who also serves as chaplain of the Episcopal Church at Yale, believes otherwise. De Lanerolle recalls a story about Niels Bohr—the father of quantum mechanics—and his first inklings about the nature of the universe. As a child, Bohr would spend hours gazing into a fishpond, contemplating the unawareness of the fish that they were being watched and that any reality, such as the source of sunlight or rain that penetrated the surface, existed outside the pond. Bohr wondered if humans were like these fish, being acted upon by multiple dimensions of reality, but aware of only a limited frame of reference. Following this reasoning, de Lanerolle expands that "Religion and philosophy are tools for acquiring knowledge of the other dimensions of reality that cannot yet be explored with the tools of science."

The Religious Scientist

In every area of his life, de Lanerolle exhibits a passion for solving problems, whether the problem happens to be the decline of brain function or the decline of a church congregation. This mentality allows him to see his religion and his scientific career as equal and intertwined parts of his life: "It's all one to me; I don't really consciously think of myself in these separate dimensions."

De Lanerolle has been working in the Neurosurgery Department at the Yale School of Medicine, where he researches epilepsy and brain trauma, since 1979. Motivated by the death of a friend from an epileptic seizure, he began researching the causes and effects of temporal lobe epilepsy in 1985 and has since linked the condition to the hippocampus and to helper cells in the brain called astrocytes. Three years ago, his research took on a second focus: brain trauma induced by proximity to bomb explosions. Beginning with animal subjects and expanding to studies on humans, he and his colleagues have confirmed that there is some biological basis to the damage in memory, cognitive function, and emotional response exhibited by soldiers returning from war.

Expanding his problem-solving skills beyond the medical realm, de Lanerolle also "provide[s] spiritual resources" as a chaplain. He has been involved at the Episcopal Church since first coming to Yale, serving on the Board of Governors for many years and eventually becoming the vice president, which involved running the church's ministry for nine years. After leaving briefly to serve as College Chaplain at Trinity College in Hartford, he returned to Yale in 2002 to find the Episcopal Church struggling with membership and finances. It was then that he took up his post as chaplain of the Episcopal Church at Yale, determined to "put the house back in order." Since then, he has recruited an organist and choir singers, reached out to increase membership, and arranged for regular dinners to follow services. As much time and effort as it requires, de Lanerolle does not consider his religious work his profession: "I do it as a sort of avocation, rather than a vocation."

A Rational Faith

De Lanerolle describes the typical dialogue between science and religion as having two sides: scientists who have a "simplistic understanding of theological thinking" and theologians who "haven't taken the trouble to understand the entire breadth of a scientific field." While he does not claim expertise in both, de Lanerolle submits these as the major shortcomings of each side.

These shortcomings are particularly evident, de Lanerolle says, when he acts as a counselor to Yale students who have questions about their faith. He comments that when students come into Yale with "fundamentalist" beliefs that take every word of the Bible literally, they begin to see contradictions between their faith and academics, particularly in the sciences. Students often come to Yale with the notion that faith and reason must be treated separately. As a result, when they are forced to confront conflicts such as "creation versus evolution" and "randomness versus divine intervention" at the university level, some students become distraught and may give up their faith entirely. To prevent this distress, he encourages them to see the Bible not as a rulebook, but as an exemplary story about people in the past interacting with God. True to his tradition, this view allows him to integrate faith and reason in his own daily life.

> *De Lanerolle believes that just as science consists of both verified laws and theories that are continually proposed, tested, and adjusted, religion should maintain its basic framework over time while still being open to new developments.*

De Lanerolle describes his faith as rational: "Some think I am a heretic, but I challenge them to think in ways that are truthful." In other words, he asks others to question what is generally accepted. He does not see religion and science as dead-end contradictions, but as more of a "two-way street," with scientific discovery sometimes causing him to "rethink [his] religious understanding." He adds, "A lot of our religious understanding has been passed down, and they didn't have the scientific information I have." De Lanerolle believes that just as science consists of both verified laws and theories that are continually proposed, tested, and adjusted, religion should maintain its basic framework over time while still being open to new developments.

Revising the Blueprints

When asked about the debate over evolution and creation, de Lanerolle answers that the writers of the Old Testament formulated an explanation for how the world came about using the limited knowledge that was available to them. He suggests that the creation story at its core implies the same general theme as evolution, with order and complexity developing from formless chaos. Holding this theme as the central significance of the story, rather than the detail of creation in seven days, he describes the Old Testament as a collection of "stories told in a simplified form so we can grapple with the big questions of life." He also explains that while scripture and tradition provide a strong foundation for faith, natural reason and experience play an integral role as well—without them, "God would cease to exist for each individual."

Evolution aside, one of the most common questions people tend to ask is, "How do you know there is a God?" De Lanerolle's first answer is simply "I don't know"—but he goes on to explain that exploring the character of God is not unlike exploring a scientific question; both call upon the scientific method. "So, let's assume God is like my big daddy," he poses as an example. "If I pray in a certain way, such-and-such should happen, right? If I ask my daddy for something I really want desperately, then maybe I should get that. And so, I might pray that way. Then I probably don't get what I want, right? So does that mean God doesn't exist? Well, it could mean God doesn't exist; that's one possibility. Or it could be that my notion of God is not what it should be. Or it could be my experiment was wrong. . . . I constantly keep evolving my understanding about God." De Lanerolle would investigate a neuroscience question, such as how thoughts are formed, in the same manner: hypothesizing, experimenting, analyzing, revising, and concluding. The scientific method is universal in that "every time, even in science, an experiment fails, you learn something from it. You grow from it. The same thing happens with religion—you grow from grappling with this notion of God."

Even more pressing than the debate over God's existence, is the search for a purpose in life. Whether you tackle this quest from a scientific perspective or from a religious one, it is evident that each individual must discover the answer for him- or herself. De Lanerolle encourages seeking an answer through both perspectives, using faith as a starting point and science as a guide, so as to evaluate life's purpose not just through a single dimension of reality—the world of our senses and conscious experience—but also through other dimensions of reality of which we are less aware. While many people see science and religion as tools of different trades, he sees them as tools of the same kit for constructing reality. "Whether that reality is true or not, we don't know," he concludes. "But it's the impact [it] has on your life that I think matters."

Jessica Hahne is a freshman English major in Silliman College. She works as a copy editor for the Yale Scientific *Magazine.*

Acknowledgments

The author would like to thank Dr. Nihal de Lanerolle for taking the time to explain his work and share his perspective.

Further Reading

de Lanerolle, N.C., Lee, T.S. and Spencer, D.D. (2010) Astrocytes and Epilepsy. *Neurotherapeutics* 7: 424–438. PMID: 20880506.

Neurononsense

Why Brain Sciences Can't Explain the Human Condition

By Roger Scruton
ABC: Australian Broadcast Company, May 9, 2012

There are many reasons for believing the brain is the seat of consciousness. Damage to the brain disrupts our mental processes; specific parts of the brain seem connected to specific mental capacities; and the nervous system, to which we owe movement, perception, sensation and bodily awareness, is a tangled mass of pathways, all of which end in the brain. This much was obvious to Hippocrates.

Even Descartes, who believed in a radical divide between soul and body, acknowledged the special role of the brain in tying them together.

The discovery of brain imaging techniques has given rise to the belief that we can look at people's thoughts and feelings, and see how "information" is "processed" in the head. The brain is seen as a computer, "hardwired" by evolution to deal with the long vanished problems of our hunter-gatherer ancestors, and operating in ways that are more transparent to the person with the scanner than to the person being scanned.

Our own way of understanding ourselves must therefore be replaced by neuroscience, which rejects the whole enterprise of a specifically "humane" understanding of the human condition.

In 1986, Patricia Churchland published *Neurophilosophy*, arguing that the questions that had been discussed to no effect by philosophers over many centuries would be solved once they were rephrased as questions of neuroscience. This was the first major outbreak of a new academic disease, which one might call "neuroenvy."

If philosophy could be replaced by neuroscience, why not the rest of the humanities, which had been wallowing in a methodless swamp for far too long? Old disciplines that relied on critical judgment and cultural immersion could be given a scientific gloss when rebranded as "neuroethics," "neuroaesthetics," "neuromusicology," "neurotheology" or "neuroarthistory" (subject of a book by John Onians).

Michael Gazzaniga's influential study *The Ethical Brain* has given rise to "Law and Neuroscience" as an academic discipline, combining legal reasoning and brain imagining, largely to the detriment of our old ideas of responsibility. One by one, real but non-scientific disciplines are being rebranded as infant sciences, even though the only science involved has as yet little or nothing to say about them.

It seems to me that aesthetics, criticism, theology, musicology and law are real disciplines, but not sciences. They are not concerned with *explaining* some aspect of the human condition but with *understanding* it, according to its own internal procedures. Rebrand them as branches of neuroscience and you don't necessarily increase knowledge: in fact you might lose it.

Brain imaging won't help you to analyze Bach's *Art of Fugue* or to interpret *King Lear* any more than it will unravel the concept of legal responsibility or deliver a proof of Goldbach's conjecture; it won't help you to understand the concept of God or to evaluate the proofs for His existence, nor will it show you why justice is a virtue and cowardice a vice. And it cannot fail to encourage the superstition which says that I am not a whole human being with mental and physical powers, but merely a brain in a box.

The new sciences in fact have a tendency to divide neatly into two parts. On the one hand there is an analysis of some feature of our mental or social life and an attempt to show its importance and the principles of its organization. On the other hand, there is a set of brain scans. Every now and then there is a cry of "Eureka!"—for example, when Joshua Greene showed that dilemmas involving personal confrontation arouse different brain areas from those aroused by detached moral calculations. But since Greene gave no coherent description of the question, to which the datum was supposed to suggest an answer, the cry dwindled into silence.

The example typifies the results of neuroenvy, which consist of a vast collection of answers, with no memory of the questions. And the answers are encased in neurononsense of the following kind (courtesy of Patricia Churchland):

"The brains of social animals are wired to feel pleasure in the exercise of social dispositions such as grooming and co-operation, and to feel pain when shunned, scolded, or excluded. Neurochemicals such as vasopressin and oxytocin mediate pairbonding, parent-offspring bonding, and probably also bonding to kith and kin . . ."

As though we didn't know already that people feel pleasure in grooming and co-operating, and as though it adds anything to say that their brains are "wired" to this effect, or that "neurochemicals" might possibly be involved in producing it. This is pseudoscience of the first order, and owes what scant plausibility it possesses to the fact that it simply repeats the matter that it fails to explain. It perfectly illustrates the prevailing academic disorder, which is the loss of questions.

Traditional attempts to understand consciousness were bedeviled by the "homunculus fallacy," according to which consciousness is the work of the soul, the mind, the self, the inner entity that thinks and sees and feels and which is the real me inside. We cast no light on the consciousness of a human being simply by redescribing it as the consciousness of some inner homunculus. On the contrary, by placing that homunculus in some private, inaccessible and possibly immaterial realm, we merely compound the mystery.

As Max Bennett and Peter Hacker have argued, this homunculus fallacy keeps coming back in another form. The homunculus is no longer a soul, but a brain, which "processes information," "maps the world," "constructs a picture" of reality, and so on—all expressions that we understand, only because they describe conscious processes with which we are familiar.

To describe the resulting "science" as an explanation of consciousness, when it merely reads back into the explanation the feature that needs to be explained, is not just unjustified—it is profoundly misleading, in creating the impression that consciousness is a feature of the brain, and not of the person.

Perhaps no instance of neurononsense has been more influential than Benjamin Libet's ingenious experiments which allegedly "prove" that actions which we experience as voluntary are in fact "initiated" by brain events occurring a short while before we have the "feeling" of deciding on them. The brain "decides" to do X, and the conscious mind records this decision some time later.

Libet's experiments have produced reams of neurobabble. But the conclusion depends on forgetting what the question might have been. It looks significant only if we assume that an event in a brain is identical with a decision of a person, that an action is voluntary if and only if preceded by a mental episode of the right kind, that intentions and volitions are "felt" episodes of a subject which can be precisely dated. All such assumptions are incoherent, for reasons that philosophers have made abundantly clear.

So just what can be proved about people by the close observation of their brains? We can be conceptualized in two ways: as organisms and as objects of personal interaction. The first way employs the concept "human being," and derives our behavior from a biological science of man. The second way employs the concept "person," which is not the concept of a natural kind, but of an entity that relates to others in a familiar but complex way that we know intuitively but find hard to describe.

Through the concept of the person—and the associated notions of freedom, responsibility, reason for action, right, duty, justice and guilt—we gain the description under which human beings are seen, by those who respond to them as they truly are. When we endeavor to understand persons through the half-formed theories of neuroscience we are tempted to pass over their distinctive features in silence, or else to attribute them to some brain-shaped homunculus inside.

For we understand people by facing them, by arguing with them, by understanding their reasons, aspirations and plans. All of that involves another language, and another conceptual scheme, from those deployed in the biological sciences. We do not understand brains by facing them, for they have no face.

We should recognize that not all coherent questions about human nature and conduct are scientific questions, concerning the laws governing cause and effect. Most of our questions about persons and their doings are about interpretation: what did he mean by that? What did her words imply? What is signified by the hand of Michelangelo's David? Those are real questions, which invite disciplined answers. And there are disciplines that attempt to answer them.

The law is one such. It involves making reasoned attributions of liability and responsibility, using methods that are not reducible to any explanatory science, and not replaceable by neuroscience, however many advances that science might make. The invention of "neurolaw" is, it seems to me, profoundly dangerous, since it cannot fail to abolish freedom and accountability—not because those things don't exist, but because they will never crop up in a brain scan.

Suppose a computer is programmed to "read," as we say, a digitally encoded input, which it translates into pixels, causing it to display the picture of a woman on its screen. In order to describe this process we do not need to refer to the woman in the picture. The entire process can be completely described in terms of the hardware that translates digital data into pixels, and the software, or algorithm, which contains the instructions for doing this.

There is neither the need nor the right, in this case, to use concepts like those of seeing, thinking, observing, in describing what the computer is doing; nor do we have either the need or the right to describe the thing observed in the picture, as playing any causal role, or any role at all, in the operation of the computer.

> *We should recognize that not all coherent questions about human nature and conduct are scientific questions, concerning the laws governing cause and effect. Most of our questions about persons and their doings are about interpretation: what did he mean by that? What did her words imply?*

Of course, we see the woman in the picture. And to us the picture contains information of quite another kind from that encoded in the digitalized instructions for producing it. It conveys information about a woman and how she looks. To describe this kind of information is impossible without describing the content of certain thoughts—thoughts that arise in people when they look at each other face to face.

But how do we move from the one concept of information to the other? How do we explain the emergence of thoughts about something from processes that reside in the transformation of visually encoded data? Cognitive science doesn't tell us. And computer models of the brain won't tell us either.

They might show how images get encoded in digitalized format and transmitted in that format by neural pathways to the centre where they are "interpreted." But that centre does not in fact interpret—interpreting is a process that we do, in seeing what is there before us.

When it comes to the subtle features of the human condition, to the byways of culpability and the secrets of happiness and grief, we need guidance and study if we are to interpret things correctly.

That is what the humanities provide, and that is why, when scholars who purport to practice them, add the prefix "neuro-" to their studies, we should expect their researches to be nonsense.

Roger Scruton is the Visiting Professor of Philosophy at the University of Oxford and the University of St Andrews. His most recent book is The Face of God.

3

The Politics of Religion and Science

(AP Photo)

Hundreds gather outside the state capitol in Richmond, Virginia, on Saturday, March 3, 2012, to protest legislation that would require women to undergo ultrasound exams before receiving abortions.

The Bible, the Beaker, and the Ballot Box: Faith, Science, and American Politics

By Paul McCaffrey

To those who believe that science and religion are eternally at odds, the United States would seem to be something of a contradiction. The nation is both one of the most religiously devout, especially when compared with other developed democracies, and a world leader in technological and scientific research. A 2007 study by the University of Michigan found that 44 percent of Americans attended religious services at least once a week. The rate in Great Britain was 27 percent; France, 21 percent; and Japan, 3 percent. More than half of US respondents, 53 percent, said that religion was very important to them, as opposed to only 16 percent in Great Britain and 14 percent in France.

Meanwhile, a key gauge of a nation's scientific contributions is the number of research papers its scientists publish each year. In 2008, the United States led the world with 316,317, while China came in a distant second at 184,080. Though China's output has increased rapidly over the past generation and is expected to eclipse that of the United States in the near future, the American scientific community is in no danger of losing its prestige or influence any time soon.

At first glance, the American public is largely comfortable with this combination of religiosity and scientific endeavor. For the vast majority of the population—84 percent, according to a 2009 poll by the Pew Forum on Religion and Public Life—science is not viewed as an ominous influence but seen to have a generally positive effect on society.

Yet a closer examination reveals that the interplay of science and religion is not always so harmonious, and often the discord between the two disciplines plays out in the political realm. The scientific community diverges from the general public in both religious and political affiliation. As a demographic, scientists do not display the same level of religious devotion as the population as a whole. Analysis conducted by the Pew Forum in 2009 revealed that 83 percent of the American people believed in God, 12 percent in a higher power, and 4 percent in neither. Among US scientists, only one in three claimed to believe in God, 18 percent in a higher power, and 41 percent in neither. Though they draw a striking contrast with the general population, these figures were not drastically different from those in a 1914 survey of scientists conducted by the psychologist James Leuba. According to Leuba's findings, 42 percent of scientists believed in God and 42 percent did not.

Based on Pew Research Center data from 2009, voter registration numbers in the United States broke down as follows: 35 percent of the electorate identified as Democrats, 23 percent as Republicans, 34 percent as independents, and 4 percent as either none or "other." In terms of ideology, 37 percent of voters considered themselves conservative, 20 percent liberal (with 5 percent claiming to be very liberal), and 38 percent moderate. Among scientists, the numbers skewed considerably more Democratic and more liberal: 55 percent were Democrats, 32 percent were independents, a mere 6 percent were Republicans, and another 4 percent had no affiliation or opted for the "other" designation. A majority of scientists—about 52 percent—described themselves as liberal, with 14 percent as very liberal. Another 35 percent claimed to be moderates, and only 9 percent held conservative views.

While scientists incline toward progressive politics and the Democratic Party, religious voters show a notable preference for conservatism and the Republicans. In a 2011 Gallup survey, 41 percent of voters described themselves as very religious. Of these, 48 percent identified as Republican or Republican leaning, compared to only 38 percent as Democrat or Democrat leaning and 13 percent as independent. Among white evangelical Christians, the trend is even more pronounced; according to Pew Research statistics, 70 percent of these voters labeled themselves Republicans. In the 2012 Republican presidential primaries, according to press reports, about half of voters were white evangelicals.

This divide between a comparatively nonreligious and Democratic-leaning scientific community and a Republican-leaning faith-oriented segment of the population has created fertile ground for political friction. How the issue of climate change has been handled within the scientific and political communities demonstrates the twin drawbacks of this troubling dynamic: a distrust of government among scientists and a distrust of science among conservatives and the more religious.

That the earth's climate has changed over time is not a matter of dispute. That it is changing in whole or in part due to human activity, through deforestation or the burning of fossil fuels, for example, is a subject of intense political debate. In the scientific community, however, there is a broad prevailing consensus. In a 2009 Pew survey, 84 percent of the scientists polled believed that the earth is warming as a result of human activity, and 70 percent saw the phenomenon as a very serious problem. The general public did not perceive the issue in the same way, with only 49 percent accepting that humans influence climate change and only 47 percent perceiving it as a major problem. The figures for Republicans were even lower, with just 16 percent believing that humans are contributing to climate change in 2010.

During the presidency of George W. Bush, there was concern within the scientific community that the Republican administration was preventing government scientists from reporting findings that conflicted with the administration's policies. For example, one of the leading government researchers on climate change, James E. Hansen, who heads the National Aeronautic and Space Administration (NASA) Goddard Institute for Space Studies, claimed that the Bush administration, skeptical of climate change, tried to restrict his commenting on the issue. Other researchers alleged that nonscientist political appointees edited drafts of scientific climate reports to downplay the severity of their findings on global warming. Rick Piltz, a member of the federal government's Climate Change Science Program, stated that an administration official altered his work. "He would put in the word *potential* or *may* or weaken or delete text that had to do with the likely consequence of climate change, pump up uncertainty language throughout," Piltz said.

These controversies hit the scientific community hard. According to surveys by the Pew Research Center, 85 percent of scientists heard about these allegations, 77 percent thought they were true, and 71 percent believed that such practices occurred more often under George W. Bush than under previous presidents. At the same time, 56 percent of the public was unaware of the dispute.

As the disagreement over climate change alienated the scientific community from the government, other factors created doubts about the accuracy of scientists' global-warming claims in the minds of the general public and especially Republican and religious voters. For some, this skepticism has a biblical component. Responding to concerns about climate change at a March 2009 hearing on the matter in the House of Representatives, Republican representative John Shimkus of Illinois quoted two verses from the biblical book of Genesis in which God states, "Never again will I curse the ground because of man even though every inclination of his heart is evil from childhood and never again will I destroy all living creatures as I have done. As long as the earth endures, seed time and harvest, cold and heat, summer and winter, day and night, will never cease." Based on his reading of the passage, Shimkus declared that climate change is not a threat to the planet. "Man will not destroy this earth," he avowed. "This earth will not be destroyed by a flood."

But the religious component is only one aspect of global-warming skepticism. In conservative political circles, the belief that climate-change theories are part of an elaborate conspiracy is widespread. Former Pennsylvania senator Rick Santorum declared, "[Global warming is] just an excuse for more government control of your life, and I've never been for any scheme or even accepted the junk science behind the whole narrative." Texas representative Ron Paul referred to climate change as "the greatest hoax . . . that has been around in many, many years if not hundreds of years."

Those who believe in such climate-change conspiracy theories often refer to a November 2009 incident that has come to be known as "Climategate." The controversy developed when hackers accessed thousands of e-mails and documents from the Climatic Research Unit at the University of East Anglia in Great Britain. Soon after, the material began to appear on various websites and was widely promoted by global-warming skeptics. The stolen e-mails, the Associated Press reported, showed that certain climatologists "stonewalled skeptics and discussed hiding data." Some of the material "suggests an effort to avoid sharing scientific data with critics skeptical of global warming." For global-warming doubters, the hacked documents revealed a vast conspiracy among climatologists. For the general public, the scandal created confusion about the scientific validity of global-warming research.

A number of investigations ensued in both the United Kingdom and the United States. The general consensus that emerged from these inquiries was that contrary to the views of climate-change doubters, there was no evidence to support allegations of fraud or data manipulation. Though the scientists in question could have been more transparent, investigators noted, many of the incendiary quotes were taken out of context or misapplied. After a comprehensive review of the hacked e-mails, the Associated Press concluded that "the messages don't support claims that the science of global warming was faked." These findings notwithstanding, Climategate did little to increase public trust in the scientific community.

Research shows that faith in science among conservative voters has been diminishing for decades. The debate over climate change, as well as the controversy concerning the theory of evolution, has likely hastened this trend. According to a study published by the *American Sociological Review* in April 2012, the percentage of conservatives professing trust in science declined by 25 percent between 1974 and 2010, while among moderates and liberals, the rate held steady. Of the three ideological groupings, conservatives have gone from having the most faith in science to having the least. Liberals, in turn, have become the most trusting. Gordon Gauchat, who carried out the study, observed that his research "shows that the public trust in science has not declined since the mid-1970s except among self-identified conservatives and among those who frequently attend church." He expects that this pattern will continue in the years ahead and that conservatives, and presumably the religiously devout, will grow increasingly alienated from the scientific community.

Assuming Gauchat is correct, it is not difficult to envision how the current trends, played out to their extremes, might further polarize an already-fractured electorate. The end result might be a political system divided not only along ideological lines but between those who embrace faith and those who embrace science, with the religious estranged from one party and the empirically inclined from the other. Such an outcome would hardly be good for faith, science, or the political system.

Unholy Alliance

The Controversy over the Catholic Church and Health Care Goes beyond Birth Control

By Jonathan Cohn
The New Republic, February 22, 2012

When the Obama administration decided that birth control coverage would be mandatory for all insurance policies, even those provided to employees by large religious institutions, the outcry from Catholic leaders and social conservatives surprised a lot of people. But conflicts between health care and religion, particularly Catholicism, are not news in many parts of the country. Just ask physicians in Sierra Vista, Arizona.

Sierra Vista is a rural community about 80 miles southeast of Tucson and about 20 miles north of the Mexican border. It has one hospital: the Sierra Vista Regional Health Center. In 2010, administrators announced that their secular institution would be joining the Carondelet Health Network, a system of Catholic hospitals. The intention was to make the hospital more financially viable, the administrators explained, but it would also entail some changes: The obstetrics service would have to abide by care directives from the Catholic Church. Although the merger would not be official for another year, staff would begin observing Catholic medical guidelines right away.

The hospital did not perform elective abortions, which is typical for small conservative communities. But the obstetricians were accustomed to terminating pregnancies in the event of medical emergencies. And just such a case presented itself one November morning, when a woman, 15 weeks pregnant, arrived at the emergency room in the middle of a miscarriage. According to a deposition later obtained by *The Washington Post*, the woman had been carrying twins and passed the first fetus at home in the bathtub. When she arrived via ambulance, she was stable and not bleeding. But the umbilical cord from the first fetus was coming out of her vagina, while the second fetus was still in her uterus.

Robert Holder, the physician on duty who gave the deposition, said the odds of saving the second fetus were miniscule. Doctors would need to tie off the umbilical cord and put the woman at severe risk of infection. After discussing the options, the family, with some difficulty, opted for a medical termination. But, under the new rules, Holder had to get approval from a nurse manager and eventually a more senior administrator. When Holder briefed the administrator, she asked whether the fetus had a heartbeat. It did, he said. "She replied that I had to send the patient out for treatment," Holder later recalled. He arranged for the woman to get the procedure at the nearest major medical institution—in Tucson. According to his account, the 90-minute trip put her at risk of hemorrhaging and infection, which did not happen, and "significant emotional distress," which did.

Holder said that an official from Ascension Health, which oversees Carondelet, told him earlier that the rules permit terminating a pregnancy when a spontaneous abortion seems inevitable. (Officials from Ascension and Sierra Vista were not available for comment.) But Bruce Silva, another obstetrician on staff and an early skeptic of the merger, told me that confusion over the rules was common. "We couldn't get a straight answer," Silva says. "There was so much gray area. And sometimes you need to make these decisions quickly, for medical reasons." Even when the new rules were clear, Silva adds, they sometimes prevented physicians from following their best clinical judgments, not to mention their patients' wishes. A prohibition on tubal ligations, a surgical form of sterilization that severs or blocks the fallopian tubes, meant women had to go elsewhere for this procedure. However, physicians routinely perform this operation as part of a cesarean section, either when patients have requested the procedure or when it's medically recommended, in order to avoid a second invasive surgery and the attendant medical risks. "I had a patient who was blind. She and her husband were working but poor, and she was diabetic, too," Silva told me. "She was having her second baby, and that's all she wanted and she's got these medical issues. She asked for a tubal ligation. And I can't do it."

> But sometimes the dual mandates of these institutions—to heal the body and to nurture the spirit, to perform public functions but maintain private identities—are difficult to reconcile. That was the issue with the recent contraception controversy. The whole point of the new health care law is to make insurance a public good to which every citizen is entitled, regardless of where he or she works.

Catholic hospitals have been a bulwark of U.S. health care since the early twentieth century, when orders of nuns from Europe came to tend to the immigrant communities powering the industrial revolution. Many of these hospitals provided care to people of all faiths. But their first order of business was to help fellow Catholics, particularly those of the same ethnicity, who required care—and, frequently, last rites—delivered in a language they understood. In this respect, the Catholic institutions were like religious hospitals from other faiths that provided services for their own followers, whether it was Lutheran hospitals that could communicate with patients in their native German or Jewish hospitals that provided only kosher food on the wards.

We now depend upon Catholic hospitals to provide vital services—not just direct care of patients, but also the training of new doctors and assistance to the needy.

In exchange, these institutions receive considerable public funding. In addition to the tax breaks to which all nonprofit institutions are entitled, Catholic hospitals also receive taxpayer dollars via public insurance programs like Medicare and Medicaid, as well as myriad federal programs that provide extra subsidies for such things as indigent care and medical research. (Older institutions also benefited from the 1946 Hill-Burton Act, which financed hospital construction for several decades.)

But sometimes the dual mandates of these institutions—to heal the body and to nurture the spirit, to perform public functions but maintain private identities—are difficult to reconcile. That was the issue with the recent contraception controversy. The whole point of the new health care law is to make insurance a public good to which every citizen is entitled, regardless of where he or she works. And, because employers have traditionally been the source of insurance for most working Americans, the law effectively deputizes employers to provide this public good. In some cases, that means forcing religious institutions to pay for benefits—such as birth control—that violate the terms of their faith. Even Sister Carol Keehan, president of the Catholic Health Association and a staunch supporter of health care reform, protested the contraception rule, arguing, "The explicit recognition of the right of Catholic organizations to perform their ministries in fidelity to their faith is almost as old as our nation itself."

This tension has implications that go far beyond birth control. In 2004, during the Terri Schiavo controversy, Pope John Paul II decreed that Catholic health care providers had obligations to provide food and water intravenously—even to patients in vegetative states, as long as doing so would keep them alive indefinitely. The U.S. Conference of Catholic Bishops interpreted that as a mandate to provide life-sustaining treatment except in cases where treatment would be "unduly burdensome to the patient"—prompting ethicists at different hospitals to debate when, and whether, that prohibited physicians from removing feeding tubes for patients with no hope of recovery. When President Obama early in his term announced a new policy for stem-cell research, leaders of Catholic hospitals hinted their institutions were not likely to allow such projects, clinical value notwithstanding.

Still, reproductive health is the area that has given rise to the most public controversies. In 2007, a physician wrote an essay in the *Journal of the American Medical Association* about a woman, also pregnant with twins, whose pregnancy was failing, threatening infection that could jeopardize her ability to have future children and perhaps her life. Distraught, she and her husband decided to terminate the pregnancy—only to learn the Catholic hospital would not perform the procedure. The physician, Ramesh Raghavan of St. Louis, knew about the case because he was the husband.

A few years later, according to an article in *Ms.* magazine, a New Hampshire waitress named Kathleen Prieskorn went to her doctor's office after a miscarriage—her second—began while she was three months pregnant. Physicians at the hospital, which had recently merged with a Catholic health care system, told her they could not end the miscarriage with a uterine evacuation—the standard procedure—because the fetus still had a heartbeat. She had no insurance and no way to get to another hospital, so a doctor gave her $400 and put her in a cab to the closest available hospital, about 80 miles away. "During that trip, which seemed endless, I was not only devastated but terrified," Prieskorn told *Ms.* "I knew that, if there were complications, I could lose my uterus—and maybe even my life."

Probably the most notorious incident occurred in 2009, when a 27-year-old woman with "right heart failure" came to the emergency room of St. Joseph's Hospital and Medical Center, a Catholic hospital in Phoenix, while eleven weeks pregnant. Physicians concluded that, if she continued with the pregnancy, her chances of mortality were "close to 100 percent." An administrator, Sister Margaret McBride, approved an abortion, citing a church directive allowing termination when the mother's life is at risk. Afterward, however, the local bishop, Thomas Olmsted, said the abortion had not been absolutely necessary. He excommunicated the nun and severed ties with the hospital, although the nun subsequently won reinstatement when she agreed to confess her sin to a priest.

There's reason to think these kinds of conflicts are becoming more common. Like every other industry in health care, hospitals are consolidating to strengthen their financial positions or merely to survive. "There are a lot of rural places that now have only a Catholic hospital," says Lois Uttley, director of MergerWatch, a research and advocacy group based in New York City. "We hear regularly from doctors there who are just distraught at not being able to provide the care they want." Silva, from Sierra Vista, notes that such arrangements can be particularly tough on poor patients: "If you're wealthy, you go up to Tucson and you get a hotel. But a lot of people can't even pay for the gas to get up there."

Catholic ownership of a hospital can mean different treatment for the patients— a recent study in the journal *Women's Health Issues* found Catholic-run hospitals tended to offer different counseling and different medical remedies than secular institutions—but it can also mean different training for the doctors. Standards for training obstetricians and gynecologists include instruction on medical contraception and tubal ligations, as well as abortion techniques (although residents may opt out), but most Catholic teaching hospitals will not provide it. "Residents will have to take the time to do it as an elective, and sometimes they just end up taking one or two lectures a year on it, which really isn't adequate," says Debra Stulberg, a family physician and assistant professor at the University of Chicago Medical School.

Sometimes, the tensions are too great to resolve. The deal to bring Sierra Vista under Carondelet fell apart, following protests that Silva, working with MergerWatch and the National Women's Law Center, helped lead. In December, the governor of Kentucky, acting on the recommendation of his attorney general and in response to community lobbying, rejected a proposed merger that would have put two major hospitals under the control of a Colorado-based Catholic hospital system. Not long after, Catholic Healthcare West, a network of 38 hospitals, voluntarily severed ties with the Church and renamed itself "Dignity Health."

But sometimes institutions have been able to reconcile religion and medicine with creative solutions. When a secular hospital in Kingston, New York, merged with a Catholic institution, in effect reducing the community's hospitals from three to two, administrators set up a separate maternity unit in the parking lot. It provides a full range of reproductive services, including abortion. In Troy, New York, leaders of a newly merged secular-Catholic hospital came up with a different solution: The maternity unit operates on the second floor, as a "hospital within the hospital"— complete with its own financial operations.

These distinctions may seem artificial or meaningless, which is precisely what some people have said about President Obama's proposal for contraception coverage. Under that proposal, insurers are supposed to provide coverage of birth control directly to the employees of institutions who believe contraception is a sin. Although it satisfied some of the critics, like Sister Carol, it infuriated critics like columnist Charles Krauthammer, who called it "an accounting trick." But what's the alternative? For better or worse, the government depends on Catholic hospitals to provide vital services—and the hospitals depend on the government for money to provide them. Convoluted solutions may be the only way for this convoluted mix of public purpose and private institution to survive.

Jonathan Cohn is a senior editor at The New Republic. *This article, which was first published on tnr.com, later appeared in the March 15, 2012, issue of the magazine.*

New Poll: Even Religious Voters Overwhelmingly Want Candidates to Debate Science

By Shawn Lawrence Otto
Neorenaissance, April 3, 2012

"Whenever the people are well informed," Thomas Jefferson wrote, "they can be trusted with their own government." But what happens now, two centuries later, when science has become so complex and so powerful that it influences every aspect of life, while most politicians' last science class was in high school? Are the people still well-enough informed to be trusted with their own government?

This is the subject of my new book, *Fool Me Twice*. But it's also the subject of a larger conflict over the nature and role of government, and the role of science as the best basis for determining public policy that is fairest to all Americans.

Every major policy challenge the United States is facing today is either wholly or partly driven by science, and yet this year in particular we have seen every mainstream candidate for president adopt one or more positions that run contrary to the best available evidence science has to offer.

This isn't just a Republican problem. The current president has also taken policy positions that run contrary to advice from scientists on bipartisan panels, such as his position restricting the over-the-counter sale of the emergency contraceptive known as Plan B.

Many of the campaign season's most memorable moments—from Michele Bachmann's campaign-ending assertion that HPV vaccine causes mental retardation, to Rick Perry's comparing himself to Galileo, to Mitt Romney' flip-flop on global warming, to Jon Huntsman's tweet heard round the world, to more by Newt Gingrich and Rick Santorum, all seem to be pivoting on science.

Why? The conventional political wisdom is that Evangelical voters and Tea Party libertarians, who form large portions of the American voting block and even larger portions of the new Republican base, are increasingly anti-science, in the words of Jon Huntsman. In other words, you can't run from anti-science and hope to get nominated or even elected president, as Huntsman himself seemed to demonstrate.

Democratic campaign operatives seem to agree with this view. Stunningly, in 2008 the candidates for president twice turned down a nationally televised science debate, but twice participated in nationally televised faith forums—one at Messiah

College in Harrisburg, Pennsylvania, between Clinton and Obama, and one at Saddleback Church in Lake Forest, California, between McCain and Obama.

At the time, campaign operatives told me that they thought science was a "niche debate," with few voters interested in it and too much to lose. I explained that we weren't interested in whether they could name the third digit of pi—we wanted to know where they stood on the big science issues that affect everyone's lives. Still they wouldn't do it. But when Obama and McCain did eventually answer our questions online, it made more than 850 million media impressions—hardly a niche topic. But they wouldn't do it on TV.

So this year I and my colleagues at ScienceDebate.org decided to test the prevailing political wisdom. We worked with our friends at Research! America and commissioned JZ Analytics, with Senior Analyst John Zogby, to do a national poll on American's attitudes about faith and science. The results were stunning.

It turns out that the presidential campaign staffers have it completely, one hundred and eighty degrees wrong when it comes to science—maybe because most of them skipped science classes in college and went into things like law and journalism.

Overwhelming majorities of American voters want the candidates to debate the big science issues facing the country. In fact, overwhelming majorities of *religious* voters want the candidates to debate these big science issues. For Pete's sake, even overwhelming majorities of *born again religious voters* want the candidates to do this, and rank it as *even more important* than their debating faith and values.

How could this be? It's possible that many in journalism and the political class, who largely come out of the humanities and ducked college science classes, believe Americans aren't interested in science because they themselves aren't interested. This is called the confirmation bias. But it's just simply wrong.

Or maybe it's because scientists have been silent in the public dialogue for so long—about two generations—that politicians wrongfully assume the public doesn't care about American science or engineering as public values or part of our national dialogue. Wrong again.

And not only wrong—but bad for America. To arrive at balanced public policy, America needs a plurality of voices in the public dialogue: foreign relations, business, religion and science, and the overwhelming majority of likely voters want the candidates to engage on the topics of healthcare, climate change, energy, education, and innovation and the economy.

They also say they want public policies to be based on the best available science, not the personal opinions or beliefs of elected officials. This indicates a certain willingness to tolerate views one might not fully personally agree with in order to achieve the fairest outcome for all Americans. That used to be a cherished American value, but these days it's something you don't hear very often in the press.

These same voters say it's wrong for elected officials to hold back, alter, or disregard scientific reports if they conflict with their own views. Surprisingly, eighty-three percent of Republicans feel this way, while just seventy-five percent of Democrats do. This suggests mainstream Republican voters may be unhappy with Republican politicians who deny the conclusions of mainstream science on topics like climate change, HPV vaccine, and the like.

Americans also seem to be heavily weighing alternative energy and want the federal government to be spending more on alternative energy research. Fifty-three percent of all likely US voters rank developing alternative energy as a top US spending priority, second only to paying down the federal deficit. This is about twice the number of voters that think

It's possible that many in journalism and the political class, who largely come out of the humanities and ducked college science classes, believe Americans aren't interested in science because they themselves aren't interested. This is called the confirmation bias. But it's just simply wrong.

the government is not spending enough on national defense. Funding science and math education came in fourth, just behind investing in roads and bridges, and scientific research was fifth.

The survey reveals deep concerns among Americans about their country's ability to maintain leadership in science. Just forty-two percent of likely voters believe the United States will remain the world leader in science just eight years from now. Isn't that worth a debate? Eighty-five percent of voters are concerned that an uncertain future for science funding in the US will cause scientists to leave their jobs or move to other countries, but the candidates aren't talking about it much.

Voters also think candidates for congress should participate in science debates—this would seem to be a no-brainer since this is where the legislation to tackle the country's major challenges is supposed to originate.

Thomas Jefferson thought it would require "no very high degree" of education for voters to discern their own best interests. In 1787 he wrote to James Madison:

> And say, finally, whether peace is best preserved by giving energy to the government, or information to the people. This last is the most certain, and the most legitimate engine of government. Educate and inform the whole mass of the people. Enable them to see that it is their interest to preserve peace and order, and they will preserve them. And it requires no very high degree of education to convince them of this. They are the only sure reliance for the preservation of our liberty.

Today, we live in a different world. Science has grown so advanced and its ability to amplify the power of the individual has grown so profound that there is a much higher burden of education and responsibility placed upon the individual than there was in Jefferson's time. Both democracy and the environment are threatened by this gap.

US voters seem intrinsically to recognize the importance of such a discussion. The least the candidates for president could do is submit to the will of the people, and participate in a nationally televised presidential science debate to discuss the real challenges facing the nation and, directly or indirectly, affecting the lives of each of her citizens. Such an historic recognition could be just what the country needs to climb out of its tailspin of loudly asserted rhetoric and reengage in evidence-based problem-solving, the way Jefferson envisioned it would.

How Science Can Lead the Way

What We Lose When We Put Faith over Logic

By Lisa Randall
Time, October 3, 2011

Today's politicians seem more comfortable invoking God and religion than they do presenting facts or numbers. Of course, everyone is entitled to his or her own religious beliefs. But when science and reason get shortchanged, so does America's future. With science, we put together observations with explanatory frameworks whose predictions can be tested and ultimately agreed on. Empirically based logic and the revelatory nature of faith are very different methods for seeking answers, and only logic can be systematically improved and applied. As we head toward the next election, it's important to keep an eye on how our political leaders view science and its advances, because their attitudes frequently mirror their approaches toward rational decision-making itself.

When Rick Perry, who defends teaching creationism in school, says evolution is merely "a theory that's out there, it's got some gaps in it," he's demonstrating a fundamental misunderstanding of scientific theory. And when he chooses to pray for the end of a drought rather than critically evaluate climate science, he is displaying the danger of replacing rational approaches with religion in matters of public policy. Logic tries to resolve paradoxes, whereas much of religious thought thrives on them. Adherents who want to accept both religious influences on the world and scientific explanations for its workings are obliged to confront the chasm between tangible effects and unseen, imperceptible influences that is unbridgeable by logical thought. They have no choice but to admit the inconsistency—or simply overlook the contradiction.

What we are seeing in the current presidential race is not so much a clash between religion and science as a fundamental disregard for rational and scientific thinking. All but two of the Republican front runners won't even consider that man-made global warming might be causing climate change, despite a great deal of evidence that it is. We know CO_2 warms the planet through the greenhouse effect, and we know humans have created a huge increase in CO_2 in the atmosphere by burning coal and oil. That man-made climate change is not proved with 100% certainty does not justify its dismissal.

In fact, an important part of science is understanding uncertainty. When scientists say we know something, we mean we have tested our ideas with a degree of accuracy over a range of scales. Scientists also address the limitations of their

> *Adherents who want to accept both religious influences on the world and scientific explanations for its workings are obliged to confront the chasm between tangible effects and unseen, imperceptible influences that is unbridgeable by logical thought. They have no choice but to admit the inconsistency—or simply overlook the contradiction.*

theories and define and try to extend the range of applicability. When the method is applied properly, the right results emerge over time.

Public policy is more complicated than clean and controlled experiments, but considering the large and serious issues we face—in the economy, in the environment, in our health and well-being—it's our responsibility to push reason as far as we can. Far from being isolating, a rational, scientific way of thinking could be unifying. Evaluating alternative strategies; reading data, when available, either in the U.S. or other countries, about the relative effectiveness of various policies; and understanding uncertainties—all features of the scientific method—can help us find the right way forward.

In 2009 I testified at a congressional hearing about the importance of basic science—something the Obama Administration made a focal point after years of unscientific and sometimes antiscientific policies by the Bush Administration. The hearing was in a room dedicated to the House Committee on Science, Space and Technology in the Rayburn House Office Building. As I looked over the heads of the seated Representatives, I saw a plaque that read, WHERE THERE IS NO VISION, THE PEOPLE PERISH. It is a noble and accurate sentiment to display, and its origin is Proverbs 29: 18.

Randall, one of 2007's TIME 100, is a professor of physics at Harvard and the author of Knocking on Heaven's Door: How Physics and Scientific Thinking Illuminate the Universe and the Modern World.

A Day in Heaven

By Joe Murphy
The Humanist, May 2011

It's a beautiful day in heaven, as all days are. Renowned scientists and mathematicians are lodged here, in a special section of paradise (and quite a few engineers have managed to infiltrate down through the eons.)

On this particular day a visitor might note several ethereal residents floating around in a cloud-speckled field of blue. This particular group includes: Eratosthenes, who measured the circumference of earth with a stick, the sun, and a deep well; Galileo Galilei, who made his own telescopes, defined the early solar system, and founded the science of mechanics; Marie Curie (Madame, if you please); Isaac Newton; Albert Einstein; and Michael Faraday, among many others. The last is sitting on a small, comfortable cloud relating an anecdote about a nearsighted laboratory assistant and his misadventure with a visiting dignitary's hat that he mistook for a storage vessel for spent acids.

As he approaches his punchline, the authoritative voice of Saint Peter reverberates across the sky. As the official gatekeeper and majordomo of the Kingdom, Peter carries a lot of clout.

In a roaring baritone, Peter bellows out: "All right, you people! I've had it with you. Some of you have been hanging around here for over a thousand years and all you do is loaf and tell jokes. Also, I haven't seen a lot of you at heavenly choir practice lately. There are big problems down on earth, what with the planet heating up and the demand for energy outpacing its supply. If something isn't done about it, everybody down there will die. That would give us an overload problem here that we couldn't handle. The boss is calling for a Cosmic-Council Conclave to vote appropriations to finance expansion of our facilities. The other place, down below, will be facing a similar problem housing their share of the crowd. The boss wants several of you to form an ad hoc committee to come up with some ideas to solve earth's problems. Some of you will probably have to go down there for a closer look. I'll arrange travel documents and passes. Let me know what you come up with, so I can brief the boss. You know where to find me—in the little house by the pearly gates."

Newton: "It appears that master Peter is having a problem with his liver again."

Galileo (a contentious and cranky old codger—you'd be too if you'd been interviewed by the Inquisition on their executive model rack): "The last time he got this way, we all caught . . ."

"Don't use that word around here!" bellows Peter.

Galileo: "I don't think there's going to be a quick fix on this one."

Marie Curie, who has a flair for organization, suggests a meeting of all several million scientists currently registered in heaven. Her organizational skills don't include practicality.

Newton: "Marie, by the time everyone gets to speak, we'll be well past final judgment day." (Newton, standing in his seventeenth-century hose, velvet doublet, and pleated collar strongly resembles a figure from a deck of playing cards. Peter once suggested that he wear a linen gown like most of the other inhabitants. But Newton wouldn't hear of it and insisted that what he'd worn on earth should be quite acceptable in the hereafter.)

"Besides, Wolfgang Pauli was telling me the other day that he was thoroughly convinced that his famous Exclusion Principle applies to heavenly beings on the astral plane as well as to the electrons in an atom. Be that so, it might be impossible to crowd all those souls into one heavenly system. Let us study the problem from our perspective and come up with a few possible solutions. *The London Times* should have some pertinent information. Let's send one of the cherubs down to fetch a copy. Louis, you pay the angel for the paper and be sure to give him a tip."

Louis de Broglie (Nobel Prize winner and legitimate pretender to the Bourbon throne of France): "Why do I always get stuck with the bill?"

Faraday: "Because you owned your own castle in the middle of the Seine. Besides, you won your Nobel Prize for something you wrote in your Ph.D. dissertation—which no one else has ever done."

De Broglie: "Does that mean that I'm made of money?"

Newton: "Yes."

Einstein: "Why not get some input from two of our youngest members: Evariste Galois and Neils Abel. As you all know, Galois was killed in a duel at age twenty, soon after he'd created the mathematical field of group theory and before he could possibly solve the quintic equation problem that has baffled mathematicians for centuries."

"Big deal," mutters Galileo.

"Shut up," whispers Curie.

"As I was about to say, before being so rudely interrupted," continues Einstein, "Young Abel died of starvation and tuberculosis before he could win acclaim for his proof that the quintic equation couldn't be solved by formula. These two may have a fresh outlook on the situation."

Enrico Fermi: "No matter how you slice this loaf of bread, it's going to involve atomic energy. I didn't work myself to death at an early age so my achievement of nuclear fission would be junked because the corporate hyenas and their bought-and-paid-for politicians tried to exploit it for quick profit before all aspects such as waste disposal and effective safety procedures were worked out. I have an idea about deactivating radioactive waste using some of the energy released by the fission."

"By recycling just a small portion of the energy now wasted by inadequate insulation, most if not all of these troublesome radioactive isotopes could be accelerated along their normal decay paths to their final, natural, nonradioactive states, such as lead."

Walther Nernst: "Yes, but what about the second law of thermodynamics?"

Fermi: "You and Nicholas Carnot did a fine job of defining entropy, Walther, but you have trouble applying it. The radioactive wastes won't be restored to their original forms but will be accelerated along to their final, natural end-products: non-radioactive, non-harmful to man. What would have taken thousands of years will be achieved in minutes, days, or perhaps weeks.

"This nontoxic trash could be placed anywhere without radiation danger to anyone. We might even be able to fill in some of the potholes in the American interstate system. Something the politicians are doing nothing about."

Faraday: "Enrico, you know it is improper to make political statements or to voice such agenda here."

A slight rumble comes from the sky. Newton: "It appears that 'evolution' is still a bad word around here." Fermi: "It wasn't a very loud rumble, perhaps the word is gaining acceptance."

Fermi: "There can be no technical fix without first a political one, for the simple reason that the politicians control the money. And they in turn are controlled by the for-profit corporations. Unless they get their hands on it, somehow, nothing will happen."

Curie: "The world's two biggest polluters, China and the United States, are controlled by small, elite segments of their respective populations: in China a self-serving bureaucracy—in the United States, self-serving corporate executives."

Galileo: "The rotten selfish bastards." (A clap of thunder sounds.)

Authoritarian voice: "Watch your language."

Galileo: "Sorry, boss."

Curie: "It seems there can be no scientific fix until the dual cancers of corporate greed and political corruption are eliminated."

Edward Jenner (the "Father of Immunology"): "Perhaps if the world went back to single-celled life-forms without the corrupt and deviant human species—he who fouls his own environment as well as those of all other lifeforms—the next time around evolution might produce a dominant form that's more in line with reality."

A slight rumble comes from the sky.

Newton: "It appears that 'evolution' is still a bad word around here."

Fermi: "It wasn't a very loud rumble, perhaps the word is gaining acceptance."

Faraday: "It's important that we establish an agenda before we go flying down to earth. We must appraise the problem before we apprise the Boss."

Galileo: "What are we going to do about the politicians and their corporate bosses?"

Curie: "To recite our not well-established mantra, 'If there is to be a technical fix, it must be implemented through a political fix.'"

Thomas Edison: "I wonder if Elizabeth I had any idea what a monster she was unleashing on the world when she issued the first patents of corporation to the Honorable East India Opium and Tea Company."

Newton: "'Tis a sad state, but we must get around it."

Nernst: "In the nineteenth century, when Mount Krakatau detonated, a lot of debris was blasted into the stratosphere. For five years much of it remained aloft, reflecting sunlight back into space. The result was some of the coolest years experienced in modern times. If we could use hydrogen bombs to trigger off a string of volcanoes along the earth's equator, we might be able to cool down the planet until a permanent fix can be made."

Curie: "Walther, stick to thermodynamics."

Galileo: "To get back to my point: It won't do a bit of good to talk to the politicians unless we offer them something. Currently, systems are so corrupt, at least one of them has gone so far as to give the instruments of the very wealthy—that is, corporations—legal personhood. This way, when corporate executives do something criminal, they can hide behind the corporation that takes the blame, gets slapped on the wrist, and gets fined some paltry amount."

Joseph Priestly (controversial clergyman and chemist): "I must echo Isaac's lament, 'tis a sad affair. I was chased out of England and my house burned to the ground because I said that English coal miners should be treated with respect and their labors fairly rewarded."

"I ended up in the colonies, where I met and befriended Thomas Jefferson and Benjamin Franklin. While living in the colony of Pennsylvania I performed my experiments by means of which I discovered anti-phlogiston, which most people now call oxygen, except the Germans, who call it Sauerstoff. I too agree that a technical solution won't work until the power brokers and the politicians they own allow it. That won't happen until the corporation can exploit it for quick profit, which of course would be done in the cheapest possible way—probably causing more economic and environmental damage than before."

Fermi: "On a technical note, in 1956 Alvarez and Teller published a little-noticed letter in *Physical Reviews* describing the fusion of two deuterium atoms in the gas phase. The electrons in these atoms had been replaced by two negatively charged mesons (pions); an enormous amount of energy was released, which could probably be controlled. If the pions could be produced economically, this could be the key to almost unlimited energy. But it's back to the politicians, as always."

Evariste Galois: "I got killed in a stupid duel over a woman I didn't even like. I will estimate the temperature changes on earth that will result if the planet's tilt is changed slightly by the judicious application of hydrogen bombs so that . . ."

Galileo: "Nonsense. If anything, the average temperature would increase and the tilt would have to be changed every six months."

Galois: "It was just a thought."

Galileo: "Not a very good one."

Ferdinand de Lesseps: "I discovered certain things about cloud formations above construction sites and how they moderated temperatures when I was building the Panama Canal. If that bastard Teddy Roosevelt [sky rumbles again] hadn't interfered and stirred up resistance among the indigenous people, I would have completed the canal and worked out the weather patterns. Of course, yellow fever and those gutless financiers withdrawing their support because Teddy huffed and puffed had a lot to do with my failure."

Faraday: "I never dreamed I would say it, but we must bribe the politicians—offer them something the corporations can't."

Curie: "What are you talking about?"

Faraday: "You're standing on it. Or perhaps I should say floating in it. We all know that a great many politicians never end up here; they often go to the other place, along with greedy corporate executives and lobbyist-bagmen. Let us get authority from the boss to offer key politicians access to heaven, if they play ball with us on our agenda."

Newton: "Good! It's settled then. First we get Peter to intercede about immigration quotas for politicians. Then some of us should go down to the hot place to get input from the pols down there. We'll need fireproof passports and refrigerated space suits."

All: "Let's go!"

Joe Murphy, PhD, is a former research chemist and one-time disc jockey who says he grew up oblivious to the desperation and financial devastation wreaked by corporate game-play. In retirement he's discovered two things about himself: 1) He hates television and 2) he's a lot more liberal—politically and socially—than he used to be. Ultimately both factors have steered him toward writing.

Some Ojibwe Tribal Members Object to Wolf Hunting, Trapping

By Tom Robertson
Minnesota Public Radio, March 13, 2012

White Earth Indian Reservation, Minnesota—Some Ojibwe in Minnesota are worried about the fate of the state's wolf population as state lawmakers consider a hunting and trapping season for the animals.

Wolves were removed from the federal endangered species list last year, and that upsets some tribal members. For many Ojibwe, wolves are important to traditional culture. Some believe wolves are sacred, and they want to see protections continue.

A painting of two wolves hangs prominently on the living room wall in Mary Favorite's home in Wauben on the White Earth Indian Reservation.

Favorite is a tribal elder and a member of the wolf clan. That means many in her large, extended family associate themselves very closely with the animal. Favorite considers wolves among her relatives.

"It's very special to me. When I read that in the paper that they were thinking about . . . passing a law about killing the wolves," Favorite said. "It broke my heart."

Favorite remembers decades ago when gray wolves nearly disappeared. Now there are an estimated 3,000 gray wolves in Minnesota.

The Department of Natural Resources proposes to let hunters and trappers kill 400 wolves this fall. Favorite hates the idea.

"I thought, 'Oh my God,'" she said. "It's like they want to come in here and they want to shoot my brothers and my sisters."

It's not just members of the wolf clan who are upset about a possible wolf hunting season. Favorite's husband, Andy, is a historian and retired tribal college teacher. For traditional Ojibwe across the upper Midwest, wolves are sacred, Andy Favorite said.

"In our creation stories and a lot of our other legends, the wolf is very prominent. A lot of our spirits come in the form of these creatures, so it's a very spiritual thing," he said. "If the tribes have the spiritual moxie, they will step in and do something to protect the wolves."

Some Minnesota tribes have already done that. In 2010, the Red Lake Band of Ojibwe was the first to adopt a wolf management plan. They designated the band's 843,000 acres of land as a wolf sanctuary.

Red Lake is unique because it's considered a closed reservation. That means most of the land is owned and controlled by the tribe.

In most of Minnesota's other reservations, regulating hunting is more complicated because there's a checkerboard of land ownership. Those tribes regulate what happens on tribal land, but the state regulates hunting licenses for state land or land owned by non–American Indians.

> *"Indians and wolves have always been a political sore point here in America," [tribal activist Bob Shimek] said. "It has always been about clearing the howling wilderness of those savages and those wolves and making it safe for pilgrims and settlers."*

In February, tribal officials at White Earth passed a resolution banning hunting and trapping on tribal lands. The tribe will only allow a wolf hunt for specific ceremonial purposes, or if wolves are causing problems with livestock or humans. Tribal natural resource managers said it's unclear how many wolves are on the reservation, but there are only a few known packs.

Other Minnesota tribes are drafting their own wolf policies.

Tribal activist Bob Shimek has been involved in the politics of wolves since the 1980s. He said many Ojibwe people believe there is a strong historic parallel between wolves and Indians that has been foretold in tribal legends—what happens to one, happens to the other. He compares bounties on wolves to government policies of the past that tried to exterminate American Indians.

"Indians and wolves have always been a political sore point here in America," he said. "It has always been about clearing the howling wilderness of those savages and those wolves and making it safe for pilgrims and settlers."

Shimek and others are unhappy the state has not consulted with the tribes about managing wolves.

DNR officials say they plan to talk with the tribes once the Legislature establishes a framework for a hunting season. Dan Stark, a large carnivore specialist for the DNR, said the goal is to balance wide-ranging interests in wolves. Farmers and ranchers who lose livestock to wolves support keeping the wolf population in check. In 2011, there were more than 100 verified complaints of wolves attacking livestock or pets.

There are also sporting groups that want a chance to hunt or trap wolves for recreation, Stark said.

"It's a pretty emotional topic for a lot of people," Stark said. "But I think that the wolf population in Minnesota is secure and we're going to make sure that however this develops, that we have wolves in the state and that wolves continue to thrive."

For Shimek, convincing the state to scrap plans for wolf hunting and trapping is an uphill battle.

"I honestly believe that a thousand Indians could show up in St. Paul to testify against this wolf legislation and it would not matter one single bit in terms of the outcome," Shimek said. "That's just the nature of politics."

On Thursday, Shimek and others at White Earth will begin a series of public education "wolf talks" on the reservation, although opposition to a wolf hunting season has not seemed to slow the bills that are advancing through the Legislature.

4

Evolution and Public Education

A sixth-grade science class in Wellsville, New York. The teaching of evolution continues to generate vehement debate on the authority of science and the place of creationism in the classroom. The most recent debates center on the scientific legitimacy of intelligent design.

Evolution in the Classroom:
From Monkey Laws to Intelligent Design

By Paul McCaffrey

On March 21, 1925, Governor Austin Peay of Tennessee signed the Butler Act into law. Otherwise known as the Tennessee Anti-Evolution Act or the Tennessee Monkey Law, the measure outlawed in all publicly-funded state schools the teaching of "any theory that denies the story of the Divine Creation of man as taught in the Bible, and to teach instead that man has descended from a lower order of animals." In addition, the act mandated a fine of between $100 and $500 for each offense on anyone who taught such material. Named for and written by Representative John Washington Butler, the bill had been passed by overwhelming margins in both houses of the Tennessee state legislature: The state house of representatives approved it by a vote of 71 to 5, and the state senate by a vote of 24 to 6. Though it had been over sixty years since Charles Darwin's initial introduction of the theory of evolution with his publication of *On the Origin of Species*, the Tennessee statute was the first anti-evolution measure enacted in the United States.

Questioning the law's constitutionality, the American Civil Liberties Union (ACLU) sought to challenge it in court. The ACLU set out to find someone in Tennessee willing to admit to teaching evolution in the public schools and to stand as a defendant in the case. Hearing of the ACLU's search, George Rappleyea, a resident of Dayton, Tennessee, met with community leaders, among them the schools' superintendent Walter White, in a local drug store on May 5, 1925. Opposed to the Butler Act, Rappleyea explained that challenging the law in Dayton could end up being a boon for the town. He said the national interest created by the story would help local businesses and earn Dayton some much-needed publicity.

Rappleyea made a strong case, and the town leaders agreed to pursue the matter. They subsequently invited John Scopes, a young science teacher and football coach, to talk with them. While filling in as a substitute for a biology teacher, Scopes told Rappleyea and his associates that he had taught from the state-approved biology textbook, *Hunter's Civic Biology*, which had a section on evolutionary theory. Based on that, the Dayton notables determined that Scopes had probably violated the law; Scopes said that he would be willing to go on trial for the offense in order to bring down the Butler Act. Soon after, on May 25, he was indicted by a Dayton grand jury.

After considerable preparation, on July 10, 1925, *The State of Tennessee v. John Thomas Scopes*, popularly known as the Scopes Monkey Trial, commenced at the Rhea County Courthouse in Dayton. A circus-like atmosphere reigned as spectators and journalists from across the country came to town to witness the proceedings, broadcast throughout the world via radio, telegraph, and movie reels. Scopes's defense team was led by the legendary attorney Clarence Darrow, and the prosecution by William Jennings Bryan, three-time Democratic presidential candidate and former secretary of state.

Following three days of jury selection, the trial began. The dueling attorneys laid out the magnitude of the case. Speaking for the state, Bryan claimed that "if evolution wins, Christianity goes," while on behalf of the defendant, Darrow stated, "Scopes isn't on trial; civilization is on trial," and called on Judge John Raulston to declare the Butler Act unconstitutional.

Two days later, on July 15, Judge Raulston upheld the constitutionality of the law, stating that it "gives no preference to any particular religion or mode of worship." Subsequently, after entering a not-guilty plea on behalf of Scopes, the defense called a zoologist who told the court that evolution was not a controversial doctrine among the biologists of the day and was widely accepted in the scientific community. Soon after, ruling on a motion by the prosecution, Raulston decided to bar this testimony, stating that the question before the court was not whether evolution had a scientific basis but whether Scopes taught evolution in violation of state law.

The drama climaxed on July 20, when Darrow called Bryan to testify. Bryan willingly took the stand to answer questions based on his knowledge of the Bible, setting up one of the most storied exchanges in legal history. The confrontation took place outside, the sweltering summer heat having persuaded Raulston to move the trial there. Inquiring about the account of creation in Genesis, Jonah and the whale, and other biblical narratives, Darrow sought to pin Bryan down on whether the Bible ought to be taken literally. The two clashed, with the avowed agnostic Darrow criticizing Bryan, telling him, "You insult every man of science and learning in the world because he does not believe in your fool religion." Bryan accused Darrow of attempting to "slur at the Bible," and declared, "I want the Christian world to know that any atheist, agnostic, unbeliever, can question me anytime as to my belief in God, and I will answer him." Despite Bryan's best efforts, the conventional assessment of the exchange is that Darrow got the better of it, with some accounts suggesting that Bryan embarrassed himself.

The next day, the trial concluded. Intent on having the law declared unconstitutional rather than getting Scopes acquitted, Darrow encouraged the court to find his client guilty so that the defense could appeal the decision. After nine minutes of deliberation, the jury complied and Judge Raulston ordered Scopes to pay a fine of $100. After his sentencing, Scopes addressed the court, stating that he would continue "to oppose this law in any way I can. Any other action would be in violation of my ideal of academic freedom—that is, to teach the truth as guaranteed in our constitution, of personal and religious freedom."

Scopes's appeal was heard by the Tennessee Supreme Court, which rendered its ruling on January 15, 1927. The court upheld the Butler Act's constitutionality but overturned Scopes's conviction. According to the court, the jury, not Judge Raulston, ought to have been tasked with determining the fine.

Based on Darrow's dramatic questioning of Bryan, the Scopes trial has often been interpreted as a victory for science over religious fundamentalism and of evolution over creationism. But the outcome did not make it any easier to teach evolution in Tennessee schools. Indeed, the Butler Act stayed on the books in the state for the next forty-two years and was not repealed until 1967. Moreover, other states passed similar statutes. Mississippi forbade teaching evolution in the classroom in 1926 and Arkansas followed suit in 1928. Soon, textbook companies began avoiding explicit mention of evolution in their scientific volumes to steer clear of any potential controversy.

Following the repeal of the Butler Act, how the legal system approached evolution in education started to shift. In 1968, in the case of *Epperson v. Arkansas*, the US Supreme Court unanimously overturned Arkansas's anti-evolution law, with seven justices ruling that it violated the Establishment Clause in the First Amendment to the Constitution, which reads, "Congress shall make no law respecting an establishment of religion."

These legal setbacks led evolution skeptics in the state legislatures to revise their tactics. Since outlawing the teaching of evolution in the schools had been ruled unconstitutional, some states enacted statutes requiring that evolution and creationism be taught side by side. In Tennessee, for example, just six years after repealing the Butler Act, the state passed a law mandating that any biology textbook used in the state's schools—if it dealt with evolution and other theories about the origins of humanity and the world—had to note that they were only theories and should not be construed as fact. In addition, the volumes had to place "equal emphasis on . . . other theories, including but not limited to, the Genesis account in the Bible." Like the Butler Act before it, the 1973 law was challenged in the courts, and in 1975, in the case of *Daniel v. Waters*, the law was struck down as unconstitutional in US District Court for violating the Establishment Clause.

The Tennessee law in *Daniel v. Waters* had a broader influence than the Butler Act. It did not just address evolution—how humans and other species developed—but also how the world was created. This is an important distinction. In 1961, John C. Whitcomb and Henry M. Morris authored *The Genesis Flood*, in which they marshaled evidence to suggest that Noah's flood did in fact occur. From this, they turned to the geological age of the earth. Scientific research had established that the world was quite a bit older than a literal interpretation of biblical accounts would seem to indicate. But Morris and Whitcomb made the case for a "young earth," theorizing that the planet was not as old as mainstream geologists thought, but could very well be as young as a strict reading of Genesis would imply.

The Genesis Flood marked the emergence of creation science, a movement that seeks to provide scientific support for the Bible's account of creation and to refute Darwinian evolution and other theories that conflict with creationism. Morris went on to found the Institute for Creation Research in 1970 to foster the effort. As laws meant to counter evolution in the classroom fell to legal challenges, whether in *Daniel v. Waters* or *Epperson v. Arkansas*, some state lawmakers turned to creation science as a way to offer a counternarrative to evolution. In 1981, the state of Louisiana passed the Balanced Treatment for Creation-Science and Evolution-Science in Public School Instruction Act. Also known as the Creationism Act, this measure mandated "equal time" for instruction in evolution and creation science. Arkansas passed a similar statute, Act 590, the same year. Act 590 was overturned in the US District Court the following year. Like its predecessors, Act 590, the judge determined, violated the Establishment Clause. In 1987, the Supreme Court ruled on the Louisiana law in the case of *Edwards v. Aguillard*, declaring that the statute was religiously motivated and thus did not adhere to the Establishment Clause either.

Again, the courtroom defeats did not deter evolution opponents. In *Of Pandas and People* (1989), Percival Davis and Dean H. Kenyon offered a critique of evolution and proposed that the complexity of biology and biological processes is evidence of "intelligent design" in the universe and an intelligent designer, presumably God. The next year, in 1990, the Discovery Institute was founded and soon became a leading proponent of intelligent design (ID) as an alternative to evolution. One of its major campaigns, Teach the Controversy, encouraged schools to inform students of the alleged shortcomings and criticisms of evolutionary theory.

In later clashes over evolution in the classrooms, the states, which had led the opposition since the Butler Act, took a back seat to local school boards. Certainly, some states have required that disclaimers be read to students instructing them to be critical in their analysis of evolution. Others mandate such statements accompany science textbooks. Still, these measures, some of which have fallen to court challenge, are a far cry from earlier outright bans or "equal time" provisions.

Across the nation, ID has become a new means of challenging evolution, with its proponents characterizing it as a competing theory. School boards have sought to introduce ID material into their science curricula. These efforts, like earlier state initiatives, have not fared well in the courts. In the 2004 case of *Kitzmiller v. Dover Area School District*, a federal judge struck down a Pennsylvania school board's requirement that ID be featured in the biology programs at public high schools. The judge concluded that "ID is not science" and is "a mere relabeling of creationism, and not a scientific theory." Based on such determinations, the judge ruled that the school board's actions had violated the Establishment Clause.

Though the Scopes Trial ended in a technical defeat for Darrow, Scopes, and the proponents of evolutionary theory, the court cases concerning evolution in education since *Epperson v. Arkansas* in 1968 have shown a remarkable about-face. Whether states or school boards sought to prevent evolution from being taught or required that instructors give "equal time" to creationism or simply make note of ID, the courts have struck them down. But while evolution has won this string of victories, it has not won over the public. In a May 2012 Gallup poll, nearly half of all Americans (46 percent) rejected evolution, stating their belief that God had created humans in their present form sometime in the past ten thousand years. Another 32 percent held the view that humans evolved over time with the guidance of a supreme being. Fifteen percent held that humans evolved as a result of natural processes only. Combined with the adaptable tactics of evolution opponents, such statistics suggest that more than a century and a half since Darwin proposed his theory and eighty-seven years after the Scopes trial, the debate over teaching evolution in schools is far from settled.

A Spiritual Approach to Evolution

By Michael Lerner
Tikkun Magazine, November 2010

Don't worry, we are not about to join the creationists with their rejection of evolution and insistence that God planted all those dinosaur bones to test your faith. The set of articles you are about to read are written by people who accept the notion that the earth evolved in the past five billion years in roughly the ways that current evolutionary biologists describe it, but some of them argue that the force driving evolution is not adequately described within the terms of contemporary scientism.

We don't expect that reading these essays is going to be easy on you. The fact is that most liberals and progressives, in fact, most people who have completed high school, have been heavily indoctrinated into the dominant religion of this historical period, the religion of scientism, and as can be expected, will feel deeply uneasy—if not feeling that they are outright disloyal—if they consider the possibility that another worldview is not only possible but plausible.

Why We Strongly Support Science

But please keep in mind that we are strongly supportive of the enterprise of science itself. Science is one of the great advances in human history, and the information it has produced through careful empirical observation and measurement has allowed us to cure many diseases, improve the material conditions of our lives, and gain insight into the complexity of the universe. Science offers us a degree of control over the natural world and hence a heightened sense of security in the face of real dangers.

We are strong believers in the need for increased funding for science and for freeing science from its current subservience to military ends (to which our government deflects scientific research by offering funding from the bloated defense department budget) and from the capitalist marketplace (which often deflects scientific research toward the needs of corporations to make short-term profits without regard to the well-being of the earth or most of its inhabitants). We advocate for more monies dedicated to environmental science, which has already helped us understand the irrationality of the current ways we treat the earth, and toward health promotion and illness prevention (including prevention of the environmental impacts by corporations that increase susceptibility to a wide variety of illnesses, including cancer and Alzheimer's disease).

Taught correctly, science can also be a stimulus to a heightened sense of awe and wonder at the grandeur and beauty of the universe. Read *The Faith of Scientists*

Michael Lerner, "A Spiritual Approach to Evolution," in *Tikkun*, Volume 25, no. 6, pp. 33–37. Copyright 2010, Tikkun Magazine. All rights reserved. Reprinted by permission of the publisher, Duke University Press. www.DukeUPress.edu

by Nancy H. Frankenberry (Princeton University Press, 2008) to get a sense of the range of scientists who have developed an inner spiritual life. As Einstein famously quipped, "Science without religion is lame; religion without science is blind." One can be a passionate advocate of science, as I am, and yet be a strong opponent of scientism, just as I am a strong advocate for the right of Jews to a state in the Middle East and yet a strong opponent of creating a religion of Zionism. It is similar to how one can be

> *Scientism thus extends science beyond its valuable role as a way to understand those parts of our world that are subject to empirical verification: it makes claims that are either dismissive or reductive of those aspects of our lives that are not subject to empirical verification or measurement.*

a strong advocate for egalitarianism and democratic control of the economy without being a communist in the sense that existed in various totalitarian societies of the twentieth century, or a strong lover of the United States without being a believer that our current economic and political system is just or desirable.

Scientism: When Science Becomes a Religion

Scientism is the belief that nothing is real and nothing can be known in the world except that which can be observed and measured. A person who adopts a scientistic perspective believes that science can in principle answer every question that can be answered. Any claim about the world that cannot be validated, at least in principle, or at least falsified on the basis of empirical data or measurement is dismissed as meaningless.

So, take a claim that we at *Tikkun* and the Network of Spiritual Progressives, our education arm, frequently make: "Caring for other people is an ethical imperative." From a scientist's perspective, this claim cannot be verified or falsified through any set of observations, so it really isn't a claim about the world at all but merely a statement of our personal tastes, choices, or proclivities. Similarly, claims about God, ethics, beauty, love, and any other facet of human experience that is not subject to empirical verification—all these spiritual dimensions of life—are dismissed by the scientistic worldview as inherently unknowable and hence nothing by which we can ever agree to run our civilization, or they are reduced to some set of observable behaviors (sexual love gets measured by erections, vaginal secretions, orgasms, or changes in brain states; and all ethical and aesthetic claims are treated in a similarly reductive way).

Scientism thus extends science beyond its valuable role as a way to understand those parts of our world that are subject to empirical verification: it makes claims that are either dismissive or reductive of those aspects of our lives that are not subject to empirical verification or measurement. Scientism makes a power jump, appropriating the honorable associations of the word "know" to a narrowly constructed definition and thereby excluding all kinds of knowledge labeled as "merely subjective," which it deems inappropriate for public discourse. Over the course of several centuries of modernity, scientism not only redefined knowledge, it also built economic, educational, and political institutions that accepted this understanding of knowledge. These institutions proceeded to impose the religion of scientism on most thinking people, leaving resistance to it in the hands of those who had little respect for intellectual life and who could thereby be ridiculed as fundamentalist know-nothings.

Thus scientism became the dominant religion of the contemporary Western world, and increasingly of the entire world. Yet it is a belief system that has no more scientific foundation than any other religious system. Consider its central religious belief: "That which is real and can be known is that which can be verified or falsified by empirical observation." The claim sounds tough-minded and rational, but what scientific experiment could you perform to prove that it is either true or false? The fact is that there is no such test. By its own criterion, scientism is as meaningless as any other metaphysical claim.

Secular people frequently respond by saying that scientism is simply what it is to be rational in the modern world. But spiritual people respond by saying: Why should we adopt that particular standard of rationality? Is there some scientific test that can prove that this is indeed the rational way to think? Absolutely not. Even the view that "one should not multiply entities beyond necessity"—a view that early scientists took from William of Occam, whose famous "razor" makes the correct point that, when doing science, one should seek the simplest possible explanation of a phenomenon—has no empirical foundation beyond the enterprise of science. It is not a guide to how to live or to define rationality.

If scientism appears intuitive to many, it is largely because we live in a society where this is the dominant religious belief. In fact, we even describe ideas that are of no intellectual value as "non-sense" (that is, without foundation in sense data) and ideas that are obvious to everyone as "common sense" (as though all that can be shared knowledge comes from our sensations). We don't notice these peculiar usages, because that's what it means to be part of a religious system—its peculiar ideas suddenly seem so obvious that we can only shake our heads in disbelief that anyone would think something else.

I actually don't believe most scientists are believers in scientism. But like the rest of us, they live in a society in which scientism predominates, so only the most reflective of them tend to make a point of distinguishing themselves from the dominant religion, and then usually only when they've achieved tenure or financial success and don't worry about being dismissed as a kook. For many of them, as well as for other intellectuals and members of liberal and progressive circles, the fear of the know-nothings taking over and imposing their fundamentalist perspective drives them into a vigorous piety about scientism.

Scientism and the Left

The vigorous adherence of many on the left to this religion is explained in detail in my book *The Left Hand of God: Taking Back Our Country from the Religious Right.* What is important to say here is that this dominant religion leads to a marginalization of ethical and spiritual values in the public sphere. Since those values are not verifiable through scientistic criteria, we get a bizarre distortion in our society in which professionals who bring radically caring values into their work are seen as subjective, moralizing, unprofessional, and inappropriate "ideologues" who may rightly be subject to dismissal from their work. In contrast, we spiritual progressives want a change in the public sphere so that the values we articulate as part of a New Bottom Line do in fact shape our public life together. That New Bottom Line seeks to define rationality, progress, and productivity not only in terms of things that are easy to measure or observe (money and power) but also in terms of those that cannot be measured through empirical science: love, kindness, generosity, ethically and ecologically sensitive behavior, awe and wonder at the grandeur of the universe, and caring for all people.

In *The Left Hand of God* I try to explain why so many men in liberal and progressive circles, and the women who are trying to become like them, eschew anything "soft" like values or spirituality because it makes them feel too vulnerable to the assault of right-wingers. Having grown up in a culture that validates "real men" as being tough and dominating others, these liberal and progressive men retain in their unconscious the traumatic experience of being put down as kids and called "sissies" when they showed caring for the powerless or eschewed fights and aggressive behavior. So as adults, they feel the need to show that if they are championing something "soft" like caring for others around the planet or eliminating poverty or war they will again be subject to humiliating put-downs unless they can show that they are "tough-minded"—and that translates into rejecting anything spiritual or the language of love, caring, generosity, or awe and wonder. They reject anything that can be dismissed as soft because it is not verifiable through the "hard data" of empirical science. Ironically, right-wing men have no such problem, since the policies of war and supporting the interests of the rich are already seen as tough-minded, so they have the psychic space to embrace spiritual or religious language without fear of being dismissed as "girly men" (the ultimate put-down in a male chauvinist culture).

It's an easy step from this pathological fear of softness to the head-oriented and heart-aversive and religiophobic language of the Democratic Party liberals and much of the independent Left. That's why they need spiritual progressives so badly.

Once we open the door to other approaches to the world than the one based on scientism, it becomes possible to understand the relationship between mind and body in a different way. Scientism led to two opposing views: first, the idea that the mind is nothing more than a particular arrangement of material reality; and second, a kind of dualism that radically separates mind from body and sees consciousness or mind as some kind of separately existing reality—perhaps a very ghostly reality that has nothing to do with the "hard" category of matter.

What the World Really Looks Like

I, on the other hand, view matter as a materialist construct that has no application in the real world, though it may be useful for certain approaches to science. In the real world, matter, spirit, consciousness, awareness, *nous*, and mind are all one integrated whole. Matter never exists without some level of awareness, consciousness, or yearning. All matter yearns for greater levels of interconnectedness, freedom, awareness, consciousness, love, generosity, cooperation, and beauty, and what moves evolution is this yearning of all being to be more fully actualized. Matter seeks this actualization by playfully exploring every possibility and intentionally seeking to enjoy itself through this play. And it is through this intentional play that matter ultimately discovers how to fulfill this deepest yearning. God is the totality of this process: the yearning, and the growing awareness, and the self-awareness of the universe as a whole. This view does not posit God as separate from the universe with a preexisting plan, but rather as the entirety of all that is, because there is nothing else but God—"and you shall know in your heart, that the transformative power is the ruling force of all this creation, there is nothing else" (Deuteronomy 4:39).

This view is derived from the Jewish mystical tradition known as Kabbalah, and the subsequent development of consciousness in the eighteenth- and nineteenth-century versions of Hasidism. It is no longer mainstream in contemporary Judaism, because so many Jews have abandoned God to worship the State of Israel. But it is the direction emerging from many of us in the Jewish Renewal movement, which originally played a central role in the development of *Tikkun* magazine. Jewish Renewal is also the movement in which I received my rabbinical ordination. I articulated a version of this view in my book *Jewish Renewal* (Putnam, 1994), when I described my relationship to God as analogous to a liver cell's relationship to the totality of a person's consciousness. The liver cell is not separate from the person (i.e., God), who can at times become aware of it, and the cell can receive communications from the person (within the limits of what a liver cell can receive), but the person is more than its liver cells, or any other part of its body: it is the consciousness of the totality, and yet is not constrained by the totality. I'll get back to this in the next issue of *Tikkun*.

So I strongly agree with Arthur Green that evolution of species is the greatest sacred drama of all time. But what I am adding to Green's argument is this: that what drives evolution is the spiritual yearning of all being that is manifest in every particular and that comes together as the consciousness of the entire universe. It is a yearning for greater consciousness, love, generosity, complexity, cooperation, playfulness, gratitude, and forgiveness. Of course, this is a faith statement in the same way that scientism is a faith statement—because no amount of data is ever going to conclusively prove either this view or a more materialist and mechanistic view of what drives the evolutionary process forward.

Most of the authors in this section on evolution are not rooted in that particular tradition, but some do share with Jewish mysticism this commitment to a fundamental unity of all being and a rejection of the radical disjunction between matter and spirit. As Christian de Quincey insists, consciousness (or mind or awareness) is part of every aspect of being "all the way down" to the tiniest component of being, despite the fact that such a claim is so counter to the "common sense" of post-Enlightenment thought (though not to what Dave Belden imaginatively describes from the future as the second Enlightenment in which scientism has been abandoned). It is Peter Gabel, my close friend for the past thirty-five years, and *Tikkun*'s indispensible associate editor, who takes this position and most forcefully defends the notion that evolution can best be understood as powered and directed by this spiritual aspect of all being.

I hope you'll carefully read these essays and allow yourself to imagine what the world would look like if the perspective being developed here were in fact as true as I believe it to be. And imagine how much more powerful a progressive movement would be if it considered challenging global capitalism on the grounds that it stands in conflict with the developing evolutionary consciousness of the universe and God.

Intelligent Design or Intelligible Design?

By Frederick Grinnell

The Chronicle of Higher Education, January 9, 2009

Whether the topic is embryos or evolution, religious interests sometimes try to influence how science is taught and practiced. Frequently the perceived conflict between religion and science is understood as a debate about matters of factual observation. As a philosopher friend commented, "If your religion requires six literal days of creation, then it clashes with science." I find that the difference between the claims of religion and of science can be far subtler—a reflection of distinct human attitudes toward experience based on different types of faith.

By religion, I mean William James's inclusive description—the religious attitude as belief that the world has an unseen order, coupled with the desire to live in harmony with that order. James's description encompasses what we typically call religion: communal beliefs and practices as well as spirituality, the person's individual quest for meaning through spiritual encounter with the world.

Some years ago, I heard the following example used to illustrate the ability of scientific and religious attitudes to divide the me/here/now of everyday life experience into distinct potential domains of understanding and action. Imagine walking along a beach and coming upon a large and unusual rock. Two sets of possible questions arise. First set: What kind of rock is this? How did it get here? What can be done with it? Second set: What does it mean that this rock and I are sharing the beach together at this moment in time? What can this moment (or rock) teach me about the meaning of life?

The first set represents science and technology. Knowing the answers enables the control essential to obtain and use the rock according to one's needs and desires. The second set represents religion and spirituality. It concerns the meaning and purpose of the individual and of life. If your religion requires six literal days of creation, then it clashes with science. But if your religion teaches that the unseen order of the world has purpose and meaning, then is it at odds with science?

A conventional way to contrast scientific and religious thinking attributes reason to the former and faith to the latter. That approach obscures what seems to me to be a central element in trying to understand the relationship. Science, too, requires faith. The British empiricist philosophers emphasized that point in their critique of the possibility of knowledge. We have no assurance of our own existence or of matters of fact beyond immediate sense experience and memories. The idea of cause and effect, a central tenet of scientific thinking, depends on one's belief that the course of nature will continue uniformly tomorrow the same as today, a belief that cannot be proved.

Such ideas presented a potential challenge to the development of modern science—a challenge that science ignored completely. Instead, commented Alfred North Whitehead, we have an instinctive faith in the "order of nature." Einstein described that as faith in the rationality of the world, which he attributed to the sphere of religion. How ironic! I call it faith in intelligible design—faith that nature's patterns and structures can be understood.

Those of us who practice science share a faith in intelligible design. But when we do our work, how do we go beyond the me/here/now of personal experience, along with its potential for misinterpretation, error, and self-deception? The answer is that by sharing our experiences with one another, we aim to transform personal subjectivity into communal intersubjectivity. Through that transformation, the discovery claims of individual researchers become the credible discoveries of the scientific community—knowledge good for anyone/anywhere/anytime. Of course, the credible knowledge of science always remains truth with a small "t," open to the possibility of challenge and modification in the future. Nevertheless, given the extent to which humankind has succeeded in populating and controlling the world, science's faith in intelligible design appears to be well justified.

> *Those of us who practice science share a faith in intelligible design. But when we do our work, how do we go beyond the me/here/now of personal experience, along with its potential for misinterpretation, error, and self-deception?*

Just as science requires faith, religion requires reason. A provocative image of reason in religion is the analogy pointed out by Rabbi Joseph B. Soloveitchik between the development of Jewish religious law and the formulation of a mathematical system: Validity depends on logical rules applied correctly to starting assumptions, but the starting assumptions need not be grounded in the shared experiential space in which we all live. For instance, at the time mathematicians developed non-Euclidean geometry, the world was experienced as fully Euclidean. Although science and mathematics are frequently taught together, mathematics, unlike science, is a closed, deductive system in which conclusions can be derived from assumptions even if the assumptions do not correspond to any known reality. In short, it is not the absence of reason that distinguishes religion from science, but rather the willingness to accept starting assumptions from outside of shared experiential space—James's unseen order—sometimes including the miraculous. Those starting assumptions can be found in every religion—for instance, the elaborate revelations of such great leaders as Buddha, Krishna, Moses, Jesus, and Muhammad.

Because each religion embraces a different set of revelations and assumptions about the unseen order, fragmentation is inevitable. We have not one but many unique, reasoned frameworks that provide guidance about values, meaning, and purpose of life. To maintain the differences, the religious attitude depends on a credibility process much different from that of science. Credibility in religion requires certification at the outset that an individual's insights are consistent with a particular religion's unique understanding of itself. Unlike the scientific attitude that settles for truth with a small "t," the religious attitude begins with certain everlasting Truths. Through acceptance of those Truths, an individual chooses to become part of a particular religious community.

Intelligent design offers a good example with which to distinguish faith in religion from faith in science. The ID movement has received widespread attention as a result of the legal battles over what should be taught in the science curriculum regarding evolution. The question has been turned into a political issue. Underlying the ID argument is a discovery claim called irreducible complexity, which denies the possibility of a common ancestry of life forms as described by modern evolutionary biology. ID proponents say that because of the limits imposed by irreducible complexity, the possibility of evolution depends on intervention of a hypothetical force outside the known laws of nature.

Supporters of ID are not interested in further investigation of irreducible complexity or of this hypothetical force. Instead they appear to be satisfied that they have arrived at the Truth of the matter. ID supporters would agree with Einstein about "the sublimity and marvelous order which reveal themselves both in nature and in the world of thought." However, rather than Einstein's "cosmic religious feeling but no anthropomorphic conception of God," ID supporters follow the glance of Isaiah 40:26: "Lift up your eyes on high and see: Who created these?" Whatever one might think of the merit or failure of intelligent design in terms of religion, having faith in the Truth of the matter situates the movement outside of science. Consequently, ID has no place in science education.

What is the relationship between scientific and religious attitudes when viewed as different kinds of faith? Bicycle riding frequently is offered as a metaphor to describe these attitudes as complementary. Having a bike makes riding possible. Other factors influence the direction in which the rider will choose to go. Science provides the technology for doing things. Religion provides the values to determine what things should be done. Notwithstanding the importance of the functional sense of complementary relationships implied by the bicycle metaphor, a different and more profound sense of complementary relationships can also be found.

The physicist Niels Bohr introduced complementarity in 1927 to account for the failure of classical physics to explain the nature of light. Two sets of evidence and two theories—waves and particles—had become associated with light propagation. Bohr argued that, at the quantum level, there could be no distinction between the object and the experimental circumstances that permitted the object to be observed. Unlike the conventional notion of complementary perspectives, in which observer and object remain separated, in complementarity, observer and object make up an interacting unit. Two observations that exhibit complementarity exist side by side, mutually exclusive, yet each adequate within its own experimental framework. Both are required for a comprehensive understanding of the phenomenon under investigation. When he was knighted, Bohr symbolically expressed his commitment to complementarity by choosing the yin-yang symbol as his family crest.

Bohr suggested that complementarity might be extended beyond physics to other domains of experience, including science and religion: materialism (science) and spiritualism (religion) as two aspects of the same thing. Although he did not develop that idea, one can imagine the religious and scientific attitudes as filters that reveal distinct domains of knowledge—domains that cannot be observed or inferred or negated from the other perspective. The religious attitude gives us James's unseen order, to which the individual seeks to conform. The scientific attitude gives us the anyone/anywhere/anytime of intersubjectivity. The domains are separate but not separated. Rather, they merge into a holistic yin-yang framework that cannot be harmonized or resolved further. They exist in dynamic tension, constantly bouncing off each other and inevitably offering distinct types of answers to fundamental questions about the self and the world.

Recognizing the limitations of our understanding is one of the most important insights from Bohr's complementarity. Perhaps there is no single correct path. Solving the world's problems may require both scientific and religious attitudes—two types of faith, not just one or the other.

Frederick Grinnell is a professor of cell biology at the University of Texas Southwestern Medical Center, in Dallas. His book Everyday Practice of Science: Where Intuition and Passion Meet Objectivity and Logic *is being published this month by Oxford University Press.*

Religion Doesn't Belong in Public Schools, but Debate Over Darwinian Evolution Does

By Casey Luskin
The Christian Science Monitor, December 16, 2010

Critical inquiry and freedom for credible dissent are vital to good science. Sadly, when it comes to biology textbooks, American high school students are learning that stubborn groupthink can suppress responsible debate.

In recent weeks, the media have been buzzing over a decision by the Louisiana State Board of Elementary and Secondary Education to adopt biology textbooks. A Fox News summary read "Louisiana committee rejects calls to include debate over creationism in state-approved biology textbooks. . . ." There was one problem with the story. Leading critics of evolution in Louisiana were not asking that public schools debate creationism, or even that they teach intelligent design. Rather, they wanted schools to simply teach the scientific debate over Darwinian evolution.

The controversy began because the biology textbooks up for adoption in Louisiana teach the neo-Darwinian model as settled fact, giving students no opportunity to weigh the pros and cons and consider evidence on both sides.

So Much for Critical Thinking

One textbook under review ("Biology: Concepts and Connections") offers this faux critical thinking exercise: "Write a paragraph briefly describing the kinds of evidence for evolution." No questions ask students to identify evidence that counters evolutionary biology, because no such evidence is presented in the text. If the modern version of Charles Darwin's theory is as solid as most scientists say, textbooks shouldn't be afraid to teach countervailing evidence as part of a comprehensive approach. Yet students hear only the prevailing view.

Is this the best way to teach science? Earlier this year a paper in the journal *Science* tried to answer that question, and found that students learn science best when they are asked "to discriminate between evidence that supports . . . or does not support" a given scientific concept. Unfortunately, the Darwin camp ignores these pedagogical findings and singles out evolution as the only topic where dissenting scientific viewpoints are not allowed.

Courts have uniformly found that creationism is a religious viewpoint and thus illegal to teach in public school science classes. By branding scientific views they dislike as "religion" or "creationism," the Darwin lobby scares educators from presenting contrary evidence or posing critical questions—a subtle but effective form of censorship.

The media fall prey to this tactic, resulting in articles that confuse those asking for scientific debate with those asking for the teaching of religion. And Darwin's defenders come off looking like heroes, not censors.

Those who love the First Amendment should be outraged. In essence, the Darwin lobby is taking the separation of church and state—a good thing—and abusing it to promote censorship. But one can be a critic of neo-Darwinism without advocating creationism.

Valid Doubts

Eugene Koonin is a senior research scientist at the National Institutes of Health and no friend of creationism or intelligent design. Last year, he stated in the journal *Trends in Genetics* that breakdowns in core neo-Darwinian tenets such as the "traditional concept of the tree of life" or "natural selection is the main driving force of evolution" indicate that the modern synthesis of evolution "has crumbled, apparently, beyond repair."

Likewise, the late Phil Skell, a member of the US National Academy of Sciences, considered himself a skeptic of both intelligent design and neo-Darwinian evolution. He took issue with those who claim that "nothing in biology makes sense except in the light of evolution" because, according to Dr. Skell, in most biology research, "Darwin's theory had provided no discernible guidance, but was brought in, after the breakthroughs, as an interesting narrative gloss."

Courts have uniformly found that creationism is a religious viewpoint and thus illegal to teach in public school science classes. By branding scientific views they dislike as "religion" or "creationism," the Darwin lobby scares educators from presenting contrary evidence or posing critical questions—a subtle but effective form of censorship.

In a 2005 letter to an education committee in South Carolina, Skell wrote: "Evolution is an important theory and students need to know about it. But scientific journals now document many scientific problems and criticisms of evolutionary theory and students need to know about these as well."

Skell was right, and polls show that more than 75 percent of Americans agree with him. The Louisiana textbook debate reflects the public's gross dissatisfaction with the quality of evolution instruction in biology textbooks.

The Louisiana Board should be applauded for rejecting censorship and adopting the disputed textbooks despite their biased coverage of evolution. Students need to learn about the evidence supporting the evolutionary viewpoint, and the textbooks present that side of this debate. But the books themselves should not be praised because they censor from students valid scientific questions about neo-Darwinian concepts—concepts that are instead taught as unquestioned scientific fact.

Students are the real losers here, because they are not taught the critical thinking skills they need to evaluate questions about evolution and become good scientists. When we start using the First Amendment as it was intended—as a tool to increase freedom of inquiry and promote access to scientific information—then perhaps these divisive controversies will finally go away.

Casey Luskin, an attorney with a graduate science background, works at the Discovery Institute in public policy and legal affairs, and is co-founder of the Intelligent Design and Evolution Awareness (IDEA) Center. His writings can be found at intelligentdesign.org.

Evolution Still Debated on Religious Grounds in the Public Domain

By Susan Barreto
Covalence Magazine, March 2012

Dating as far back as the 1880s, Charles Darwin's Theory of Evolution began its controversial history among Christians. While much has changed since then in terms of both the science and the theological discussion of human origins, there still is an element of traditional creationism that troubles the waters of pondering how humans came to be and where they are going.

The current controversy is playing out in US state legislatures, where new bills are posing the question of whether evolution should be taught in public schools. According to Michael Dowd, founder of the Clergy Letter Project, new bills have surfaced in Alabama, Missouri and Oklahoma. Similar bills in Indiana and New Hampshire failed to garner the essential support to become law.

The distrust of evolution on religious grounds in the United States is of course not news. However, many do not know that Christians have been in anything but agreement on how the evolution story fits with the creation story found in Genesis. Just a little more than 20 years after Darwin's publishing of *On the Origin of Species* in 1859, controversy began to blossom. The editor of a prominent American religious weekly wrote that roughly half of educated ministers in leading evangelical denominations believed that Genesis was no more a record of actual occurrences than the parable of the Prodigal Son, according to Ronald L. Numbers, author of *The Creationists*, which provides a detailed account of the history of the creationist movement.

A central issue is whether Genesis represents a historical and scientifically valid account of how creation came about. Creationists historically questioned how God's word could be wrong about the creation of world. The major question creationists ask is—How is God involved if science is right?

The other questions are many. Evolution suggests that the age of the earth was much older than depicted in the story of the first humans Adam and Eve. How could Genesis be wrong about that? Where does the creative spark of consciousness come through evolution? Where does God come into the picture? How does the story of the Fall play into our evolutionary heritage? Did we have a single common ancestor that was created by God?

A little research shows such topics are being discussed in churches and in other instances at religiously affiliated universities. Last month 556 congregations participated in Evolution Weekend by including Charles Darwin readings in the liturgy while pastors delivered sermons on the broader topics of religion and science with the aim of revealing how little conflict there needs to be between religion and science. Sponsored by the Clergy Letter Project during the week of Darwin's birthday, congregations in 10 countries participated.

A recent survey from the Clergy Letter Project, shows that an overwhelming majority of clergy (85% of those surveyed) from various faith communities do support biologists' view that evolution is a supported by scientific evidence. These findings though are in direct contradiction with what has been going on politically on a national level.

> *According to the National Center for Science Education (NCSE), six legislative bills dealing with evolution have been introduced in 2012, with legislatures in New Hampshire, Oklahoma, Missouri and Indiana considering bills against the teaching of evolution in the public school system.*

According to the National Center for Science Education (NCSE), six legislative bills dealing with evolution have been introduced in 2012, with legislatures in New Hampshire, Oklahoma, Missouri and Indiana considering bills against the teaching of evolution in the public school system.

In Oklahoma, the Senate bill does not push for teaching of intelligent design or promoting a certain belief system, but allows for open discussion of scientific theories and directs teachers to teach certain material and allow supplemental material to be taught. If the bill were to become law, it would require the Oklahoma State Board of Education to assist teachers and administrators to promote "critical thinking, logical analysis, open and objective discussion of scientific theories including, but not limited to, evolution, the origin of life, global warming, and human cloning."

Local school districts in Indiana would have been required to teach "various theories concerning the origin of life, including creation science." In the late 1980s, teaching of creationism in the schools was struck down by the Supreme Court. Numerous newspaper editorials across the state have been highly critical of the proposed bill. In late January, the bill was passed in the state Senate Education Committee, but by mid-February failed to garner the support to move farther.

The focus is back on intelligent design being taught alongside evolution in Missouri. The legislator who proposed that House bill has been quoted as saying, "The jury is still out on evolution." Previous versions of this bill were introduced and died in 2004, according the NCSE.

Two bills were filed early this year in the New Hampshire legislature. One would have charged the state board of education to require teachers to instruct pupils that proper scientific inquiry results from not committing to any one theory or hypothesis, no matter how firmly it appears to be established. The second bill would require evolution to be taught in the public schools as a theory, including the theorists' political and ideological viewpoints and their position on the concept of atheism.

These bills seemed to have gotten the support of creationist legislators and prominent lobbying groups such as the Discovery Institute—the group that initially backed efforts to teach intelligent design in public schools. According to policy outlined on its website, officials now are no longer mandating intelligent design but are supporting the teaching of evolution to students in the hopes that students also learn more about the "unresolved issues" of evolutionary theory.

Seven states (Alabama, Minnesota, Missouri, New Mexico, Pennsylvania, South Carolina and Texas) have science standards that require learning about some of the scientific controversies relating to evolution, according to the Discovery Institute. Additionally, Louisiana has a statewide law that allows teachers "to help students understand, analyze, critique, and review scientific theories in an objective manner," specifically naming evolution as an example. Texas's science standards require that students "analyze, evaluate and critique scientific explanations . . . including examining all sides of scientific evidence of those scientific explanations so as to encourage critical thinking." Texas also requires students to "analyze and evaluate" core evolutionary claims including "common ancestry," "natural selection," "mutation," and the formation of "long complex molecules having information such as the DNA molecule for self-replicating life."

These efforts are often supported by Christians who identify themselves as conservatives or "creationists," even though it is important to note that among them there are very many ways of looking at evolution's impact on our faith. For many there are non-legislative developments that go hand in hand: The latest development is the construction of a park in Kentucky to celebrate the story of Noah's Ark.

The last piece of land for the 800-acre site has been purchased in Williamstown, Kentucky (just south of Cincinnati). The attraction is expected to draw over a million people in its first year to see a full-scale replica of Noah's Ark, according to the group Answers in Genesis, which also is the entity behind Kentucky's Creation Museum. The group says that the Creation Museum attracts 300,000 visitors a year and there is work underway to build a 1,000-seat auditorium that has a new observatory with high-power telescopes. Since its opening in 2007, the Creation Museum has reported more than 1.5 million visitors.

The story is very different for most scientists, who happen also to be Christian. They find evolution's tenets as anything but controversial or puzzling. Gayle Woloschak, a molecular biologist at Northwestern University's Feinberg School of Medicine and a leader in the religion and science dialogue, finds richness in realizing the interconnectivity of humanity and the rest of creation.

A denial in evolution leads to a denial of an understanding of humanity's impact on the environment and on the processes that shape ecology, she says. "Evolution is a creative and changing force in nature that renews, restores and rekindles life," she says.

The topic of evolution is not something that theologians are shying away from either, even as congregations have some confusion on the topic. In fact in a recent

Q&A with *Covalence*, Dr. Philip Hefner in exploring transhumanism pointed out that there are three components that biology contributes to our understanding of who we are: "complex composition of our bodies, our evolutionary natural history, and our ecological connectedness." He adds that the idea that our spiritual nature is embedded in the natural process is a very recent emphasis.

Given the very different takes on evolution among those who are Christian, it is not surprising the public may be confused about how Christianity relates to evolution. This is not new. Still, for now though it seems that the religion and evolution dialogue needs to 'evolve' in the public square to confidently discuss whether belief in evolution truly needs to alter a person's view of religion.

Susan Barreto is a journalist who has been following religion and science since 2003 with articles appearing in various newsletters and The Lutheran *magazine. She is also a deputy editor of a monthly hedge fund magazine owned by Euromoney Institutional Investor. Susan is a long-time member of Luther Memorial Church in Chicago, where she lives with her husband and son.*

The Light of the World

By Michael Reiss
New Statesman, April 5, 2010

Creationists and evolutionists are bitterly divided over the origins of life, but teachers should not take sides, argues Michael Reiss.

To some people's incredulity and others' satisfaction, creationism's influence is growing across the globe. Definitions of creationism vary, but roughly 10–15 per cent of people in the UK believe that the earth came into existence exactly as described in the early parts of the Bible or the Quran, and that the most that evolution has done is to change species into other, closely related species.

The more recent theory of intelligent design agrees with creationism, but makes no reference to the scriptures. Instead, it argues that there are many features of the natural world—such as the mammalian eye—that are too intricate to have evolved from non-living matter, as the theory of evolution asserts. Such features are simply said to be "irreducibly complex."

At the same time, the overwhelming majority of biologists consider evolution to be central to the biological sciences, providing a conceptual framework that unifies every disparate aspect of the life sciences into a single, coherent discipline. Most scientists also believe that the universe is about 13–14 billion years old.

The well-known schism between a number of religious worldviews—particularly Judeo-Christian views based on Genesis and mainstream Islamic readings of the Quran—and scientific explanations derived from the theory of evolution is exacerbated by the way people are asked in surveys about their views on the origins of human life. There is a tendency to polarize religion and science: questions focus on the notion that either God created everything, or God had nothing to do with it. The choices erroneously imply that scientific evolution is necessarily atheistic, linking acceptance of evolution with the explicit exclusion of any religious premise.

In fact, people have personal beliefs about religion and science that cover a wide range of possibilities. This has important implications for how biology teachers should present evolution in schools. As John Hedley Brooke, the first holder of the Andreas Idreos Professorship of Science and Religion at Oxford University, has long pointed out, there is no such thing as a fixed relationship between science and religion. The interface between them has shifted over time, as has the meaning of each term.

Most of the literature on creationism (and intelligent design) and evolutionary theory puts them in stark opposition. Evolution is consistently presented in creationist books and articles as illogical, contradicted by scientific evidence such as the fossil record (which they claim does not provide evidence for transitional forms), and as the product of non-scientific reasoning. The early history of life, they say, would require life to arise from inorganic matter—a form of spontaneous generation largely rejected by science in the 19th century. Creationists also accuse evolutionary theory of being the product of those who ridicule the word of God, and a cause of a range of social evils (from eugenics, Marxism, Nazism and racism to juvenile delinquency).

Creationism has received similarly short shrift from evolutionists. In a study published in 1983, the philosopher of science Philip Kitcher concluded that the flat-earth theory, the chemistry of the four elements and medieval astrology were all as valid as creationism (not at all, that is).

After many years of teaching evolution to school and university students, I have come to the view that creationism is best seen by science teachers not as a misconception, but as a worldview. A worldview is an entire way of understanding reality: each of us probably has only one.

Life Lessons

Evolutionary biologists attack creationism—especially "scientific creationism"—on the grounds that it isn't a science at all, because its ultimate authority is scriptural and theological, rather than the evidence obtained from the natural world.

After many years of teaching evolution to school and university students, I have come to the view that creationism is best seen by science teachers not as a misconception, but as a worldview. A worldview is an entire way of understanding reality: each of us probably has only one. However, we can have many conceptions and misconceptions. The implications of this for education is that the most a science teacher can normally hope to achieve is to ensure that students with creationist beliefs understand the basic scientific position. Over the course of a few school lessons or a run of university lectures, it is unlikely that a teacher will be able to replace a creationist worldview with a scientific one.

So how might one teach evolution in science lessons to 14- to 16-year-olds? The first thing to note is that there is scope for young people to discuss beliefs about human origins in other subjects, notably religious education. In England, the DCSF (Department for Children, Schools and Families) and the QCA (Qualifications and Curriculum Authority) have published a non-statutory national framework for religious education and a teaching unit that asks: "How can we answer questions about creation and origins?" The unit focuses on creation and the origins of the universe and human life, as well as the relationships between religion and science. As you might expect, the unit is open-ended and is all about getting young people to learn about different views and develop their own thinking. But what should we do in science?

In summer 2007, after months of behind-the-scenes meetings, the DCSF guidance on creationism and intelligent design received ministerial approval and was published. As one of those who helped put the guidance together, I was relieved when it was welcomed. Even the discussions on the RichardDawkins.net forum were positive, while the *Freethinker,* an atheist journal, described it as "a breath of fresh air" and "a model of clarity and reason."

The guidance points out that the use of the word "theory" in science (as in "the theory of evolution") can be misleading, as it is different from the everyday meaning—that is, of being little more than an idea. In science, the word indicates that there is substantial supporting evidence, underpinned by principles and explanations accepted by the international scientific community. The guidance makes clear that creationism and intelligent design do not constitute scientific theories.

It also illuminates that there is a real difference between teaching something and teaching *about* something. In other words, one can teach about creationism without advocating it, just as one can teach in a history lesson about totalitarianism without advocating it.

This is a key point. Many scientists, and some science teachers, fear that consideration of creationism or intelligent design in a science classroom legitimizes them. That something lacks scientific support, however, doesn't seem to me a sufficient reason to omit it from a science lesson.

I remember being excited, when I was taught physics at school, that we could discuss almost anything, provided we were prepared to defend our thinking in a way that admitted objective evidence and logical argument. I recall one of our A-level chemistry teachers scoffing at a fellow student, who reported that she had sat (outside the lesson) with a spoon in front of her while Uri Geller maintained he could bend viewers' spoons. I was all for her approach. After all, I reasoned, surely the first thing was to establish if the spoon bent (it didn't for her), and if it did, to start working out how.

Free Expression

When teaching evolution, there is much to be said for allowing students to raise any doubts they have in order to shape and provoke a genuine discussion. The word "genuine" doesn't mean that creationism and intelligent design deserve equal time with evolution. They don't. However, in certain classes, depending on the teacher's comfort with talking about such issues, his or her ability to deal with them, and the make-up of the student body, it can and should be appropriate to address them.

Having said that, I don't pretend to think that this kind of teaching is easy. Some students become very heated; others remain silent even if they disagree profoundly with what is said. But I believe in taking seriously the concerns of students who do not accept the theory of evolution while still introducing them to it. Although it is unlikely that this will help them resolve any conflict they experience between science and their beliefs, good teaching can help students to manage it—and to learn more science.

My hope is simply to enable students to understand the scientific perspective with respect to our origins, but not necessarily to accept it. We can help students to find their science lessons interesting and intellectually challenging without their being a threat. Effective teaching in this area can help students not only learn about the theory of evolution, but also better appreciate the way science is done, the procedures by which scientific knowledge accumulates, the limitations of science and the ways in which scientific knowledge differs from other forms of knowledge.

Michael Reiss is professor of science education at the Institute of Education, University of London. His PhD was in evolutionary biology, and he is a priest in the Church of England.

Faith and the Cosmos

By Ila Delio
America Magazine, April 4, 2011

Can Catholic universities foster dialogue between religion and science?

When I started teaching in 1996, I was hired by Trinity College in Hartford, Connecticut, to teach a course on science and religion. With degrees in both areas, I felt well prepared; but I soon learned that the amount of literature on the relationship between these two topics had swelled enormously. The growth rate of scientific progress in our time is astounding. Rapid advances in technology make it difficult to keep abreast of progress in such areas as genetics, robotics, molecular biology and neuroscience. Discoveries in cosmology, astronomy and physics continue to disclose a universe that is ancient, dynamic, interconnected and expanding.

As technology advances at an exponential rate, it drives other areas of modern life to accelerate exponentially as well. The rapidity of technological change, writes the philosopher Nick Bostrom, suggests that continued innovation will have an even larger impact on humanity in future decades. With these changes come new moral and religious questions, and the Catholic Church needs theologians willing to address them. Unfortunately, few Catholic universities have devoted resources to educating theologians willing to engage with the scientific world. This is a loss for both academic disciplines.

If the secular, scientific culture behaves like a rabbit, leaping across vast areas of discovery and invention, the Catholic Church too often behaves like a turtle, crawling up from behind, hesitant to accept new scientific discoveries. The slow pace of the church's embrace of science is not because of a hesitant pope. Benedict XVI has worked to connect the two disciplines, establishing within the Vatican, under the Pontifical Council of Culture, a department dedicated to dialogue between science and theology. The pope has issued various statements on the sciences and their impact on humanity and the earth and has expressed to Catholic youth his support of new computer technologies, when used correctly, to connect with others. Overall, though, many theologians are reluctant to engage developments in science. It does not help that within the universities theology has been isolated from the sciences.

The mechanization and specialization of higher education has rendered the university a multiversity. Instead of educating students to know the universe and stars "turning together as one," academic disciplines, including theology and philosophy, have become highly specialized, competitive fields. If the modern church is reluctant to embrace insights from modern science as integral to revelation, part of the hesitancy may be due to the place theology holds within the academy.

In his book *The Soul of America*, the historian George Marsden recounts how and when higher education in general became hostile to religion. By the 1920s many universities, despite their religious roots, had grown increasingly secular, sidelining or even scorning religion. The separation of science from such humanistic fields as religion, history and literature created a model of university life that did not allow any positive role for religious people, institutions or ideas on campus. One had to leave religion at the door or privatize it. As a result, students did not learn how to connect science with areas of meaning and value. Elaine Ecklund, a sociologist at Rice University and the author of *Science vs. Religion: What Scientists Really Think*, suggests that by separating religion from the rest of university education, the American university lost its soul.

An Uneasy Relationship

The church has been a patron of the sciences throughout the ages, although not consistently. Major events like the Galileo affair and the rise of Protestantism "caused a psychic trauma for the church," write Peter Hess and Paul Allen in their excellent book, *Catholicism and Science*. Although the church did not shut the door to scientific research, events like these also stifled openness to scientific innovations.

Theology, however, entered the 20th century as a closed set of neo-Thomistic discourses with questions and rules set by neo-scholastic philosophy with few, if any, other intellectual or cultural sources, says Paul Crowley, S.J., the chair of religious studies at Santa Clara University, that did not cohere with existing papal efforts to support scientific research. Still, in the 1930s the Vatican had moved its astronomical observatory out of the city of Rome to Castel Gandolfo and outfitted it with modern equipment and in 1979 established the Pontifical Academy of Sciences to demonstrate the church's commitment to scientific research. "The Pontifical Academy," declared Pope John Paul II, "is a visible sign, raised among the people of the world, of a profound harmony that can exist between the truths of science and the truths of faith."

Some theologians have worked to connect these truths. Karl Rahner, S.J., did not shy away from exploring connections between matter and the soul or from considering the theological implications of life on other planets. Another Jesuit priest, Bernard Lonergan, drew on the scientific method to develop a method of theology. Today, some Catholic theologians (like John F. Haught) engage the sciences to illuminate areas of systematic theology like divine action; others (like Denis Edwards) are trying to deepen theological insight on questions in ecology, such as climate change. But on the whole, Catholic theology remains a product of Augustinian, Thomistic and Aristotelian ideas. Few Catholic theologians are grappling with the sciences on their own terms as a means of theological reflection.

In the late 20th century, as theology entered into dialogue with the cultural pluralities of gender, race, history and philosophy, it nonetheless settled into the university system as an academic silo, just as the sciences sequestered themselves into specialized disciplines. Religion and science grew more estranged.

Theology students are trained in departments independent of a broader integration with the sciences in the university. As a result, according to William Stoeger, S.J., of the Vatican observatory, "there are few theologians or theologically interested philosophers at universities where the most significant scientific work is done." Even the annual meeting of the Catholic Theological Society of America, where attention is given to major currents in theology, does not show much engagement with the sciences. Of its 16 topical areas of discussion, only one is devoted to theology and the natural sciences.

In his book *Religion and Science*, Ian Barbour laid out four types of relationships between science and religion: conflict, independence, dialogue and integration. While scientists tend to see the relationship between the two disciplines as one of either conflict or independence, theologians, when they are interested, tend toward dialogue and integration. Undoubtedly, science and religion are independent disciplines, each with its own language, methods and tools of analysis, but the academic structure has kept them intellectually as well as spatially apart.

Reforming this structure to promote dialogue is key, since scientific language is technical and objective, and the descriptions of scientific findings do not readily invite theology-minded students into discussion without a teacher. Both disciplines present unique challenges, but it is not difficult to see why a theologian may more readily delve into the familiar theses of St. Thomas Aquinas over the unfamiliar formulas of Albert Einstein, or why the reverse might be true for scientists. Scientists who are interested in religion or express religious belief often have little opportunity in the academy to discuss religion as it relates to their work. Some universities, like Santa Clara, are making a concerted effort to engage scientists and theologians in discussion on meaning and value, but such initiatives are rare.

The Role of the Catholic University

The term "Catholic sacramental imagination" has long been used for the typically Catholic view that the material world can bring people into intimate relationship with God. The term captures the heart of the Catholic intellectual tradition, which is rooted in the richness of the material cosmos as a fit dwelling for the divine. While the church recognizes the importance of science for the development of faith, it also recognizes the limits of science as the ultimate horizon of meaning. The value of science, Pope John Paul II wrote, is that it can "purify religion from error and superstition," just as "religion can purify science from idolatry and false absolutes."

Although the church continues to bridge science and religion, the significance of this dialogue for the life of faith cannot be left to the institutional church alone. Theologians are needed to reflect on the big questions of meaning and purpose in light of evolution, ecology and technology, as well as to comment on the moral questions raised, especially by the biomedical sciences. Science and religion make their best contributions when each can speak to the other of the truth of reality. As Paul Crowley, S.J., observes, "If theology cannot engage a culture that has been framed

> *Undoubtedly, science and religion are independent disciplines, each with its own language, methods and tools of analysis, but the academic structure has kept them intellectually as well as spatially apart.*

by the paradigms of science, then theology itself risks self-marginalization." It has "no voice at the table concerning the significant issues facing humanity today" and becomes an exercise in history and hermeneutics. On the other hand, unbridled science can become "scientism," making broad philosophical claims without the development of philosophical foundations.

Catholic universities must become leaders in integrating science and religion. John Haughey, S.J., writes that the Catholic intellectual tradition is one of making wholes. Yet few Catholic universities offer courses or programs in science and religion, and those that do attract relatively few students, not all of whom are adequately prepared for such discussions.

Several years ago, a colleague and I initiated a certificate program in religion and science at Washington Theological Union, a graduate school of theology and ministry in Washington, D.C., but the program was eventually discontinued for lack of student interest. At the Gregorian University in Rome, Gennaro Auletta and colleagues have developed a program called Science and the Ontological Quest, which is responsible for coordinating science and religion courses in six Roman pontifical universities. Although only a small number of seminarians are taking such courses, the engagement of seminarians in the dialogue between science and religion may be one of the most crucial pastoral needs of our time.

Catholic universities need an invigoration of the Catholic imagination, for which dialogue between science and religion is a rich source. Theology cannot continue to develop apart from 21st-century cosmology and ecology, nor can science substitute for religion. The dialogue between science and religion has been developing in the last few decades, but Catholic universities have been slow to support this mutual enrichment. Developing collaborative structures of interaction between science and religion on the university level can benefit students and faculty alike, not only academically but also spiritually. While the current structure of academic specialization makes dialogue difficult as an integral part of university life and thought, universities must support existing centers of dialogue, like the Woodstock Theological Center at Georgetown University. Centers like these serve as bridge-builders and integrators, bringing together faculty, students and professionals across the disciplines.

To restore soul to the university may require a re-imagining of education, including a search for new ways to develop dialogue between science and religion. Development of this relationship can enrich personal life, community life and the life of the planet. As John Paul II wrote, "The things of the earth and the concerns of faith derive from the same God," for it is one and the same Love "which moves the sun and the other stars." Both the light of faith and the insights of science can help humanity evolve toward a more sustainable future.

Ilia Delio, O.S.F., is a senior fellow at Woodstock Theological Center, Georgetown University, where she concentrates on the area of science and religion.

5

The Greening of Faith

Texas State Park Police Officer Thomas Bigham walks across the cracked lake bed of O.C. Fisher Lake, Aug. 3, 2011, in San Angelo, Texas. A combination of long periods of 100-plus degree days and a lack of rain in the drought-stricken region has dried up the lake that once spanned over 5400 acres. The year 2011 brought a record heat wave to Texas, massive floods in Bangkok, and an unusually warm November in England.

Silent Spring: Faith and the Environment

By Paul McCaffrey

The birth of the modern environmental movement is often traced back to the publication of Rachel Carson's seminal 1962 book *Silent Spring*. Prior to writing *Silent Spring*, Carson, a Johns Hopkins University–trained marine biologist, worked for the US Fish and Wildlife Service for many years, during which time she rose to become the editor in chief of the organization's publications. While carrying out her duties for the government, she also pursued science writing on the side. Her 1951 book *The Sea around Us* became a best seller and earned Carson a National Book Award. Based on the book's success, Carson left her government position and dedicated herself to writing. In 1953, she moved to a seaside cottage on Maine's Sheepscot Bay, where she authored another best seller, *The Edge of the Sea* (1955).

In 1958, a friend of Carson's, Olga Owens Huckins, wrote a letter to the *Boston Herald* to report a disturbing pattern and forwarded a copy of the correspondence to Carson. At the time, the insecticide dichlorodiphenyltrichloroethane (DDT) was being widely and indiscriminately used to kill mosquitoes and other disease-carrying pests. First deployed during World War II to prevent outbreaks of malaria, typhus, and other insect-borne illnesses among military and civilian populations, DDT had earned Swiss chemist Paul Hermann Müller the 1948 Nobel Prize in Physiology or Medicine for conducting the research that first uncovered the substance's value as an insecticide. By the late 1950s, hundreds of millions of pounds of DDT were being released into the environment in the United States every year, with little thought for the potential consequences.

In her letter, Huckins observed that soon after local authorities in Massachusetts sprayed her neighborhood with DDT, dead birds started to appear on her lawn. "All of these birds died horribly, and in the same way," she wrote. "Their bills were gaping open, and their splayed claws were drawn up to their breasts in agony." Despite government assurances that the substance was harmless, Huckins had her doubts, and she encouraged Carson to investigate the matter and use her status as an author and scientist to persuade the state to stop its spraying program. Carson started to look into the effects of DDT and related substances on wildlife. "The more I learned about the use of pesticides, the more appalled I became," she said in an interview. "I realized that here was the material for a book." Despite legal threats from chemical companies, the *New Yorker* agreed to serialize *Silent Spring*, publishing the first installment in June of 1962.

Citing various scientific studies and other documentation, Carson detailed how pesticides are absorbed into the body and build up in fatty tissue. These chemicals, she observed, "destroy the very enzymes whose function is to protect the body from harm, they block the oxidation processes from which the body receives its energy, they prevent the normal functioning of the various organs, and they may initiate in certain cells the slow and irreversible change that leads to malignancy." She also referenced the toll that DDT and other substances took on the environment. These chemical cocktails not only killed pests but also, as they were absorbed into the water and soil and entered the food chain, contaminated and eliminated other species. Meanwhile, after a time, the targeted pests built up immunity, requiring stronger and stronger concentrations of chemicals to kill. This resulted in the use of ever-increasing amounts of pesticides.

The "silent spring" evoked in the title of the book refers to a vision of nature devoid of birds, insects, and other creatures, which Carson proposed could be the ultimate result of pesticide overuse. In addition to its scientific background, Carson's larger argument has theological overtones. "Just as in the biblical story of the Garden of Eden, Carson's tale of rampant poisoning of nature was a morality tale of mankind's hubris," Andrew P. Morriss observed for *The Freeman* in 2012, connecting *Silent Spring* with Carson's Presbyterian upbringing as well as with American Puritanism.

The reaction to *Silent Spring* was immediate. The book quickly became a best seller, but it also generated a backlash, especially from chemical companies, and critics dismissed Carson's argument as overwrought and "emotional." Not long after the publication of *Silent Spring*, however, US president John F. Kennedy tasked his Science Advisory Committee with investigating Carson's claims about DDT. In its final report, the committee confirmed that the indiscriminate use of pesticides and poisonous chemicals "was potentially a much greater hazard" than nuclear fallout. Soon, governments at the local, state, and federal levels began instituting measures to monitor and regulate the use of pesticides and other potentially harmful chemicals. The use of DDT as a pesticide was largely banned in the United States in the early 1970s.

As the environmental movement took shape in the aftermath of the publication of *Silent Spring*, other factors helped to elevate ecological concerns in the public consciousness. In 1969, for example, an oil spill in the Santa Barbara Channel polluted beaches and killed wildlife up and down the California coast, generating widespread media attention and intense public outrage. That same year, the highly polluted Cuyahoga River in Cleveland, Ohio, caught fire, creating further indignation and helping to spur clean water regulations and the creation of the US Environmental Protection Agency (EPA) in 1970.

In the midst of these developments, some observers saw theological causes for the environmental crisis. Though Morriss perceived a distinctly Christian undercurrent to Carson's conservation efforts, others had a different take, arguing that Christianity itself may be perceived as having given humankind carte blanche to abuse the environment and take from it whatever can be taken. In an article entitled "The Historical Roots of Our Ecological Crisis," published in the journal *Science* in 1967, the medieval historian Lynn White Jr. observed, "What people do about their ecology depends on what they think about themselves in relation to things around them. Human ecology is deeply conditioned by beliefs about our nature and destiny—that is, by religion." In the transition from paganism to Christianity in the West, White theorized, the relationship between humanity and nature was transformed. During the pre-Christian era, he claimed, "every tree, every spring, every stream, every hill had its own *genius loci*, its guardian spirit." Such doctrines imbued nature with divine qualities and placed it on a relatively equal footing with humanity. "Before one cut a tree, mined a mountain, or dammed a brook," White wrote, "it was important to placate the spirit in charge of that particular situation, and to keep it placated."

Christianity, White argued, created a completely different dynamic. In the Bible's book of Genesis, for example, humanity is said to have been made in God's image and given "dominion over the fish of the sea, and over the fowl of the air, and over every living thing that moveth upon the earth." To White, such doctrines "not only established a dualism of man and nature but also insisted that it is God's will that man exploit nature for his proper ends." Thus, according to White, Christian doctrine is in part responsible for rampant DDT and pesticide use as well as, should it come, the apocalyptic "silent spring" envisioned by Carson. White concluded that the only way to address the environmental crisis was through a fundamental restructuring of how Christianity perceives the relationship between humankind and nature. "Our present science and our present technology are so tinctured with orthodox Christian arrogance toward nature that no solution for our ecologic crisis can be expected from them alone," he declared. "Since the roots of our trouble are so largely religious, the remedy must also be essentially religious, whether we call it that or not." White encouraged revisiting the example of Saint Francis of Assisi, the patron saint of animals, who preached that humanity has a duty to exercise responsible stewardship over the natural world.

Not everyone agreed with White's assessment that Christianity bears responsibility for the degradation of the environment. In the 1994 essay "Biblical Views of Nature: Foundations for an Environmental Ethic," for example, scholar Marcia Bunge contended that "the Bible contains insights that can help form the basis of a sound environmental ethic." She noted that the name of the biblical Adam was derived from the Hebrew *adamah*, which means "earth" and "ground," implying a connection between humanity and nature. She also highlighted the story of Noah's ark, wherein Noah is charged with gathering two of every species, to imply that God is concerned with the fate not only of humankind but also of the animals. Bunge also quoted the letters of the apostle Paul, certain passages from which, she argued, "indicate that Christ's redemptive power affects the whole creation."

White's critique notwithstanding, both Carson's example and Bunge's biblical analysis suggest that attributing pollution and other environmental excesses to Christianity—or to any religion—is problematic. Still, Rachel Oliver observed for CNN that "within each belief system, there lie subtle differences that, many argue, give an indication as to how we view our position in relation to [the earth]." The major theological dividing line, Oliver contended, is whether a faith views humanity as part of the natural world or the natural world as something created to serve humanity. As White's and Bunge's competing interpretations suggest, the answer to this question is not always clear.

Nevertheless, mindful of the ecological concerns that sprang up in the wake of *Silent Spring*, religious leaders have come to grasp the importance of the health of the natural world and place a greater emphasis on conservation and environmental protection, often turning to scripture to establish a theological rationale for such perspectives. The Assisi Declarations of September 1986 demonstrate the depth of this understanding. In honor of the twenty-fifth anniversary of its founding, the World Wildlife Fund called together leaders from five of the world's major faiths: Buddhism, Islam, Hinduism, Christianity, and Judaism. Gathered together in Assisi, Italy, the birthplace of Saint Francis, the invitees crafted statements detailing their individual religions' commitment to preserving the environment. Despite their divergent doctrines and beliefs, their messages echo one another, emphasizing both humanity's union with nature and its duty to protect it. The Hindu declaration, for example, concludes with a quotation from one of the faith's holy texts: "The Earth is our mother, and we are all her children." The Jewish declaration ends with the entreaty, "We are now all passengers, together, in this same fragile and glorious world. Let us safeguard our rowboat—and let us row together." The lesson was clear: preventing a "silent spring" is not only a task for environmentalists but also a religious duty.

Environment and the New Humanism

By Edward O. Wilson
Humanist, November 2007

Adapted from an address given on April 22, 2007, as part of "The New Humanism" conference held at Harvard University.

I want to begin by paying two personal tributes, first to Paul Kurtz, one of the global champions of this freedom movement we call humanism, and second to Tom Ferrick, Harvard University's recently retired humanist chaplain and our local champion and pioneer. Both led us through the period in which humanism was not so easily defined and its enduring merit not so easily discerned in the sea of religious belief surrounding us. Now the atmosphere is changing. America better understands secularism, but it has a long way to go to fully accept it.

According to the extensive 2006 Gallup poll sponsored by Baylor University, 25 percent of Americans are at least mildly secularist. Most of these have a view that could be called deistic or agnostic; they concede at least the remotely possible existence of a deity or deity-like creator, but they believe that this entity has no connection with us. It may have started the universe—it's a kind of cosmological god, as I call it in my 1978 book, *On Human Nature,* as opposed to a biological god, one that intervenes in our affairs at a personal or species level. Three to 4 percent of the total population is atheistic (that's within the 25 percent) and the rest are part of what we usually call the "faith community." An AOL poll, also taken in 2006, revealed that 51 percent of Americans don't believe in evolution, and probably almost all for religious reasons. Something like 15 percent more have doubts about it. A 2004*Newsweek* poll found that 55 percent of Americans, 83 percent of whom identified as evangelical Protestants, believe the Bible to be literally accurate.

Gazing out at this metaphysical landscape where America sits, I appreciate the opportunity to discuss what a few others and I like to call the "new humanism." It contrasts with the assertive and well-argued brief for atheism recently advanced, for example, by Richard Dawkins and Sam Harris. They say what has been heard before, at least in fragments, but they say it boldly and confidently. They respond to the contemporary intrusion of militant religious dogma into our political and private lives as something to be combated frontally and aggressively. It isn't my style, but I salute this newly influential military wing of secularism and humanism.

This new atheism, as it's been dubbed, is more than a defense line. It's a bold movement forward that will help validate humanism and give it a place at the table of public discourse. But what I'm interested in is the new humanism. It's an approach no less skeptical than militant atheism, but is, at least as I have conceived and practiced it, based on finding common ground. Call it the diplomacy wing if you will. The common ground comprises issues that transcend religion and personal beliefs, are vital to human welfare, and for which indisputable fact can be made manifest. The religious faithful, including fundamentalist evangelicals, can't simply be dismissed as stupid people. Like everyone else, they are human and therefore are more likely to listen if an argument is given with courtesy and respect, and accompanied with a request for help. Likewise, they are more likely to consider reading about a different worldview if it is linked to a transcendent issue, offered in a spirit of friendship and collaboration. The great issue of our time, the environment, is such a transcendent issue.

Pastor, we need your help. The Creation—living Nature—is in deep trouble. Scientists estimate that if habitat conversion and other destructive human activities continue at their present rates, half the species of plants and animals on Earth could be gone or at least fated for early extinction by the end of the century.

It is also, as you know, the topic of my 2006 book, *The Creation: An Appeal to Save Life on Earth*, for which I took a decidedly new humanist approach. To the believers I said, let us talk. Let us try to be friends and, without proselytizing, find common ground.

Since publishing *The Creation*, I have in fact formed many new friends within the faith community, including evangelical leaders and laity, and in other Judeo-Christian denominations. I've lectured at one Baptist university, and I've met leaders of the Mormon Church, at their invitation, in Salt Lake City. I've also helped organize an ongoing collaboration between evangelical leaders with leaders in environmental science and activism to address issues of the environment jointly.

One reason I put a lot of hope into forming this alliance was because I was reared in the Southern Baptist Church and know the culture. But equally, I had in mind what I call "the New York effect." If you can make it in New York, the song goes, you can make it anywhere. So I thought of the evangelicals as the place to start. (Not with those doctrinally easygoing and quasisecular Unitarian Universalists!) The evangelicals have a strong ethic but one farthest removed from secularism. We may not like what it's based on or where it leads them on many social issues, but it is a passion ideally independent of ordinary ambitions and economic greed. It is one group you can count on, once they're committed to an ethical position, for intense and sincerely felt and expressed support.

In the course of this venture, I've been enormously impressed by the variety of religious opinion, even across what one considers conservative groups, and the fluctuation, stopping short of course of the fundamental dogmas of religious faith. There is wiggle room, for example, in the split now occurring in the evangelical community between hard-right conservatives versus centrists and liberals (of course the latter must be relatively defined). The split is against some of the leaders, a relatively small group of rigidly dogmatic evangelicals who have acquired a lot of power through megachurches and radio and television talk shows. But I don't believe they are typical of the evangelical movement as a whole.

Although its positive impact was much wider than I had expected, I'll admit that my primary purpose in writing *The Creation* wasn't to promote humanism. I had an entirely different ambition: to save biodiversity by bringing people of all beliefs into the environmental movement; to get them to pay particular attention to the rest of life on Earth. Speeches and books even by the "greenest" of our spokesmen in this country are usually directed to climate change, to shortages of water, and to other looming crises for humankind. They have relatively little to say about the rest of life, a large part of which is vanishing before our eyes.

I have felt an urgent need to help correct this imbalance. I thought conservationists ought to be able to recruit the faith community in doing so, sidestepping or at least postponing the differences that have led to the culture wars. After all, Judeo-Christians have every reason—it's written right there in the Bible—to regard stewardship of the living world as part of their magisterium. They just haven't paid much attention to it. So I spoke to them about biology and conservation. Then I held my breath, so to speak, and waited. The effort has proved successful for the most part. The response from much of the religious community has been strong and encouraging. Among humanists, Paul Kurtz, to my relief, gave *The Creation* a wonderful review (the closest equivalent we might expect to a papal imprimatur), and I've had no objection at all yet from fellow scientists, most of whom are secularists.

So now let me present the opening paragraphs of the book, *The Creation*, published in September 2006. It's intended to abate the culture wars, including perhaps even the contentious issues surrounding evolution. To recall an old evangelical hymn, let us meet at the river.

Dear Pastor,

We haven't met, yet I feel I know you well enough to call you friend. First of all, we grew up in the same faith. As a boy in Alabama and Florida, I too answered the altar call; I went under the water. Although I no longer belong to that faith, I'm confident that if we met and spoke privately of our deepest beliefs, it would be in a spirit of mutual respect and goodwill. I know we share many precepts of moral behavior.

I write to you now for your counsel and help.

[Let me break here to say, parenthetically, that if you want to enter a discourse with the religious majority and really make them listen to biology and the fact of evolution, you don't say, "You poor, ignorant fools, you're harming America!"]

Of course, in doing so, I see no way to avoid the fundamental differences in our respective worldviews. You are a strict interpreter of Christian Holy Scripture. I am a secular humanist. For you, the glory of an unseen divinity; for me, the glory of the universe revealed at last. For you, the belief in God made flesh to save mankind; for me, the belief in Promethean fire seized to set men free. You found your final truth, I'm still searching. I may be wrong, you may be wrong, we may be both partly right.

Does this difference in worldviews separate us in all things? It does not. You and I and every other human being strive for the same imperatives of security, freedom of choice, personal dignity, and a cause to believe in larger than ourselves.

Let's see then, if we can, and you are willing, to meet on the near side of metaphysics and declare a truce in the culture wars in order to deal with the real world we share. I put it this way because you have the power to help solve a great problem about which I care deeply. I hope that you have the same concern. I suggest that we set aside our differences in order to save the Creation. The defense of living Nature is a universal value. It doesn't rise from, nor does it promote, any religious or political dogma. Rather, it serves without discrimination the interests of all humanity.

Pastor, we need your help. The Creation—living Nature—is in deep trouble. Scientists estimate that if habitat conversion and other destructive human activities continue at their present rates, half the species of plants and animals on Earth could be gone or at least fated for early extinction by the end of the century. A full quarter will drop out to this level during the next half-century as a result of climate change alone.

Surely we can agree that each species, however inconspicuous and humble it may seem to us at this moment, is a masterpiece of biology, and well worth saving. Each species possesses a unique combination of genetic traits that fits it more or less precisely to a particular part of the environment. Prudence alone dictates that we act quickly to prevent the extinction of species and, with it, the pauperization of Earth's ecosystems— hence, of the Creation.

You may well ask at this point, Why me? Because religion and science are the two most powerful social forces in the world today, including especially the United States. If religion and science could be united on the common ground of biological conservation, the problem would soon be solved. If there is any moral precept shared by people of all beliefs, it is that we owe ourselves and future generations a beautiful, rich, and healthful environment.

Well, having spoken thus to the pastor as the book opens, I then invite him (and the general reader as well) to examine the full panoply of biology, including evolution. Will this work? It already has in ways I find more than a little encouraging.

Shortly after the book came out my friend Eric Chivian, a cofounder of the Nobel prize–winning Physicians for Social Responsibility, thought it might be a good idea to carry the message directly and physically to the evangelicals. So he got together with his friend, Richard Cizik, vice president for governmental affairs of the National Association of Evangelicals, to discuss this approach to the environment. He and Cizik then invited me for lunch at the Cosmos Club in Washington to discuss the issues. We soon agreed, "Let's have a retreat with a larger group." And so in late 2006 a dozen of the principal evangelical leaders in this country and a dozen scientists, including Jim Hansen, head of NASA's Goddard Institute for Space

Studies; Peter Seligmann, chairman and CEO of Conservation International; and Peter Raven, director of the Missouri Botanical Garden, met at Melhana Plantation near Thomasville, Georgia, for two days of intense discussion.

We were all nervous at first, but soon located the common ground we sought. Friendships were made. And I helped write a covenant—yes, we call it that—with a brilliant young Baptist professor of theology from Union College in Jackson, Tennessee whose name is David Gushee. That was edited and signed by everyone present. We next held a press conference in Washington, DC, on December 17, 2006, to launch a joint environmental initiative. Meanwhile the volume of mail I've received from the faith community has been large and almost completely favorable. I've been invited to speak at special events within the evangelical world and at conferences that are bringing scientists and evangelicals together. This personal response, I knew, amplified efforts already underway among some evangelicals and members of other Judeo-Christian denominations, to promote environmental activism.

In particular, during the year following the publication of *The Creation*, I visited Samford University in Birmingham, Alabama, which has been called Ivy League of the Southern Baptist Conference. It is, in fact, a strongly sectarian college based upon the faith, just as Notre Dame and Holy Cross were based upon Catholicism, and Harvard University was long ago based upon a strict puritan doctrine. They all have evolved. Even Samford is said to be less tied nowadays to fundamentalist Baptist doctrine than in its early days. For several years previously, as a native son, my name had come up to give a principal lecture at Samford, but I was turned down as "too controversial an atheist." With *The Creation*, however, I was welcomed. It was marvelous to see this happen. We stayed away from doctrinal differences and talked about what the religious can do, what Southern Baptists can do, what scientists can do, and what both might accomplish together. As at the Melhana conference, we discussed what needs to be added to the evangelical activities and teachings of denominations like Southern Baptism to help save the living environment. The moral argument for saving the creation might be added to the ordinary agenda for regular sermons at all churches, a step that has rarely occurred until now.

Consider this: once you put on the table that you don't agree with evangelicals in many basic beliefs but that you have something deeply in common with them on which we should all be working together, the mood changes entirely. I've found it wonderful to form friendships with people that I thought would otherwise stiffen up when I got close to them.

We can all evolve, and now with added impetus perhaps we can also coevolve.

Edward O. Wilson is a world authority on biodiversity and the evolution of social behavior. He is Pellegrino University Research Professor Emeritus and Honorary Curator in Entomology at Harvard University, a Pulitzer–prize winning author, and the 1999 Humanist of the Year.

Environmentalism as Religion

By Joel Garreau
New Atlantis: A Journal of Technology & Society, Summer 2010

Traditional religion is having a tough time in parts of the world. Majorities in most European countries have told Gallup pollsters in the last few years that religion does not "occupy an important place" in their lives. Across Europe, Judeo-Christian church attendance is down, as is adherence to religious prohibitions such as those against out-of-wedlock births. And while Americans remain, on average, much more devout than Europeans, there are demographic and regional pockets in this country that resemble Europe in their religious beliefs and practices.

The rejection of traditional religion in these quarters has created a vacuum unlikely to go unfilled; human nature seems to demand a search for order and meaning, and nowadays there is no shortage of options on the menu of belief. Some searchers syncretize Judeo-Christian theology with Eastern or New Age spiritualism. Others seek through science the ultimate answers of our origins, or dream of high-tech transcendence by merging with machines—either approach depending not on rationalism alone but on a faith in the goodness of what rationalism can offer.

For some individuals and societies, the role of religion seems increasingly to be filled by environmentalism. It has become "the religion of choice for urban atheists," according to Michael Crichton, the late science fiction writer (and climate change skeptic). In a widely quoted 2003 speech, Crichton outlined the ways that environmentalism "remaps" Judeo-Christian beliefs:

> There's an initial Eden, a paradise, a state of grace and unity with nature, there's a fall from grace into a state of pollution as a result of eating from the tree of knowledge, and as a result of our actions there is a judgment day coming for us all. We are all energy sinners, doomed to die, unless we seek salvation, which is now called sustainability. Sustainability is salvation in the church of the environment. Just as organic food is its communion, that pesticide-free wafer that the right people with the right beliefs, imbibe.

In parts of northern Europe, this new faith is now the mainstream. "Denmark and Sweden float along like small, content, durable dinghies of secular life, where most people are nonreligious and don't worship Jesus or Vishnu, don't revere sacred texts, don't pray, and don't give much credence to the essential dogmas of the world's great faiths," observes Phil Zuckerman in his 2008 book *Society without God.* Instead, he writes, these places have become "clean and green." This new faith has very concrete policy implications; the countries where it has the most purchase tend also to have instituted policies that climate activists endorse. To better understand the future of climate policy, we must understand where "ecotheology" has come from and where it is likely to lead.

From Theology to Ecotheology

The German zoologist Ernst Haeckel coined the word "ecology" in the nineteenth century to describe the study of "all those complex mutual relationships" in nature that "Darwin has shown are the conditions of the struggle for existence." Of course, mankind has been closely studying nature since the dawn of time. Stone Age religion aided mankind's first ecological investigation of natural reality, serving as an essential guide for understanding and ordering the environment; it was through story and myth that prehistoric man interpreted the natural world and made sense of it. Survival required knowing how to relate to food species like bison and fish, dangerous predators like bears, and powerful geological forces like volcanoes—and the rise of agriculture required expertise in the seasonal cycles upon which the sustenance of civilization depends.

Our uniquely Western approach to the natural world was shaped fundamentally by Athens and Jerusalem. The ancient Greeks began a systematic philosophical observation of flora and fauna; from their work grew the long study of natural history. Meanwhile, the Judeo-Christian teachings about the natural world begin with the beginning: there is but one God, which means that there is a knowable order to nature; He created man in His image, which gives man an elevated place in that order; and He gave man mastery over the natural world:

> And God blessed them, and God said unto them, Be fruitful, and multiply, and replenish the earth, and subdue it: and have dominion over the fish of the sea, and over the fowl of the air, and over every living thing that moveth upon the earth. And God said, Behold, I have given you every herb bearing seed, which is upon the face of all the earth, and every tree, in the which is the fruit of a tree yielding seed; to you it shall be for meat. [Genesis 1:28–29]

In his seminal essay "The Historical Roots of Our Ecologic Crisis," published in *Science* magazine in 1967, historian Lynn Townsend White, Jr. argues that those Biblical precepts made Christianity, "especially in its Western form," the "most anthropocentric religion the world has seen." In stark contrast to pagan animism, Christianity posited "a dualism of man and nature" and "insisted that it is God's will that man exploit nature for his proper ends." Whereas older pagan creeds gave a cyclical account of time, Christianity presumed a teleological direction to history, and with it the possibility of progress. This belief in progress was inherent in modern science, which, wedded to technology, made possible the Industrial Revolution. Thus was the power to control nature achieved by a civilization that had inherited the license to exploit it.

To White, this was not a positive historical development. Writing just a few years after the publication of Rachel Carson's eco-blockbuster *Silent Spring*, White shared in the concern over techno-industrial culture's destruction of nature. Whatever benefit scientific and technological innovation had brought mankind was eclipsed by the "out of control" extraction and processing powers of industrial life and the mechanical degradation of the earth. Christianity, writes White, "bears a huge burden of guilt" for the destruction of the environment.

White believed that science and technology could not solve the ecological problems they had created; our anthropocentric Christian heritage is too deeply ingrained. "Despite Copernicus, all the cosmos rotates around our little globe. Despite Darwin, we are not, in our hearts, part of the natural process. We are superior to nature, contemptuous of it, willing to use it for our slightest whim." But White was not entirely without hope. Even though "no new set of basic values" will "displace those of Christianity," perhaps Christianity itself can be reconceived. "Since the roots of our trouble are so largely religious, the remedy must also be essentially religious." And so White suggests as a model Saint Francis, "the greatest spiritual revolutionary in Western history." Francis should have been burned as a heretic, White writes, for trying "to substitute the idea of the equality of all creatures, including man, for the idea of man's limitless rule of creation." Even though Francis failed to turn Christianity toward his vision of radical humility, White argued that something similar to that vision is necessary to save the world in our time.

White's essay caused a splash, to say the least, becoming the basis for countless conferences, symposia, and debates. One of the most serious critiques of White's thesis appears in theologian Richard John Neuhaus's 1971 book *In Defense of People*, a broad indictment of the rise of the mellifluous "theology of ecology." Neuhaus argues that our framework of human rights is built upon the Christian understanding of man's relationship to nature. Overturning the latter, as White hoped would happen, will bring the former crashing down. And Neuhaus makes the case that White misunderstands his own nominee for an ecological patron saint:

> What is underemphasized by White and others, and what was so impressive in Francis, is the unremitting focus on the glory of the Creator. Francis' line of accountability drove straight to the Father and not to Mother Nature. Francis was accountable *for* nature but *to* God. Francis is almost everyone's favorite saint and the gentle compassion of his encompassing vision is, viewed selectively, susceptible to almost any argument or mood.
> . . . It was not the claims of creation but the claims of the Creator that seized Francis.

Other Christian writers joined Neuhaus in condemning the ecomovement's attempt to subvert or supplant their religion. "We too want to clean up pollution in nature," *Christianity Today* demurred, "but not by polluting men's souls with a revived paganism." The Jesuit magazine *America* called environmentalism "an American heresy." The theologian Thomas Sieger Derr lamented "an expressed preference for the preservation of nonhuman nature against human needs wherever it is necessary to choose." (Stephen R. Fox recounts these responses in his 1981 book *John Muir and His Legacy: The American Conservation Movement*.)

The Greening of Christianity

From today's vantage, it seems that White's counsel has been heeded far and wide. Ecotheologies loosely based on concepts lifted from Hinduism or Buddhism have become popular in some Baby Boomer circles. Neo-pagans cheerfully accept the "tree-hugger" designation and say they were born "green." And, most strikingly, Christianity has begun to accept environmentalism. Theologians now speak routinely of "stewardship"—a doctrine of human responsibility for the natural world that unites interpretations of Biblical passages with contemporary teachings about social justice.

In November 1979, a dozen years after White's essay, Pope John Paul II formally designated Francis of Assisi the patron saint of ecologists. Over the following two decades, John Paul repeatedly addressed in passionate terms the moral obligation "to care for all of Creation" and argued that "respect for life and for the dignity of the human person extends also to the rest of Creation, which is called to join man in praising God." His successor, Benedict XVI, has also spoken about the environment, albeit less stirringly. "That very ordinariness," argues a correspondent for the *National Catholic Reporter*, "seems remarkable. Benedict simply took for granted that his audience would recognize the environment as an object of legitimate Christian interest. What the matter-of-fact tone reveals, in other words, is the extent to which Catholicism has 'gone green.'"

American Protestantism, too, has gone green. Numerous congregations are constructing "green churches"—choosing to glorify God not by erecting soaring sanctuaries but by building more energy-efficient houses of worship. In some denominations, programs for recycling or carpooling seem as common as food drives. Church-sponsored Earth Day celebrations are widespread.

Even some evangelicals are turning toward environmentalism. Luis E. Lugo, the director of the Pew Forum on Religion and Public Life, speaks of their "broader environmental sensitivity":

> Once it's translated into Biblical terms, [evangelicals] pick up the environmental banner using phrases that resonate with the community—"Creation care." That immediately puts it in an evangelical context rather than the empirical arguments about the environment. "This is the world God created. God gave you a mandate to care for this world." It's a very direct religious appeal.

That said, the widely reported "greening of evangelicals" shouldn't be exaggerated. Conservative evangelical leaders remain wary of environmentalism's agenda and of any attacks on industrial prowess that could be seen as undermining American national greatness. Many evangelicals are rankled by environmentalists' critique of the Genesis depiction of man's place in the natural order. And evangelicals are alert to any hint of pagan worship. Moreover, the available poll data—admittedly rather sparse—paints a mixed picture. In a 2008 survey conducted by the Barna Group, a California-based public opinion firm that concentrates on church issues, 90 percent of the evangelical respondents said they "would like Christians to take a more active role in caring for creation" (with two thirds saying they strongly agreed with that sentiment). But the term "Creation care" had not sunk in (89 percent of the respondents who identified themselves as Christian said they had never heard of it). And both the Barna survey and another 2008 survey conducted by Pew found that evangelicals tend to be much more skeptical about the reality of global warming than other American Christians or the population at large.

To the extent that evangelicals and environmentalists are in fact reaching out to one another, there can be benefits for each side. For churches with aging congregations, green issues reportedly help attract new, younger members to the pews. And what do environmental activists hope to gain by recruiting churches to their cause? "Foot soldiers, is the short answer," says Lugo.

Carbon Calvinism

Beyond influencing—one might even say colonizing—Christianity, the ecological movement can increasingly be seen as something of a religion in and of itself. It is "quasi-religious in character," says Lugo. "It generates its own set of moral values."

Freeman Dyson, the brilliant and contrarian octogenarian physicist, agrees. In a 2008 essay in the *New York Review of Books*, he described environmentalism as "a worldwide secular religion" that has "replaced socialism as the leading secular religion." This religion holds "that we are stewards of the earth, that despoiling the planet with waste products of our luxurious living is a sin, and that the path of righteousness is to live as frugally as possible." The ethics of this new religion, he continued,

> are being taught to children in kindergartens, schools, and colleges all over the world. . . . And the ethics of environmentalism are fundamentally sound. Scientists and economists can agree with Buddhist monks and Christian activists that ruthless destruction of natural habitats is evil and careful preservation of birds and butterflies is good. The worldwide community of environmentalists—most of whom are not scientists—holds the moral high ground, and is guiding human societies toward a hopeful future. Environmentalism, as a religion of hope and respect for nature, is here to stay. This is a religion that we can all share, whether or not we believe that global warming is harmful.

Describing environmentalism as a religion is not equivalent to saying that global warming is not real. Indeed, the evidence for it is overwhelming, and there are powerful reasons to believe that humans are causing it. But no matter its empirical basis, environmentalism is progressively taking the social form of a religion and fulfilling some of the individual needs associated with religion, with major political and policy implications.

William James, the pioneering psychologist and philosopher, defined religion as a belief that the world has an unseen order, coupled with the desire to live in harmony with that order. In his 1902 book *The Varieties of Religious Experience*, James pointed to the value of a community of shared beliefs and practices. He also appreciated the individual quest for spirituality—a search for meaning through encounters with the world. More recently, the late analytic philosopher William P. Alston outlined in *The Encyclopedia of Philosophy* what he considered the essential characteristics of religions. They include a distinction between sacred and profane objects; ritual acts focused upon sacred objects; a moral code; feelings of awe, mystery, and guilt; adoration in the presence of sacred objects and during rituals; a worldview that includes a notion of where the individual fits; and a cohesive social group of the likeminded.

Environmentalism lines up pretty readily with both of those accounts of religion. As climate change literally transforms the heavens above us, faith-based environmentalism increasingly sports saints, sins, prophets, predictions, heretics, demons, sacraments, and rituals. Chief among its holy men is Al Gore—who, according to his supporters, was crucified in the 2000 election, then rose from the political dead and ascended to heaven twice—not only as a Nobel deity, but an Academy Awards angel. He speaks of "Creation care" and cites the Bible in hopes of appealing to evangelicals.

Selling indulgences is out of fashion these days. But you can now assuage your guilt by buying carbon offsets. Fire and brimstone, too, are much in vogue—accompanied by an unmistakable whiff of authoritarianism: "A professor writing in the *Medical Journal of Australia* calls on the Australian government to impose a carbon charge of $5,000 on every birth, annual carbon fees of $800 per child and provide a carbon credit for sterilization," writes Braden R. Allenby, an Arizona State University professor of environmental engineering, ethics, and law. An "article in the *New Scientist* suggests that the problem with obesity is the additional carbon load it imposes on the environment; others that a major social cost of divorce is the additional carbon burden resulting from splitting up families." Allenby, writing in a 2008 article on GreenBiz.com, continues:

> A recent study from the Swedish Ministry of Sustainable Development argues that males have a disproportionately larger impact on global warming ("women cause considerably fewer carbon dioxide emissions than men and thus considerably less climate change"). The chairman of the Intergovernmental Panel on Climate Change states that those who suggest that climate change is not a catastrophic challenge are no different than Hitler. . . . E.O. Wilson calls such people parasites. *Boston Globe* columnist Ellen Goodman writes that "global warming deniers are now on a par with Holocaust deniers."

The sheer volume of vicious language employed to recast social and cultural trends in terms of their carbon footprint suggests the rise of what Allenby calls a dangerous new "carbon fundamentalism."

Some observers detect parallels between the ecological movement and the medieval Church. "One could see Green peacers as crusaders, with the industrialist cast as the infidel," writes Richard North in *New Scientist*. That may be a stretch, but it does seem that this new religion has its share of excommunicated heretics. For example, since daring to challenge environmentalist orthodoxy, Freeman Dyson has discovered himself variously described as "a pompous twit," "a blowhard," "a cesspool of misinformation," and "an old coot riding into the sunset." For his part, Dyson remains cheerily unrepentant. "We are lucky that we can be heretics today without any danger of being burned at the stake," he has said. "But unfortunately I am an old heretic. . . . What the world needs is young heretics."

Many of those making the case that environmentalism has become a religion throw around the word "religion" as a pejorative. This disdain is rooted in an uncontroversial proposition: You cannot reason your way to faith. That's the idea behind the "leap of faith"—or the leap *to* faith, in Kierkegaard's original formulation: the act of believing in something without, or in spite of, empirical evidence. Kierkegaard argued that if we choose faith, we must suspend our reason in order to believe in something higher than reason.

So those on the right side of the political spectrum who portray environmentalism as a religion do so because, if faith is inherently not achievable through rationality, and if environmentalism is a religion, then environmentalism is utterly irrational and must be discredited and ignored. That is the essence of Michael Crichton's 2003 speech. "Increasingly," he said, "it seems facts aren't necessary, because the tenets of environmentalism are all about belief." Environmentalism, he argued, has become totally divorced from science. "It's about whether you are going to be a sinner, or saved. Whether you are going to be one of the people on the side of salvation, or on the side of doom. Whether you are going to be one of us, or one of them."

A similar attack from the right comes from Ray Evans, an Australian businessman, politician, and global-warming skeptic:

> Almost all of the attacks on the mining industry being generated by the environmentalist movement [in the 1990s] were coming out of Northern Europe and Scandinavia, and it didn't take me long to work out that we were dealing with religious belief, that the elites of Northern Europe and Scandinavia—the political elites, the intellectual elites, even the business elites—were, in fact, believers in one brand of environmentalism or another and regardless of the facts. Some of the most bizarre policies were coming out of these countries with respect to metals. I found myself having to find out—"Why is this so?"—because on the face of it they were insane, but they were very strongly held and you'd have to say that when people hold onto beliefs regarding the natural world, and hold onto them regardless of any evidence to the contrary, then you're dealing with religion, you're not dealing with science. . .
>
> Secondly, it fulfills a religious need. They need to believe in sin, so that means sin is equal to pollution. They need to believe in salvation. Well, sustainable development is salvation. They need to believe in a mankind that needs redemption, so you get redemption by stopping using carbon fuels like coal and oil and so on. So, it fulfills a religious need and a political need, which is why they hold onto it so tenaciously, despite all the evidence that the whole thing is nonsense.

Leftists also sometimes disparage environmentalism as religion. In their case, the main objection is usually pragmatic: rationalism effects change and religion doesn't. So, for instance, the Sixties radical Murray Bookchin saw the way environmentalism was hooking up with New Age spirituality as pathetic. "The real cancer that afflicts the planet is capitalism and hierarchy," he wrote. "I don't think we can count on prayers, rituals, and good vibes to remove this cancer. I think we have to fight it *actively* and *with all the power we have*." Bookchin, a self-described revolutionary, dismissed green spirituality as "flaky." He said that his own brand of "social ecology," by contrast, "does not fall back on incantations, sutras, flow diagrams, or spiritual vagaries. It is avowedly *rational*. It does not try to regale metaphorical forms of spiritual mechanism and crude biologisms with Taoist, Buddhist, Christian, or shamanistic 'Eco-la-la.'"

The Prophet and the Heretic

In the 1960s, a British chemist working with the American space program had a flash of insight. Planet Earth, James Lovelock realized, behaves like one complex, living system of which we humans are, in effect, some of its parts. The physical components of the earth, from its atmosphere to its oceans, closely integrate with all of its living organisms to maintain climatic chemistry in a self-regulating balance ideal for the maintenance and propagation of life.

His idea turned out to have scientific value. However, Lovelock would probably just be a footnote in scientific history instead of the much decorated intellectual celebrity he is, except for one thing: He named this vast planetary organism after the Greek goddess who personified the earth—Gaia—and described "Her" as "alive."

So those on the right side of the political spectrum who portray environmentalism as a religion do so because, if faith is inherently not achievable through rationality, and if environmentalism is a religion, then environmentalism is utterly irrational and must be discredited and ignored.

Not only was his Gaia Hypothesis predictably controversial in the world of science—as befits a radical rethinking of earth's complex biosphere—but it was both revered and reviled by those who saw it as fitting in perfectly with tie-dyed New Age spirituality. This was true even though he describes his time at the Jet Propulsion Laboratory in Pasadena as one in which "not all of us were hippies with our rock chicks." For both good and ill, Lovelock not only gave the planet a persona, he created one for himself, becoming "the closest thing we have to an Old Testament prophet, though his deity is not Jehovah but Gaia," as the *Sunday Times* recently noted.

Even though Lovelock continues to go to great lengths to be an empiricist, his 2009 book *The Vanishing Face of Gaia: A Final Warning*—published in the year he celebrated his ninetieth birthday—has been reviewed as a prophet's wrathful jeremiad of planetary doom, studded with parables of possible salvation for the few.

Being embraced by the spiritual left has brought Lovelock fame and attention. Yet it's a marvel the challenges Lovelock has created for himself in changing the minds of zealots. In *Vanishing Face*, for example, Lovelock, ever the scientist, open-mindedly considers the possibilities for last-ditch humans fighting global warming by intentionally reengineering the planet. One idea he discusses is retrofitting every commercial airliner on earth to allow them, as they fly, each to spray a ton or two of sulfuric acid into the stratosphere every day for the foreseeable future. The notion is that this will create molecules that will cause solar energy to be reflected back into space, replacing the reflectivity of the melting polar ice caps.

So, you say to Lovelock: You've succeeded in getting out this idea that the planet is a living organism. An awful lot of people are totally convinced by your hypothesis, and even view you as a prophet. How would you begin to sell this idea of injecting sulfuric acid into a living being that some view in religious terms?

"Yes, especially when you think about the role of the element sulfur in old theology," Lovelock replies. "The devil—the scent of sulfur reveals his presence. I hear what you're saying very clearly. I've never had to sell it to religious greens so far. I don't look forward to the job."

Of environmentalism increasingly being faith-based, Lovelock says, "I would agree with you wholeheartedly. I look at humans as probably having an evolutionary desire to have ideology, to justify their actions. Green thinking is like Christian or Muslim religions—it's another ideology."

In terms of saving Gaia, do you view carbon Calvinism as a net plus or a net minus?

"A net minus. You often hear environmentalists saying that one should do this or the other thing—like not fly—because not doing it can save the planet. It's sheer hubris to imagine we can save Gaia. It's quite beyond our capacity. What we have to do is save ourselves. That's really important. Gaia would like it."

Gaia would like it?

"Yes. I've got to be very careful here, because I get misinterpreted badly. I'm not making out Gaia to be a sentient entity and that sort of thing. It's really metaphoric. So having said that—"

Gaia would think it important for us to save ourselves?

"Exactly. Our evolution of intelligence is something of immense value to the planet. It could make, eventually, part of it, an intelligent planet. More able to deal with problems like incoming asteroids, volcanic outbursts and so on. So I look on us as highly beneficial and therefore certainly worth saving."

The good news about religious greens, Lovelock says, is that they can be led. Saints like him can change minds. "I have a personal experience here. Something like five years ago in Britain they did a big poll. There was hardly anybody" in favor of nuclear power. Now—thanks in no small part to Lovelock's lobbying, at least in his own account—the great majority of Britons favor nuclear energy.

Lovelock's faith in democracy is shared by Bjørn Lomborg. He believes that people want to do good, and if you approach them on that basis, you can get them to listen to reason. Lomborg is the Danish author of *The Skeptical Environmentalist* (published in English in 2001), and the director of the Copenhagen Consensus Center. He has been pilloried for opposing the Kyoto Protocol and other measures to cut carbon emissions in the short term because of the evidence he sees that they don't achieve their goals. Instead, he argues that we should adapt to inevitable short-term temperature rises and spend money on research and development for longer-term environmental solutions, as well as other pressing world crises such as malaria, AIDS, and hunger. He argues, for example, that getting Vitamin A and zinc to 80 percent of the 140 million children in the developing world who lack them is a higher priority than cutting carbon emissions. The cost, he argues, would be $60 million per year, yielding health and cognitive development benefits of over $1 billion.

Despite his heresy, Lomborg thinks empiricism can prevail over faith. He believes that, in a democracy, if you keep calmly and rationally and sympathetically making your case, the great majority can come to think you are making more sense than the true believers. "My sense is that most people do want to do good," he says.

> They don't just want to pay homage to whatever god or whatever religion is the flavor of the year. They actually want to see concrete results that will leave this planet a better place for the future. So I try to engage them in a rational manner rather than in the religious manner. Of course, if people's minds are entirely made up there is nothing you can do to change it. But my sense is that most people are not in that direction. My sense is that in virtually any area, you have probably 10 percent true believers that you just cannot reach. And probably also 10 percent who just disparage it and don't give a hoot about it. But the 80 percent are people who are busy living their lives, loving their kids, and making other plans. And I think those are the 80 percent you want to reach.

So why do so many people want to burn you at the stake?

> Oh sure. Certainly a lot of the high priests have been after me. But I take that as a compliment. It simply means that my argument is a lot more dangerous. If I was just a crazy guy ranting outside the religious gathering, then it might not matter. But I'm the guy who says, maybe you could do smarter. Maybe you could be more rational. Maybe you could spend your money in a better way.

> A lot of people have been after me with totally disproportionate behavior if this were really a discussion on facts. But I continuously try to make this an argument about rationality. Because when you do that, and your opponents perhaps exaggerate, and go beyond the rational argument, it shows up in the conversation. Most people would start saying, "Wow, that's weird, that they'd go this far."

> This is not to deny that global warming is also a serious problem. But then again I ask: why is it that we tackle it only in the way that current dogma talks about—cut carbon emissions right now and feel good about yourself? Instead of focusing on making new innovations that would [allow everyone] to cut carbon emissions in the long run much cheaper, more effectively, and with much greater chance of success.

> When you make those double arguments, I think the 80 percent we've talked about start saying, "That guy makes a lot of sense. Why are the other people continuously almost frothing around the mouth?"And always saying, "No, no, no, it has to be cut carbon emissions and that has to be the biggest problem in the world."

> I think that's the way to counter much of this discussion. It's not about getting your foot into the religious camp as well. It's simply to stand firmly on the rational side and keep saying, "but I *know* you want to do good in the world."

Lovelock and Lomberg, prophet and heretic, honored and reviled, one hoping for action today and the other expecting solutions tomorrow—yet each professes confidence in an eventual democratic endorsement of his plan. Talk about a leap of faith.

The New Religion and Policy

The two faces of religious environmentalism—the greening of mainstream religion and the rise of carbon Calvinism—may each transform the political and policy debate over climate change. In the former case, the growing Christian interest in stewardship could destabilize the political divide that has long characterized the culture wars. Although the pull of social issues has made the right seem like a natural home for evangelicals, a commitment to environmentalism might lead them to align themselves more with the left. Even if no major realignment takes place, the bond between evangelicals and the right might be loosened somewhat. (And beyond politics, other longstanding positions may be shaken up. Activists and scientists who long pooh-poohed evangelicals because of their views on evolution or the life questions will have to get accustomed to working with the new environmental "foot soldiers," and vice versa.)

A deeper concern is the expansion of irrationalism in the making of public policy. Of course, no policy debate can ever be reduced to matters of pure reason; there will always be fundamentally clashing values and visions that cannot be settled by rationality alone. But the rhetoric of many environmentalists is more than just a working out of those fundamental differences. The language of the carbon fundamentalists "indicates a shift from [seeking to help] the public and policymakers understand a complex issue, to demonizing disagreement," as Braden Allenby has written. "The data-driven and exploratory processes of science are choked off by inculcation of belief systems that rely on archetypal and emotive strength. . . . The authority of science is relied on not for factual enlightenment but as ideological foundation for authoritarian policy."

There is nothing unusual about human beings taking more than one path in their search for truth—science at the same time as religion, for example. Nor is there anything unusual about making public policy without sufficient data. We do it all the time; the world sometimes demands it.

The good news about making public policy in alliance with faith is that it can provoke a certain beneficial zeal. People tend to be more deeply moved by faith than by reason alone, and so faith can be very effective in bringing about necessary change—as evidenced by the civil rights movement, among others.

The bad news is that the empirical approach arose in no small part to mitigate the dangers of zeal—to keep blood from flowing in the streets. A strict focus on fact and reason whenever possible can avert error and excess in policy. But can someone who has made a faith of environmentalism—whose worldview and lifestyle have been utterly shaped by it—adapt to changing facts? For the one fact we reliably know about the future of the planet's climate is that the facts will change. It is simply too complex to be comprehensively and accurately modeled. As climatologist Gavin Schmidt jokes, there is a simple way to produce a perfect model of our climate that will predict the weather with 100 percent accuracy: first, start with a universe that is exactly like ours; then wait 14 billion years.

So what happens if, say, we discover that it is not possible to return the environment to the conditions we desire, as James Lovelock expects? What happens if evidence accumulates that we should address climate change with methods that the carbon Calvinists don't approve of? To what extent, if any, would devotees of the "natural" accept reengineering the planet? How long will it take, if ever, for nuclear power to be accepted as green?

In the years ahead, we will see whether the supposedly scientific debates over the environment can really be conducted by fact and reason alone, or whether necessary change, whatever that may turn out be, will require some new Reformation. For if environmental matters really have become matters of faith—if environmentalism has become a new front in the longstanding culture wars—then what place is left for the crucial function of pragmatic, democratic decision-making?

Joel Garreau is the author of Radical Evolution: The Promise and Peril of Enhancing Our Minds, Our Bodies—*and* What it Means to Be Human *(Doubleday, 2005); the Lincoln Professor of Law, Culture, and Values at Arizona State University; and a Senior Future Tense Fellow at the New America Foundation. This article was developed during a Templeton-Cambridge Journalism Fellowship in Science and Religion at the University of Cambridge.*

The Emerging Alliance of World Religions and Ecology

By John Grim and Mary Evelyn Tucker
Carnegie Ethics Online, September 2, 2009

Introduction

This article aims to present a prismatic view of the potential and actual resources embedded in the world's religions for supporting sustainable practices toward the environment. An underlying assumption is that most religious traditions have developed attitudes of respect, reverence, and care for the natural world that brings forth life in its diverse forms. Furthermore, it is assumed that issues of social justice and environmental integrity need to be intricately linked for creating the conditions for a sustainable future.

Several qualifications regarding the various roles of religion should be mentioned at the outset. First, we do not wish to suggest here that any one religious tradition has a privileged ecological perspective. Rather, multiple perspectives may be the most helpful in identifying the contributions of the world's religions to the flourishing of life for future generations.

Second, while we assume that religions are necessary partners in the current ecological movement, they are not sufficient without the indispensable contributions of science, economics, education, and policy to the varied challenges of current environmental problems. Therefore, this is an interdisciplinary effort in which religions can play a part.

Third, we acknowledge that there is frequently a disjunction between principles and practices: ecologically sensitive ideas in religions are not always evident in environmental practices in particular civilizations. Many civilizations have overused their environments, with or without religious sanction.

Finally, we are keenly aware that religions have all too frequently contributed to tensions and conflict among ethnic groups, both historically and at present. Dogmatic rigidity, inflexible claims of truth, and misuse of institutional and communal power by religions have led to tragic consequences in various parts of the globe.

Nonetheless, while religions have often preserved traditional ways, they have also provoked social change. They can be limiting but also liberating in their outlooks. In the 20th century, for example, religious leaders and theologians helped to give birth to progressive movements such as civil rights for minorities, social justice for the poor, and liberation for women. More recently, religious groups were instrumental in launching a movement called Jubilee 2000 for debt reduction for poor nations.[1] Although the world's religions have been slow to respond to our current environmental crises, their moral authority and their institutional power may help effect a change in attitudes, practices, and public policies.

The Challenge of the Environmental Crisis and the Role of Religions in Meeting It

The environmental crisis has been well documented as a plural reality in its various interconnected aspects of resource depletion and species extinction, pollution growth and climate change, population explosion and overconsumption.[2] Thus, while we are using the term "environmental crisis" in a singular form, we recognize the diverse nature of the interrelated problems. These problems have been subject to extensive analysis and scrutiny by the scientific and policy communities and, although comprehensive solutions remain elusive, there is an emerging consensus that the environmental crisis is both global in scope and local in impact. A major question we confront is: What are the appropriate boundaries for the protection and use of nature? The choices will not be easy as we begin to reassess our sense of rights and responsibilities to present and future generations, and to reevaluate appropriate needs and overextended greed regarding natural resources.

Many organizations and individuals have been calling for greater participation by various religious communities in meeting the growing environmental crisis by reorienting humans to show more respect, restraint, and responsibility toward the Earth community.[3] Consider, for example, a statement by scientists, "Preserving and Cherishing the Earth: An Appeal for Joint Commitment in Science and Religion," issued at a Global Forum meeting in Moscow in January of 1990. It suggests that the human community is committing "crimes against creation" and notes that "problems of such magnitude, and solutions demanding so broad a perspective, must be recognized from the outset as having a religious as well as a scientific dimension. Mindful of our common responsibility, we scientists—many of us long engaged in combating the environmental crisis—urgently appeal to the world religious community to commit, in word and deed, and as boldly as is required, to preserve the environment of the Earth." It goes on to declare that "the environmental crisis requires radical changes not only in public policy, but in individual behavior. The historical record makes clear that religious teaching, example, and leadership are powerfully able to influence personal conduct and commitment. As scientists, many of us have had profound experiences of awe and reverence before the universe. We understand that what is regarded as sacred is more likely to be treated with care and respect. Our planetary home should be so regarded. Efforts to safeguard and cherish the environment need to be infused with a vision of the sacred."[4]

Although the responses of religions to the global environmental crisis were slow at first, they have been steadily growing over the last 25 years.[5] Just as religions played an important role in creating sociopolitical changes in the 20th century (e.g., human and civil rights), so now religions are poised in the 21st century to contribute to the emergence of a broader environmental ethics based on diverse sensibilities regarding the sacred dimensions of the natural world.

Religion and Ecology

Religion is more than simply a belief in a transcendent deity or a means to an after-life. It is, rather, an orientation to the cosmos and our role in it. We understand religion in its broadest sense as a means whereby humans, recognizing the limitations of phenomenal reality, undertake specific practices to effect self-transformation and community cohesion within a cosmological context. Religion thus refers to those cosmological stories, symbol systems, ritual practices, ethical norms, historical processes, and institutional structures that transmit a view of the human as embedded in a world of meaning and responsibility, transformation and celebration. Religion connects humans with a divine or numinous presence, with the human community, and with the broader Earth community. It links humans to the larger matrix of mystery in which life arises, unfolds, and flourishes.

In this light nature is a revelatory context for orienting humans to abiding religious questions regarding the cosmological origins of the universe, the meaning of the emergence of life, and the responsible role of humans in relation to life processes. Religion thus situates humans in relation to both the natural and human worlds with regard to meaning and responsibility. At the same time, religion becomes a means of experiencing a sustaining creative force in the natural and human worlds and beyond. For some traditions this is a creator deity; for others it is a numinous presence in nature; for others it is the source of flourishing life.

This experience of a creative force gives rise to a human desire to enter into processes of transformation and celebration that link self, society, and cosmos. The individual is connected to the larger human community and to the macrocosm of the universe itself. The transformative impulse seeks relationality, intimacy, and communion with this numinous power. Individual and communal transformations are expressed through rituals and ceremonies of celebration. More specifically, these transformations have the capacity to embrace the celebration of natural seasonal cycles as well as various cultural rites of passage. Religion thus links humanity to the rhythms of nature through the use of symbols and rituals that help to establish moral relationships and patterns for social exchange.

The issues discussed here are complex and involve various peoples, cultures, worldviews, and academic disciplines. Therefore, it is important to be clear about our terms. As it is used here, the term "ecology" locates the human within the horizon of emergent, interdependent life rather than viewing humanity as the vanguard of evolution, the exclusive fabricator of technology, or a species apart from nature. "Scientific ecology" is a term used to indicate the empirical and experimental study of the relations between living and nonliving organisms within their ecosystems. While drawing on the scientific understanding of interrelationships in nature, we are introducing the term "religious ecology" to point toward a cultural awareness of kinship with and dependence on nature for the continuity of all life. Thus, religious ecology provides a basis for exploring diverse cultural responses to the varied earth processes of transformation. In addition, the study of religious ecology can give us insight into how particular environments have influenced the development of cultures. Therefore, one can distinguish religious ecology from scientific ecology just as one can distinguish religious cosmology from scientific cosmology.

The issues discussed here are complex and involve various peoples, cultures, worldviews, and academic disciplines. Therefore, it is important to be clear about our terms. As it is used here, the term "ecology" locates the human within the horizon of emergent, interdependent life rather than viewing humanity as the vanguard of evolution, the exclusive fabricator of technology, or a species apart from nature.

This awareness of the interdependence of life in religious ecology finds expression in the religious traditions as a sacred reality that is often recognized as a creative manifestation, a pervasive sustaining presence, a vital power in the natural world, or an emptiness (sunyata) leading to the realization of interbeing.[6] For many religions, the natural world is understood as a source of teaching, guidance, visionary inspiration, revelation, or power. At the same time, nature is also a source of food, clothing, and shelter. Thus, religions have developed intricate systems of exchange and thanksgiving around human dependence on animals and plants, on forests and fields, on rivers and oceans. These encompass symbolic and ritual exchanges that frequently embody agricultural processes, ecological knowledge of ecosystems, or hunting practices.[7]

Methodological Approaches to Study of Religion and Ecology

There is an inevitable disjunction between the examination of historical religious traditions in all of their diversity and complexity and the application of teachings or scriptures to contemporary situations. While religions have always been involved in meeting contemporary challenges over the centuries, it is clear that the global environmental crisis is larger and more complex than anything in recorded human history. Thus, a simple application of traditional ideas to contemporary problems is unlikely to be either possible or adequate. In order to address ecological problems properly, religious leaders and laypersons have to be in dialogue with environmentalists, scientists, economists, businesspeople, politicians, and educators. With these qualifications in mind we can then identify three methodological approaches that appear in the emerging study of religion and ecology: retrieval, reevaluation, and reconstruction. Interpretive retrieval involves the scholarly investigation of cosmological, scriptural, and legal sources in order to clarify traditional religious teachings regarding human-Earth relations. This requires that historical and textual studies uncover resources latent within the tradition. In addition, interpretive retrieval can identify ethical codes and ritual customs of the tradition in order to discover how these teachings were put into practice.

In interpretive reevaluation, traditional teachings are evaluated with regard to their relevance to contemporary circumstances. Can the ideas, teachings, or ethics present in these traditions be adopted by contemporary scholars or practitioners who wish to help shape more ecologically sensitive attitudes and sustainable practices? Reevaluation also questions ideas that may lead to inappropriate environmental practices. For example, are certain religious tendencies reflective of otherworldly or world-denying orientations that are not helpful in relation to pressing ecological issues? It asks as well whether the material world of nature has been devalued by a particular religion and whether a model of ethics focusing solely on human interaction is adequate to address environmental problems.

Finally, interpretive reconstruction suggests ways that religious traditions might adapt their teachings to current circumstances in new and creative ways. This may result in a new synthesis or in a creative modification of traditional ideas and practices to suit modern modes of expression. This is the most challenging aspect of the emerging field of religion and ecology and requires sensitivity to who is speaking about a tradition in the process of reevaluation and reconstruction. Postcolonial critics have appropriately highlighted the complex issues surrounding the problem of who is representing or interpreting a tradition. Nonetheless, practitioners and leaders of particular traditions may find grounds for creative dialogue with scholars of religious traditions in these various phases of interpretation.

Diversity and Dialogue of Religions

The diversity of the world's religions may seem self-evident to some, but it is worth stressing the differences within and between religious traditions. At the same time, it is possible to posit shared dimensions of religions in light of this diversity, without arguing that the world's religions have some single emergent goal. The world's religions are inherently distinctive in their expressions, and these differences are especially significant in regard to the study of religion and ecology. Several sets of religious diversity can be identified as being integrally related. First, there is historical and cultural diversity within and between religious traditions as expressed over time in varied social contexts. For example, we need to be sensitive to the variations in Judaism between Orthodox, Conservative, and Reform movements, in Christianity between Catholic, Orthodox, and Protestant varieties of the tradition, and in Islam between Sunni and Shiite positions.

Second, there is dialogical and syncretic diversity within and between religions traditions, which adds another level of complexity. Dialogue and interaction between traditions engenders the fusion of religious traditions into one another, often resulting in new forms of religious expression that can be described as syncretic. Such syncretism occurred when Christian missionaries evangelized indigenous peoples in the Americas. In East Asia there is an ongoing dialogue between and among Confucianism, Daoism, and Buddhism that results in various kinds of syncretism.[8]

Third, there is ecological and cosmological diversity within and between religions. Ecological diversity is evident in the varied environmental contexts and bioregions where religions have developed over time. For example, Jerusalem is the center of a sacred bioregion where three religious traditions—Judaism, Christianity, and Islam—have both shaped and been shaped by the environment. These complex interactions illustrate that religions are not static in their impacts on ecology. Indeed, throughout history the relationships between religions and their natural settings have been fluid and manifold.

Religious traditions develop unique narratives, symbols, and rituals to express their relationships with the cosmos as well as with various local landscapes. For example, the body is a vital metaphor for understanding the Daoist relationship with the world: as an energetic network of breathings-in and breathings-out, the body, according to Daoism, expresses the basic pattern of the cosmos. Another example, from Buddhism, of a distinctive ecological understanding involves Doi Suthep, a sacred mountain in the Chiang Mai valley of northern Thailand: the ancient Thai reverence for the mountain is understood as analogous to respect for the Buddhist reliquary, or stupa.

Converging Perspectives: Common Values for the Earth Community

The project of exploring world religions and ecology may lead toward convergence on several overarching principles. The common values that most of the world's religions hold in relation to the natural world might be summarized as reverence, respect, restraint, redistribution, responsibility, and renewal. While there are clearly variations of interpretation within and between religions regarding these six principles, it may be said that religions are moving toward an expanded understanding of their cosmological orientations and ethical obligations. Although these principles have been previously understood primarily with regard to relations toward other humans, the challenge now is to extend them to the natural world.

As this shift occurs—and there are signs it is already happening—religions can advocate reverence for the earth and its profound cosmological processes, respect for the earth's myriad species, an extension of ethics to include all life forms, restraint in the use of natural resources combined with support for effective alternative technologies, equitable redistribution of wealth, the acknowledgement of human responsibility in regard to the continuity of life and the ecosystems that support life, renewal of the energies of hope for the transformative work to be done.

Just as religious values needed to be identified, so, too, the values embedded in science, education, economics, and public policy also need to be more carefully understood. Scientific analysis will be critical to understanding nature's economy; education will be indispensable to creating sustainable modes of life; economic incentives will be central to an equitable distribution of resources; public-policy recommendations will be invaluable in shaping national and international priorities.

But the ethical values that inform modern science and public policy must not be uncritically applied. Instead, by carefully evaluating the intellectual resources both of the world's religions and of modern science and public policy, our long-term ecological prospects may emerge. We need to examine the tensions between efficiency and equity, between profit and preservation, and between the private and public good. We need to make distinctions between human need and greed, between the use and abuse of nature, and between the intrinsic value and instrumental value of nature. We need to move from destructive to constructive modes of production, and from the accumulation of goods to an appreciation for the common good of the Earth community.

There has been much progress in the arena of religion and ecology. Indeed, a new academic field of study has emerged with implications for public policy. This is in large measure due to a three-year conference series at Harvard's Center for the Study of World Religions from 1996–1998, which resulted in ten edited volumes, a large website, the journal *Worldviews: Global Religions, Culture, and Ecology*, and the formation of the Forum on Religion and Ecology based at Yale University. Other milestones include the *Encyclopedia of Religion*, published in 2005. Thousands of people around the globe are now participating in this work, both in the classroom and in engaged projects for a sustainable future.

Notes

1. The movement, which began in Britain, has had demonstrable influence on the decisions of the World Bank and other lending organizations to reduce or forgive debts in more than twenty countries. See http://www.jubilee2000uk.org/
2. See, for example, IPCC Fourth Assessment Report, 2007.
3. See http://www.thomasberry.org
4. "Preserving and Cherishing the Earth: An Appeal for Joint Commitment in Science and Religion," 1990.
5. For two examples of this, see: Stewardship or Sacrifice? Conference, October 2009, Rock Ethics Institute and Public Campaign on Climate Change, World Council of Churches.
6. The term "interbeing" is used in the writings of the Vietnamese monk Thich Nhat Hanh.
7. See Eugene N. Anderson, *Ecologies of the Heart: Emotion, Belief, and the Environment* (New York and Oxford: Oxford University Press, 1996) and John A. Grim, ed., *Indigenous Traditions and Ecology: The Interbeing of Cosmology and Community* (Cambridge, Mass.: Center for the Study of World Religions, Harvard Divinity School, 2001).
8. See Judith A. Berling, *The Syncretic Religion of Lin Chao-en* (New York: Columbia University Press, 1980).

Stewards of the Earth

The Growing Religious Mission to Protect the Environment

By Jim E. Motavalli
E: The Environmental Magazine, November 2002

When conservative evangelical Christians call for action on global warming, Hindu holy men dedicate themselves to saving sacred rivers and Buddhist monks work with Islamic mullahs to try to halt the extinction crisis, boundaries are clearly being redrawn in the ongoing struggle for the political hearts and minds of the world's believers. Faith-based environmental activism is soaring, and with it comes new criticism that some religious leaders are straying from church doctrine. Many of the arguments hinge on a seemingly simple point: Did God give human beings "dominion" over the Earth, to control as we see fit, or did God give us "stewardship" of creation as a sacred trust?

One factor in the resurgence of faith-based environmentalism is the 1993 founding of the National Religious Partnership for the Environment (NRPE) by a former radio talk show host and spokesperson for New York City's Episcopal Cathedral of St. John the Divine named Paul Gorman. NRPE quickly proved its effectiveness by joining together and helping educate such disparate and mainstream bodies as the U.S. Catholic Conference (the policy agency for all Catholic bishops, derby and parishes), the National Council of Churches of Christ (a federation of Protestant, Eastern Orthodox and African-American denominations), the Coalition on the Environment and Jewish Life (COEJL, an alliance across all four Jewish movements) and the Evangelical Environmental Network (a coalition of evangelical Christian agencies and institutions).

With such dynamic leadership, churches are moving environmental concerns to the heart of their ministry, and they are calling on their congregants to take increasingly radical action. "A child born in a wealthy country is likely to consume, waste and pollute more in his lifetime than 50 children born in developing nations," said the Archbishop of Canterbury in a New Year's address on the eve of 2001. "It may not be time to build an ark like Noah, but it is high time to take better care of God's creation."

In 1997, the Patriarchate of the Greek Orthodox Church, Bartholomew I, used strong language against polluters. "To commit a crime against the natural world is a sin," he said. "For humans to cause species to become extinct and to destroy the biological diversity of God's creation . . ., for humans to degrade the integrity of [the]

Earth by causing changes in its climate, stripping the Earth of its natural forests or destroying its wetlands . . ., for humans to contaminate the Earth's waters, its land, its air and its life with poisonous substances, these are sins," he said.

In a 1990 World Day of Peace message, Pope John Paul II emphasized that Christian responsibility toward nature is an essential part of faith. Statements like these are common across many denominations, but it's the concrete actions and growing faith-based activism that represents an important change. The impassioned Earth Charter, which grew out of the 1992 Rio Earth Summit, calls for an ethically based "global partnership to care for the Earth and one another."

Last June, Patriarch Bartholomew and the Pope issued a strong "Common Declaration" that affirmed their environmental commitment. "God has not abandoned the world," it said. "It is His will that His design and our hope for it will be realized through our co-operation in restoring its original harmony. In our own time we are witnessing a growth of an ecological awareness which needs to be encouraged, so that it will lead to practical programs and initiatives"

The declaration can be read as a call to action. "It's one thing to have theological arguments, but the average congregation needs to connect those with their own lives," says Rebecca Gould, professor of religion and environmental studies at Vermont's Middlebury College. "Environmental issues are a reminder that there is a connection." According to Gould, congregations are beginning to step forward and say, "Our house of worship should reflect our beliefs for creation." Some, like Ursula Goodenough, a professor of biology at Washington University, go even further and say that we may, indeed, need new houses of worship. "There are two ways the religious project can move forward," she says. "One is working within the traditions and greening them, and the other is trying to articulate new religions where environmental transformation is the whole point."

The religious reawakening has rippled across faiths, creating unlikely coalitions. NRPE's priority is to "weave the mission of care for God's creation across all areas of organized religion." Since 1993, it has incorporated environmental activities into already established social programs. Habitat for Humanity, a Christian housing organization, began identifying chemical threats in construction and promoting environmentally friendly materials; the United Jewish Appeal underwrote curricula for environmental education. The Association of Evangelical Relief and Development agencies prepared field staff to become environmental and anti-hunger campaigners.

Congregation-based projects were soon born as well: Jesus People Against Pollution in Columbia, Mississippi, has surveyed 20,000 citizens affected by the chemical dioxin and forced Superfund clean-ups. The Sisters of the Immaculate Heart in Detroit, Michigan, have turned a former crack cocaine house into a community garden and cleared 120 lots for planting trees and flowers. The Hamburg Presbyterian Church in upstate New York adopted a nearby creek, monitoring pH levels and winning it state designation as a protected habitat.

Since pollution concentrates in poor and often non-white neighborhoods, many churches see the struggle for environmental justice as ideally combining the twin missions of concern for the world's disadvantaged with concern for the Earth itself.

The United States Catholic Conference's Environmental Justice Program awards grants to help parishes develop reuse plans for abandoned brownfields, educate communities about the health problems of toxic emissions, and train teachers in land stewardship and ethics. According to Program Director Walt Grazer, some 20,000 environmental justice resource kits have been distributed to every parish in the U.S.

Target Earth, a national Christian group, has activities in 15 countries, including field stations, hands-on service projects and conservation programs. Particularly active on college campuses, Target Earth educates students and sends them on green-themed alternative spring break programs.

The environmental work of Christian churches extends far beyond the U.S., to include such exemplary projects as the tree planting organized by Zimbabwe's African Independent Churches (AIC) that has transformed what were once barren landscapes. Working with the indigenous Shona people of Zimbabwe, the churches' ZIRCON environmental arm plants more than one million native and non-native fruit trees per year.

Ultimately, the care for creation agenda will be advanced congregation by congregation, at the grassroots level. That's just the approach taken by Seattle-based Earth Ministry, which has recruited what it calls colleagues in 90 mainline Christian churches in the Puget Sound area. According to Nancy Wright, a Congregational minister and program associate with Earth Ministry, the colleagues lead book discussions, organize hikes and stream restorations, promote community-supported agriculture and conduct top-to-bottom "greenings" of church facilities.

Wright is optimistic about the chances for spreading this new gospel, but she's also realistic. "Unfortunately" she says, "the churches are declining in membership, and that is a factor. But I see wonderful developments like the Patriarch's statement and it makes me hopeful. It's not really a new thing that fellowship with God includes care for creation—it goes back to scripture. But we're awakening to new possibilities."

Science and Religion Meet

There is an uncomfortable moment during the film *Contact* in which the scientist Ellie Arroway (Jodie Foster) is asked if she believes in God. Never having been confronted with this question before, the usually voluble scientist answers evasively, and it temporarily sinks her mission as Earth's representative to other worlds.

Many of today's scientists would be more prepared for religious questions. In 1995, for example, Heinz Award–winning marine biologist Jane Lubchenco was a participant in a conference organized by the Greek Orthodox Church that marked the 1,900th anniversary of the Book of Revelations and focused on "The Apocalypse and the Environment." She says, "There's a reawakening in many different faith groups, and it's informed by science but certainly not driven by it."

In 1937, Nobel Prize–winning physicist Max Planck wrote in his essay "On Religion and Science," "Man needs science in order to know; religion in order to act." In their book *The Good in Nature and Humanity*, Stephen Kellert and Timothy

Farnham talk about the need for "a common vocabulary, a language that allows thoughtful people to cross over safely and share ideas about science, religion, spirituality and the natural world."

Science and religion were once more intimately connected. Mary Evelyn Tucker, the Bucknell University professor of religion who (with her husband John Grim) organized the "Religions of the World and Ecology" conference series at Harvard, says, "All of the religious traditions, from those of the indigenous peoples to Taoism and Confucianism, have had a sense that we live within a larger cosmos. They saw a bigger frame of time and space, with us dwelling in what you might call 'intimate immensities,' that recognized not only the vastness of the universe but also the intimacy of natural processes. For example, the beauty and mystery of a sunset will stop us all, and science alone cannot fully explain all the incredible complexity at work. For that, we developed liturgical celebrations of the solstice and equinox, but much of this fell into disuse as religions became more human-centered and neglected the connection to the Earth."

That may now be changing, in part because of the immensity of the environmental crisis we face. In a lecture delivered as part of the Harvard series in 1996, religious historian Thomas Berry noted hopefully that "perhaps a new revelatory experience is taking place, an experience wherein human consciousness awakens to the grandeur and sacred quality of the Earth process. Humanity has not participated in such a vision since shamanic times, but in such a renewal lies our hope for the future for ourselves and for the entire planet." Berry's idea of renewal is reflected in a 1992 warning signed by 1,670 scientists, including 104 Nobel laureates, that called for "a great change in our stewardship of the Earth."

George Fisher, a professor of geology at Johns Hopkins, asks, "How do those of us living in the western world share resources with the other 90 percent of the Earth's population? These are scientific questions in part, because we need to know how the Earth works, but science doesn't tell us what we should do. Those are moral and ethical questions."

Writing in a special issue of *Daedalus* magazine edited by Tucker and Grim, Columbia University Professor George Rupp notes that humanity has developed the capacity to alter the Earth, its climate and its biodiversity in a profound way, and that "the critical question is whether we have the wisdom and ethical maturity to employ our scientific and technological skills with discretion. We need to step back and take stock if we are to avoid serious mistakes." John Cobb, Jr. of the Claremont School of Theology calls for an engaged Christian church that "finds it way between leaving all to God and celebrating the human ability to create." In 1972, he wrote a book called *Is it Too Late?*, and he's still asking that question.

Religion offers a framework for that kind of analysis. And it is becoming increasingly clear to many religious denominations that environmental issues are intruding on what have traditionally been their concerns, such as alleviating the suffering of the poor. As Pennsylvania-based environmental attorney Donald Brown writes in *Daedalus*, climate change acquires a clear ethical dimension when, despite the disproportionate generation of global warming gases by wealthier nations, its biggest impact is on the health, food supplies and well-being of the world's poorest people.

NRPE's Gorman points out that the Biblical story of Noah's ark is a powerful prophetic argument for preserving biodiversity. "Noah's covenant is with all creation for succeeding generations," he says.

One of the world's most prominent scientists, entomologist E.O. Wilson of Harvard, has written eloquently about the extinction crisis, and he is heartened by the growing alliance between religious groups and scientists. "I like to think that the environmental values of secular and religious alike arise from the same innate attraction to nature," he writes in *The Future of Life*. "They express the same compassion for animals, aesthetic response to free-living flowers and birds, and wonders at the mysteries of wild environments." Marc Bekoff, the author of *Minding Animals* and a professor of animal behavior at the University of Colorado, also sees a growing concern among faith communities about the importance of preserving species. "It's amazing to me the number of religious scholars who want to know about animal behavior and animal ecology," he adds.

Energy and Climate: Galvanizing Issues

The religious community is joining a growing movement against global warming that is determined to reduce carbon dioxide emissions by building support for sustainable energy. Against a vacuum of leadership from the federal government, it is building from the bottom up.

Meeting in Oxford, England, last July, a landmark gathering of environmental scientists, theologians and policymakers issued a declaration stating very firmly that global warming is real, and that it is the duty of committed Christians to do something about it. "By reducing the Earth's biological diversity" their statement said, "human-induced climate change diminishes God's creation. . . . The call to 'love the Lord Your God and love your neighbor' (Matthew 22:37-39) takes on new implications in the face of present and projected climate change."

"This was an important breakthrough," says Climate Forum 2002 participant Reverend Jim Ball, the American Baptist minister who heads the Evangelical Environmental Network. "The meeting brought together senior climate scientists and Christian leaders, and it really helped us understand this crucial issue."

It helped that many of the participating scientists were themselves evangelical Christians, including co-convenor Sir John Houghton of the John Ray Initiative, a former science advisor to Margaret Thatcher who edited the first and second assessment reports for the UN-sponsored Inter-Governmental Panel on Climate Change (IPCC).

Among the declaration's signers was Reverend Richard Cizik, vice president of the National Association of Evangelicals, an influential body that represents between 25 and 40 million churchgoers. "Many evangelicals have been led to believe that the challenge of global warming is simply fiction, but I don't see how they could take a look at the evidence of these scientists—many of whom are also

Christians—and not be convinced. The church community is challenged to examine the evidence for global warming, and to respond to the fact of it," Cizik says.

For many environmentalists, the phrase "evangelical Christian" is likely to conjure an implacable enemy who supports Jerry Falwell, the Christian Coalition and the polluters' lobby in Congress. But in fact there is a wide spectrum of opinion—and a growing activism for the environment. "Our purpose as an organization is to help evangelical Christians understand what the Bible says about caring for all creation," says Ball, another Oxford signatory.

The Oxford Declaration was not a shot in the dark or an isolated incident. "The involvement of the religious community is growing quickly—and is essential," says climate journalist Ross Gelbspan, author of *The Heat Is On*. "When I talk about the climate crisis to policymakers, I cast it in terms of bottom line thinking because that's their vocabulary. But, at root, climate change is a moral and ethical issue."

Sally Bingham, the environmental minister at the Episcopal Grace Cathedral in San Francisco, cites the second chapter of Genesis as a motivation for her work. "God put Adam in the Garden to till it and to keep it. We haven't done a very good job of that. Christians are commanded to love their neighbors, and you can't do that by polluting their air and water."

Bingham formed California Interfaith Power and Light to convince the state's 50,000 religious congregations to become more energy-conscious. Bingham, who was briefly jailed for a nonviolent protest against proposed oil drilling in the Alaska National Wildlife Refuge, has recruited Jewish and Muslim congregations. Members are asked to sign "covenants" committing them to improving the energy efficiency of their buildings, to creating global warming education campaigns, and to using renewable energy when possible. There are now solar panels on the roofs of Gloria Dei Lutheran Church in Sacramento and Congregation Shir Hadash in Los Gatos, for instance. Volunteers like Oakland Mayor Jerry Brown have helped more than 150 member parishes install compact fluorescent lights and make other energy-saving changes. An action guide for this kind of hands-on reform, Responsible Purchasing for Faith Communities, is available from the Center for a New American Dream (www.newdream.org).

In 2001, the U.S. Catholic Bishops said in an unequivocal statement: "While some uncertainty remains, most experts agree that something significant is happening to the atmosphere. Human behavior and activity are, according to the most recent findings of international scientific bodies, contributing to a warming of the Earth's climate. . . . Consequently, it seems prudent not only to continue to research and monitor this phenomenon, but to take steps now to mitigate possible negative effects."

That same year, Congregational minister Dan Smith took to his pulpit in Lexington, Massachusetts, and asked, "What Would Jesus Drive?" Such questions are rooted in evangelical tradition, where "What Would Jesus Do?" is a common query. With help from environmental writer Bill McKibben, Smith crafted a campaign that included demonstrations at sport-utility vehicle (SUV) dealerships. "I wanted to encourage faithful people to consider how their daily decisions were either

Sally Bingham, the environmental minister at the Episcopal Grace Cathedral in San Francisco, cites the second chapter of Genesis as a motivation for her work. "God put Adam in the Garden to till it and to keep it. We haven't done a very good job of that. Christians are commanded to love their neighbors, and you can't do that by polluting their air and water."

contributing to healing God's creation or to the destruction of it," Smith told his congregants. In an interview, he added, "I felt compelled to say something about global warming, but our church parking lot is usually half full of SUVs. For me to be involved in an activist rally surprised some people, but the congregation has been supportive." The Evangelical Environmental Network hopes to launch "What Would Jesus Drive?" as a national campaign.

The Jewish Council for Public Affairs (representing 13 national and 122 local Jewish public affairs organizations) adopted a resolution advocating that Congress move toward a clean and sustainable energy system that will diminish reliance on imported oil and reduce greenhouse gas emissions. COEJL director Mark Jacobs testified before Congress in support of increasing vehicle fuel economy standards.

Interfaith global climate change campaigns have formed in 18 states, educating congregations and organizing visits with elected officials. The National Council of Churches (NCC), working with COEJL, created the Interfaith Climate Change Network, which describes global warming as "a matter of justice . . . for future generations who will inherit an unstable climate." Bob Edgar, the Methodist minister and former Congressman who is NCC's general secretary, says, "We've led efforts on climate change, and we've educated people about energy efficiency."

Active for Islam

Especially in light of the terrorist attacks of September 11, 2001, it is important to point out the deep ecological teachings inherent in Islam, and the very real on-the-ground projects that have developed from them. Although high-impact environmentalism is still not widespread in Islamic societies, some efforts have taken root. The Sultan of Oman, for instance, has worked with the World Wildlife Fund to successfully reintroduce the native oryx (an antelope that had disappeared from the wild in the 1970s). And in Saudi Arabia, King Fahd established research centers to breed endangered species, coupled with a network of nature reserves and a public education campaign.

"Allah entrusted man with the guardianship of the Earth," says the Islamic Foundation for Ecology and Environmental Sciences, founded in the mid-1980s. "We have to fulfill that ancient trust now, before it becomes too late." The foundation has set up an extensive training program in environmental teachings based on the Qur'an. It promotes self-sufficiency in farming through organic agriculture and permaculture, and it serves as a demonstration center for solar technology, water wheels, waste recycling and wind power. The foundation distributes a teaching pack entitled "Qur'an Creation and Conservation," and it is setting up the Muslim Alliance for Conservation as an international grassroots organization.

Richard Foltz, an Islamicist who teaches in the religion department at the University of Florida, says the strongest environmental activism in the Muslim world occurs in Iran, which also has the most direct Islamic rule. Although the mullahs are not themselves sponsors of green initiatives, the revolutionary constitution adapted in 1979 asserts that protection of the natural environment is "a public obligation" and that "all activities, economic or otherwise, which may cause irreversible damage to the environment are forbidden."

Despite the strong words, however, Teheran, Iran's capital city, has some of the worst air pollution in the world, killing an estimated 7,500 people a year from related illnesses. The country also faces water and population crises, and some 149 independent Iranian environmental groups have been launched in response. Among the most active is the Green Front, established by four medical students in 1989. In 1999, it organized hundreds of volunteers in a cleanup of the Caspian Sea coast.

Although many Muslim countries campaign against women's reproductive rights, Iran's Islamic government has one of the world's most extensive birth control programs. Family planning courses are mandatory for engaged couples, and birth control devices are free and widely available. According to the Population Reference Bureau, an annual growth rate of 3.9 percent in 1976 has been slashed to 1.2 percent today.

"Iran shatters all the stereotypes about Islam and the environment" says Foltz. This is due at least in part to pioneering work done by Sewed Hossein Nasr of George Washington University, author of the influential *Man and Nature*. The environmental crisis, he says, "is in reality a spiritual and religious crisis." Unfortunately, while Iran is a role model for much of the Islamic world, it has found few adherents on the environment. In most Islamic countries, population control is a taboo subject, and rigid centralized control stifles grassroots movements. Women's rights and, by most measures, freedom are the lowest in the world in Arab societies, according to the United Nations' Arab Human Development Report 2002.

The Buddhist Way

There is a strong tradition of respect for nature in Buddhism as well. As Nick Wallis of the Friends of the Western Buddhist Order explains, "All the most significant events [of Buddha's life] occur in the countryside and are associated with trees." Buddha was born as his mother grasped the branch of a sal tree, and he achieved Enlightenment beneath the Bodhi tree. "Studying Buddhism, I was taught the importance of a caring attitude toward the environment," writes the Dalai Lama. "Our practice of nonviolence applies not just to human beings but to all sentient beings or any living thing."

In practice, environmentalists face an uphill battle being heard in societies that are authoritarian and rapidly industrializing, but religious faith has manifested itself in courageous ways. Some 700 Thai monks and nuns are united in Sekiya Dhamma, a network that has fought logging and other environmental exploitation. One such monk is Pha Pachak, who in order to protect forests from loggers wrapped saffron monk's cloth around imperiled trees and blessed them. The tactic worked, since killing an ordained being is a dangerous undertaking for people of Buddhist faith. But Pha Pachak was beaten and thrown in jail for his obstruction of the powerful lumber industry. Pachak's work is carried on: in 1999, an International Solidarity Walk through Thailand ended with an Interfaith Tree Ordination.

The monk Buddhadasa Bhikkhu, who died in 1993, was a kindred spirit; he was very politically active and a strong environmentalist. "The greedy and selfish are destroying nature," he declared. Also in Thailand, writer and activist Sulak Sivaraska has helped form a number of groups, including the International Network of Engaged Buddhists. Like Pachak, he has been arrested for his work. "Not only our traditional culture, but our natural environment is in crisis," he says.

A modern Buddhist philanthropic organization, Tzu Chi, has promoted recycling efforts in Taiwan and Malaysia. Americans, too, have promoted their own form of socially engaged Buddhism, through the work of pioneers like poet Gary Snyder, author Joanne Macy and Swarthmore Professor of Religion Donald Swearer.

Hinduism's Green Tradition

Although Hinduism expresses a reverence for nature, imbuing rivers, forests and mountains with divine significance, India today is in its worst environmental crisis, facing 2.5 million premature deaths annually from air pollution alone. As *Hinduism Today* points out, "Most economic advancement during the last half century has come at severe environmental cost: falling water tables, soil loss, air and water pollution, forest degradation, overgrazing, loss of species and unmanageable municipal waste."

P. R. Trivedy, chairman of the Indian Institute of Ecology and Environment, says, "In the Vedas and other religious books there are detailed discussions and descriptions on nature and how to protect it. There is an urgent need to have a competent cadre of Hindu leaders educated and trained in religion, culture and the environment."

Suman Sahai, who campaigns for farmers' rights, points out that the 5,000-year-old Hindu tradition respects all forms of life. "Religious leaders can do wonders, but we are forgetting our traditions and have done nothing so far," she says.

Perhaps "nothing" is a little strong. Through the work of the Institute of Himalyan Environment and Development, Hindu pilgrims to mountain provinces ravaged by clear-cutting have been convinced to plant trees in God's name—with dramatically successful results. One sadhu, or holy man, 80-year-old Swami Vankhandi, personally replanted 15 acres of deforested land and fought off loggers. India's wealthiest Hindu temple, Tirumala Tirupati in Andhra Pradesh, has organized the planting of several million trees across the country. Another temple, Venkateswara, has encouraged pilgrims to plant 2.5 million trees.

One of India's foremost environmentalists, Vandana Shiva, predicts that the country will be in a severe food and water crisis by 2020. But she also points to some points of light in the form of faith-based activism. "Swami Chidanand of Hardiwar blessed the struggle against Tehri Dam [in the hills of Uttar Pradesh, the dam will submerge 100 villages and damage the Ganga River] and the Chipko movement [Indian "tree huggers" who have blocked loggers]," Shiva says.

Vasudha Narayanan, in an eloquent essay entitled "One Tree Is Equal to 10 Sons: Hindu Responses to the Problems of Ecology, Population and Consumption," summed up the reformists' message. "It is we who belong to the Earth," she wrote, "and by wrongly usurping what is not ours and what should be shared with future generations of human beings, we are indulging in adharmic, or unrighteous behavior."

Jewish Reverence for Life

Arizona State Professor Hava Tirosh-Samuelson cites the Jewish ideal of tikkun olam, or "repair of the world," as helping to promote a new Jewish concern for the environment. "The Talmudic sages express great concern about preserving the environment and preventing pollution," writes Richard Schwartz in his book *Judaism and Global Survival*. "It is forbidden," he quotes, "to live in a town which has not garden or greenery." And he cites an ancient Jewish story, in which two men who are quarreling over ownership of a piece of land go to see their rabbi, who puts his ear to the ground and proclaims, "Let us ask the land." As the rabbi straightens up, he announces, "Gentlemen, the land says it belongs to neither of you but that you belong to it."

In what has become something of a Jewish Earth Day, congregations plant trees and pursue agricultural projects on Tu B'Shevat, the 15th day of the Hebrew month of Shevat. On that day, observant Jews believe, God decides how bountiful the fruit trees will be in the next year.

Rabbi Arthur Waskow, who founded and runs the Philadelphia-based Shalom Center, writes of such traditions in books like *Trees, Earth and Torah*. "We are reviving ancient harvest festivals and integrating concern for the Earth into the fabric of Jewish life," Waskow says. "Instead of simply asking God to protect us from famine and locusts, we're asking to be saved from General Electric's pollution of the Hudson River."

The Shalom Center is on the front lines. "Focusing on the Jewish heritage of protecting trees," Waskow says, "we joined with such groups as the Redwood Rabbis and brought people to Maxaam shareholders' meetings to protest against logging ancient redwoods. We held a 'plant-in' on company land and were nearly arrested." The Redwood Rabbis also sponsored the "National Forest Protection and Restoration Act" to safeguard all national forests from commercial logging, a piece of legislation spearheaded by Christians Caring for Creation, and by the Religious Campaign for Forest Conservation.

The Coalition on the Environment and Jewish Life has 26 member organizations. Formed in 1993, the group states forcefully that "the ecological crisis hovers over all Jewish concerns, for the threat is global, advancing, and ultimately jeopardizes ecological balance and the quality of life." Energy security, global warming and forest protection are primary COEJL concerns, and members conduct letter-writing campaigns and other actions. COEJL Chair Sharon Bloome blasts efforts to drill for oil in the Alaska National Wildlife Refuge (ANWR). "We do not need to drill in ANWR to maintain our capacity to ensure Israel's oil supply," she says. "Israel's oil use is less than two percent that of the United States."

Another Jewish activist, Rabbi Fred Scherlinder Dobb of the Adat Shalom Reconstructionist Congregation in Maryland, is a co-chair of the Massachusetts-based Religious Witness for the Earth (RWE). RWE has called for religious witness against ANWR drilling, and organized a prayer vigil and nonviolent protest outside the U.S. Department of Energy, resulting in 22 arrests. "The prophets weren't always popular," says Dobb, "but their calls to justice became the enduring voices of their generations."

The increasing momentum on domestic environmental issues is unfortunately not mirrored in the Middle East. Tragically, one casualty of the intifada in Israel and the West Bank has been environmental partnerships between Jews and Muslims. For instance, a university-led project on air pollution receiving Palestinian cooperation collapsed after the recent conflicts. Nevertheless, there is a strong tradition of interfaith work on issues ranging from water distribution to pollution.

Theological Dissent

If religious campaigns for the environment were ineffective, they probably wouldn't generate much opposition. But perhaps sensing a gathering consensus, some groups have been critical, particularly the Michigan-based Acton Institute for the Study of Religion and Liberty, headed and co-founded by Catholic priest Robert A. Sirico.

Sirico denounces "this ongoing alliance between the radical environmental movement and the faith community" as "tragically unreflective." In a written response to *E* questions, he invoked the pastoral division between God's mission for humankind: stewardship or dominion. "In the first chapter of Genesis," he argues, "man is given dominion over the Earth. This clearly specifies that man—not the birds or cows—is responsible for the world and enjoys a large degree of prudential discretion in how he uses his authority."

Sirico strikes out at what he calls "the New-Ageist neo-paganism in which people ascribe divine status to animals and plants" though a huge amount of religious activism has been coming from mainstream denominations. The Acton Institute was inflamed by a television advertisement jointly sponsored by the Sierra Club and the National Council of Churches that attacked President Bush's proposal to drill for oil in ANWR as incompatible with "caring for creation." It was further incensed when the *Wall Street Journal* quoted Sierra Club Executive Director Carl Pope as saying, "the relationship with the churches gives him new clout on Capitol Hill." According to Sirico's associate, Phillip DeVous, "That kind of activist campaign serves the interests of the Sierra Club more than it does Christianity. The nuanced church message is lumped in with the green political agenda."

By being out front on a number of issues, NCC has become a lightning rod of criticism for conservative theologians. "The NCC is in the pocket of a lot of those environmental groups," says Michael Cromartie, vice president of the Washington, D. C.–based Ethics and Public Policy Center. Because he signed the Oxford

Declaration on global warming, Reverend Cizik of the National Association of Evangelicals (NAE) worries that "friends at the Heritage Foundation and on the political right" will now think him a candidate for NCC membership. But Cizik isn't going that far. "The NAE is the conservative alternative to the National Council of Churches," he says. "We represent mainline Christianity today, which the NCC does not."

Bob Edgar of NCC says the group earned its scarlet letter from conservatives 50 years ago, when it translated the Bible from the original Hebrew and Greek and helped to foster the idea of stewardship, rather than dominion, over the Earth. "We were also part of the civil rights movement, working with Martin Luther King, so that was a factor in our liberal reputation," Edgar says. "We don't agree with the Sierra Club on everything, but on some issues we have like-mindedness," he says.

Conservative theologians formed their own coalition, the Interfaith Council for Environmental Stewardship (now dormant, it spoke out against "a romantic view of nature"). In 1999, 25 of them got together in West Cornwall, Connecticut, and drew up what's known as the Cornwall Declaration. This document praises advances in human health, nutrition and life expectancy, and says that economic progress shouldn't be traded for environmental goals. "Many people mistakenly view humans as principally consumers and polluters rather than producers and stewards," the Declaration states. "Consequently, they ignore our potential, as bearers of God's image, to add to the Earth's abundance."

Paul Gorman of the National Religious Partnership says that, despite the rhetoric, it's not accurate to see the current struggle as one between the concepts of stewardship and dominion. The evidence of humankind's dominion is all around us, in our warming atmosphere, polluted seas and deforested plains. An increasing number of the faithful see that evidence, too, and that—rather than an excess of romanticism or mistaken neo-pagan beliefs—is what's turning believers all over the world into activists for the Earth.

Contact: Acton Institute, (616)454-3080, www.acton.org; Coalition on the Environment and Jewish Life, (212)684-6950, X210, www.coejl.org/home.shtml; Earth Charter, www.earthcharter.org; Earth Ministry, (206)632-2426, www.earthministry.org; National Council of Churches, (212)870-2025, www.ncccusa.org.

Making the Climate a Part of the Human World

By Simon D. Donner

Bulletin of the American Meteorological Society, October 2011

Ongoing public uncertainty about climate change may be rooted in a perceived conflict between the scientific evidence for a human role in the climate and a common belief that the weather and climate are controlled by higher powers.

Twenty years after the publication of the first Intergovernmental Panel on Climate Change report, the scientific community continues to struggle to convey the evidence for anthropogenic climate change and the argument for mitigation and adaptation. Uncertainty about climate change persists among the general public, particularly in North America (Pew Research Center 2009), despite repeated consensus statements by leading scientific organizations and groups of the world's leading scientists. In the past few years, public understanding of climate change has itself evolved into an entire subfield of research (e.g., Hulme 2009). Lingering public doubts about the basic science of anthropogenic climate change have been attributed to a wide variety of factors, including organized efforts at promoting "skepticism" (Oreskes and Conway 2010), political affiliations (Dunlap and McCright 2008), and cognitive biases (Weber 2010).

The lingering public uncertainty about anthropogenic climate change may be rooted in an important but largely unrecognized conflict between climate science and some long-held beliefs. In many cultures, the weather and climate have historically been viewed as too vast and too grand to be directly influenced by people. The structure of most agricultural societies is rooted partially in the belief that humans manage the land and the gods manage the weather (Fagan 2003; Burroughs 2005). Divine control of weather and climate is enshrined in many ancient and modern belief systems, including the Semitic religions, Eastern polytheistic religions, and some indigenous animist traditions around the world (e.g., Williams 1998). Examples of higher powers asserting control over the weather and climate are found throughout ancient and modern religious texts, including the Old Testament of the Bible (Figure 1). In these belief systems, humans may indirectly influence the climate through communication with the divine, but they cannot directly influence the climate.

From *Bulletin of the American Meteorological Society* 92.10 (October 2011): 1297–1302. Copyright © 2011 by American Meteorological Society. Reprinted with permission. All rights reserved.

> Then the Lord answered Job out of the storm. He said:
>
> Do you know the laws of the heavens? Can you set up God's dominion over the earth? Can you raise your voice to the clouds and cover yourself with a flood of water?
>
> Do you send the lightning bolts on their way? Do they report to you, "Here we are?"
>
> Who endowed the heart with wisdom or gave understanding to the mind? Who has the wisdom to count the clouds? Who can tip over the water jars of the heavens when the dust becomes hard and the clods of earth stick together?
>
> Job, 38:1, 33–37 (NIV)

Figure 1: A passage from the Old Testament describing God's power over the weather and the sky [Book of Job, chapter 38, verses 1 and 33–37 (New International Version)].

Skepticism about anthropogenic climate change may therefore be reasonable when viewed through the lens of religion or the lens of history. To create a lasting public understanding of anthropogenic climate change, scientists and educators need to appreciate that the very notion that humans can directly change the climate may conflict with beliefs that underpin the culture of the audience.

Religion and Climate

The prevalence of the human belief in divine control of the climate can be traced to the challenges faced by hunter-gatherers and early human societies. Early humans foremost required the skills to respond to immediate, local threats. There may have been an evolutionary advantage to believing that one can only affect the local environment. Regional or global patterns and trends in the environmental variables were not relevant to everyday survival (Hulme 2009).

With the development of agriculture, humans gained control of the land and became more dependent on the climate. Early city-states reliant on agricultural production in the surrounding lands were particularly vulnerable to droughts and floods (Fagan 2003). The weather god, who reigned supreme in early polytheistic belief systems, often emerged as the sole deity in later monotheistic religions; for example, the god "Yahweh" of the Old Testament has been traced to a weather god from a particular region of ancient Palestine (Neihr 1996).

In addition to physical infrastructure such as irrigation and food storage, city-states in Mesopotamia, Egypt, South America, and Mesoamerica developed complex rituals and religious infrastructure to enhance their resilience to climate variability. These activities and structures represented a means for people to indirectly influence the climate, which otherwise lay outside of the human realm (Fleming 2010). Leaders who could predict the coming rains or seasonal flood were perceived to be communicating with the divine (Fagan 2003). Contractual agreements between the people and the gods, with a set of responsibilities for each party, are depicted in religious art (Barber and Barber 2004). Prayers and sacrifices were used to prevent droughts and storms in many agricultural societies across the planet, from city-states in Mesoamerica and Mesopotamia (Fagan 2003) to the indigenous communities in the Pacific Islands (Williamson 1937). In these societies, failure of the annual rains or flood was perceived as punishment for inadequate sacrifices, sins, or a lack of devotion to the divine.

The ancient view of weather and climate is still apparent in modern behavior and language (e.g., the insurance term "act of God"). Scientific claims that human activity could influence the climate were restricted until the twentieth century to regional changes in temperature and rainfall due to the modification of the land surface (Boia 2005). Weather or climate engineering efforts over the past century were often expressed in religious language, as though humans were assuming a divine role (Fleming 2010). Some religious holidays observed in largely secular countries, such as Easter and Passover, draw directly from the ancient practice of praying for rain to nourish the soil or offering thanks for the water that provided a healthy harvest. Examples of communities who continue to interpret droughts, floods, and storms as divine acts can be found in parts of Papua New Guinea (Ellis 2003), the South Pacific (Donner 2007), Bangladesh (Schmuck 2000), and the United States (Paolisso 2003).

Though common, this belief that humans cannot directly influence the climate is not found in all cultures. Some agricultural societies, including several in the highlands of New Guinea, do not distinguish between human culture and nature (Strathern 1998). In such societies, the same word is often used (e.g., *vanua* in Fijian) to describe the land and the people that inhabit the land. These societies may include individuals who are believed to possess the magical powers necessary to command the weather (Fleming 2010). Alternatively, these societies may view the integrated human–nature realm as distinct from the sky, similar to the distinction in the Semitic religions. The practice of praying for the rains during the cultivation season in the Pacific Islands, such as Fiji, is one factor that unites the "new" religion of Christianity with the local pre-Christian animist belief system.

Believing in Climate Change

The belief that humans do not directly influence the climate is manifested in the present discourse on climate change in several ways. First, it leads to some of the extremes in public opinion. Polls find that evangelical or religious Americans are more unlikely to believe the planet is warming than the public at large, and even less likely to believe the warming is due to human activity (Pew Research Center 2009). Prominent conservative Christian political leaders in the United States, including Tom Delay, John Shimkus, and James Inhofe, have publicly questioned climate science on the basis that it is "arrogant" to think that humans can change the climate

> *There are important counterexamples in which religious groups have expressed concern about the effects of human activity on the climate. Most notably, a movement within the U.S. Christian evangelical community urges action to reduce greenhouse gas emmissions based on the Biblical concept of stewardship, as well as intergenerational equity and social justice.*

(e.g., McCammack 2007). Many residents of the atoll nations of Kiribati and Tuvalu doubt that human-included climate change could raise sea levels because, in the Book of Genesis, God promised Noah to never flood Earth again (Donner 2007; Mortreux and Barnett 2009). Even in secular communities, a broad sense that forces beyond humans control the climate may partly explain the persistence of the argument that natural forcings, such as solar activity, are the primary cause of observed twentieth-century climate change despite overwhelming scientific evidence to the contrary.

At the other end of the spectrum of the public discourse, climate change is often perceived as a punishment for sins against God or nature (Hulme 2009). In this view, humans have inspired climate change by committing immoral actions that warrant a harsh response either from the divine powers or from the integrated human–nature system. For example, some religious and environmental activist groups present climate change in apocalyptic frames (Swyngedouw 2010). These activists may approach climate change with religious fervor out of a sense that changing the climate is akin to losing Eden or betraying the "last stronghold of Nature" (Hulme 2010, p. 118). Although literature from the more "radical" environmental groups may not refer specifically to religion, the rhetoric reveals a concern that humans have disrupted the natural order and will suffer the consequences (Dunlap 2004).

Finally, the pervasive nature of the belief that humans cannot directly influence the climate may limit the confidence of the segment of the public who provisionally accept that human activity is changing the climate. The lack of conviction in people's acceptance of the science of anthropogenic climate change is typically not captured by opinion polls (Krosnick et al. 2006). Recent swings in public opinion (Pew Research Center 2009; Leiserowitz et al. 2010) suggest that a measurable portion of the population who at one time provided a positive answer to questions like "Is global warming happening?" and "Is human activity responsible for global warming?" in fact lacked conviction in those attitudes. For this portion of the public, the belief that human activity is causing climate change is weak enough to be threatened by unseasonably cool weather or other current events. Underlying doubts that human activity can influence the climate may explain some of the malleability of public opinion about the scientific evidence for climate change. It may also have an indirect influence on motivation for action to address climate change, which is a value judgment based on a number of variables, including the scientific evidence for a human role in climate change.

There are important counterexamples in which religious groups have expressed concern about the effects of human activity on the climate. Most notably, a movement within the U.S. Christian evangelical community urges action to reduce greenhouse gas emissions based on the Biblical concept of stewardship, as well as intergenerational equity and social justice (e.g., ECI 2006). The effect of this movement on the public understanding of climate change in the United States is unclear (McCammack 2007). Attitudes about climate change among evangelical Americans may be influenced more by support for conservative politicians and by the evangelical organizations urging the rejection of climate science and climate action based on the Biblical notion of "dominion" over Earth (e.g., Beisner et al. 2006) than by the stewardship movement.

Reforming Climate Change Education and Outreach

In light of the recent public scandals about climate science, there have been many calls for scientists to engage the public using different voices and frames (Jasanoff 2010; Nisbet et al. 2010). Scientists often mistakenly assume that public reluctance to take action on issues such as climate change is primarily rooted in a lack of available information (Bubela et al. 2009). Culture affects the way an audience receives information and is critical to engaging the public on controversial scientific issues (Nisbet and Mooney 2007). The emotional or affective response to information about a risk may be valued more in decision making than the cognitive or rational response (Loewenstein et al. 2001). Therefore, an audience can learn more easily or more rapidly from personal or cultural experience than from numerical or statistical evidence, which requires greater interpretative skills and effort (McCaffery and Buhr 2008; Weber 2010). For example, if embracing scientific evidence has implications for behavior and policy choices, some audiences may reasonably choose to reject either the evidence or the authority of the source in favor of past cultural or religious knowledge (Stolberg 2010).

Climate change outreach efforts need to address the perceived conflict between the scientific evidence and deeply ingrained cultural perceptions of climate. First, the development of human beliefs about climate should be added to educational materials and lesson plans. Existing education and outreach efforts rarely acknowledge any thinking about climate or climate change prior to the Arrhenius (1896) study on atmospheric carbon dioxide and temperature. For example, none of the top 50 climate change information Web sites maintained by intergovernmental bodies, governments, and nongovernmental organizations mentions historical or religious perspectives on weather, climate, or climate change (Table 1). The historical and religious context is also missing from the pedagogical philosophy and the materials of the emerging "climate literacy" movement (e.g., NOAA 2009).

Second, educators and scientists should take lessons from approaches used in the teaching of evolution, another subject in which science can appear to conflict

TABLE 1

Category	Examples	No.
Government	U.S. Global Change Research Program; U.S. Environmental Protection Agency (EPA); Met Office	24
Nongovernmental Organizations	Union of Concerned Scientists; 350.org; Environmental Defense Fund	16
International Organizations	United Nations Environment Programme; World Meteoro-logical Organization	6
Educational Institutions	University Corporation for Atmospheric Research; Woods Hole Oceanographic Institution	4

Top climate-change information Web sites, all of which contain no information on religious or his-torical perspectives on weather and climate. The sites were found with Google using the search term "climate change." The first 50 responses belonging to intergovernmental organizations (e.g., United Nations organizations); city, state, or national governments; or nongovernmental organiza-tions that contain educational material about climate change were employed in the analysis.

with preexisting beliefs. Pedagogical research on evolution finds that providing people with opportunities to evaluate how their culture or beliefs affect their will-ingness to accept scientific evidence is more effective than attempting to separate scientific views from religious or cultural views (Stolberg 2010). One approach is to hold interactive dialogues or forums, in which the audience, as well as the climate experts, has the opportunity to discuss and voice preexisting doubts about human influence on the climate. Another broader approach is to develop material that directly reconciles perceived areas of conflict between religious beliefs and scientific evidence. For example, literature distributed to religious leaders by the Pacific Council on Churches specifically addresses the perceived conflict between belief in God's covenant with Noah and the evidence for sea level rise (Pacific Council of Churches 2010). Such clear and direct explanations are missing from the "climate literacy" literature (McCaffery and Buhr 2008) and from the educa-tional literature distributed by U.S. evangelical organizations promoting climate action (ECI 2006).

Conclusions

Reforming public communication about anthropogenic climate change will require humility on the part of scientists and educators. Climate scientists, for whom any inherent doubts about the possible extent of human influence on the climate were overcome by years of training in physics and chemistry of the climate system, need to accept that there are rational cultural, religious, and historical reasons why the public may fail to believe that anthropogenic climate change is real, let alone that it warrants a policy response. It is unreasonable to expect a lay audience, not armed with the same analytical tools as scientists, to develop lasting acceptance during a 1-hour public seminar of a scientific conclusion that runs counter to thousands of years of human belief. Without addressing the common longstanding belief that human activity cannot directly influence the climate, public acceptance of climate change and public engagement on climate solutions will not persist through the next cold winter or the next economic meltdown.

Acknowledgments

The author thanks M. Oppenheimer and three anonymous reviewers for their helpful comments on earlier drafts of the manuscript. The author also thanks C. Kleinschmidt for research assistance. This research is funded by a Discovery Grant from the Natural Sciences and Engineering Research Council of Canada.
Affiliations: Donner—Department of Geography, University of British Columbia, Vancouver, British Columbia, Canada.

References

Arrhenius, S., 1896: On the influence of carbonic acid in the air upon the temperature of the ground. *Philos. Mag. J. Sci.,* 41, 237–276.

Barber, E. W., and P. T. Barber, 2004: *When They Severed Earth from Sky: How Human Myth Shapes the Mind.* Princeton University Press, 312 pp.

Beisner, E. C., P. K. Driessen, R. McKitrick, and R. W. Spencer, 2006: *A Call to Truth, Prudence, and Protection of the Poor: An Evangelical Response to Global Warming.* Interfaith Stewardship Alliance, 24 pp.

Boia, L., 2005: *The Weather in the Imagination.* Reaktion Books, 224 pp.

Bubela, T., and Coauthors, 2009: Science communication reconsidered. *Nat. Biotechnol.,* 27, 514–518.

Burroughs, W., 2005: *Climate Change in Prehistory.* Cambridge University Press, 372 pp.

Donner, S. D., 2007: Domain of the gods: An editorial essay. *Climatic Change,* 85, 231–236.

Dunlap, R. E., and A. M. McCright, 2008: A widening gap: Republican and Democratic views on climate change. *Environment,* 50, 26–35.

Dunlap, T. R., 2004: *Faith in Nature: Environmentalism as Religious Quest.* University of Washington Press, 206 pp.

ECI, 2006: Climate change: An evangelical call to action. Evangelical Climate Initiative, 5 pp.

Ellis, D. M., 2003: Changing earth and sky: Movement, environmental variability, and responses to El Niño in the Pio-Tura region of Papua New Guinea. *Weather, Climate, Culture,* S. Strauss and B. J. Orlove, Eds., Berg, 161–180.

Fagan, B., 2003: *The Long Summer: How Climate Changed Civilization.* Basic Books, 304 pp.

Fleming, J. R., 2010: *Fixing the Sky: The Checkered History of Weather and Climate Control.* Columbia University Press, 210 pp.

Hulme, M., 2009: *Why We Disagree about Climate Change.* Cambridge University Press, 432 pp.

—, 2010: Learning to live with recreated climates. *Nature and Culture,* 5, 117–122.

Jasanoff, S., 2010: Testing time for climate science. *Science,* 328, 695–696.

Krosnick, J., A. L. Holbrook, L. Lowe, and P. S. Visser, 2006: The origins and consequences of democratic citizens' policy agendas: A study of popular concern about global warming. *Climatic Change,* 77, 7–43.

Leiserowitz, A., E. Maibach, and C. Roser-Renouf, 2010: Climate change in the American mind: Americans' global warming beliefs and attitudes in January 2010. Yale University and George Mason University, Yale Project on Climate Change, 10 pp.

Loewenstein, G. F., E. U. Weber, C. K. Hsee, and N. Welch, 2001: Risks as feelings. *Psychol. Bull.,* 127, 267–286.

McCaffery, M. S., and S. M. Buhr, 2008: Clarifying climate confusion: Addressing systematic holes, cognitive gaps, and misconceptions through climate literacy. *Phys. Geogr.,* 29, 512–518.

McCammack, B., 2007: Hot damned America: Evangelicalism and the climate change policy debate. *Amer. Quart.,* 59, 645–668.

Mortreux, C., and J. Barnett, 2009: Climate change, migration and adaptation in Funafuti, Tuvalu. *Global Environ. Change,* 19, 105–112.

Neihr, H., 1996: The rise of YHWH in Judahite and Israelite religion: Methodological and religio-historical aspects. *The Triumph of Elohim: From Yahwisms to Judaisms,* D. Vikander Edelman, Ed., Eerdmans, 45–72.

Nisbet, M. C., and C. Mooney, 2007: Framing science. *Science,* 316, 56.

—, M. A. Hixon, K. Dean Moore, and M. Nelson, 2010: Four cultures: New synergies for engaging society on climate change. *Front. Ecol. Environ.,* 8, 329–331.

NOAA, 2009: Climate literacy: The essential principles of climate sciences. NOAA Guide, 14 pp.

Oreskes, N., and E. M. Conway, 2010: *Merchants of Doubt: How a Handful of Scientists Obscured the Truth on Issues from Tobacco Smoke to Global Warming.* Bloomsbury Press, 368 pp.

Pacific Council of Churches, cited 2010: Otin Taii declaration: A statement and recommendations from the Pacific churches' consultation on climate change.

Paolisso, M., 2003: Chesapeake Bay watermen, weather, and blue crabs: Cultural models and fishery policies. *Weather, Climate, Culture,* S. Strauss and B. J. Orlove, Eds., Berg, 61–82.

Pew Research Center, 2009: Fewer Americans see solid evidence of global warming. Pew Research Center for the People and the Press, 22 pp.

Schmuck, H., 2000: An act of Allah: Religious explanations for floods in Bangladesh as survival strategy. *Int. J. Mass. Emerg. Disasters,* 18, 85–95.

Stolberg, T., 2010: Teaching Darwinian evolution: Learning from religious education. *Sci. Educ.,* 19, 679–692.

Strathern, M., 1998: No nature, no culture: The Hagen case. *Nature, Culture and Gender,* C. MacCormack and M. Strathern, Eds., Cambridge University Press, 174–222.

Swyngedouw, E., 2010: Apocalypse forever? Postpolitical populism and the spectre of climate change. *Theory Cult. Soc.,* 27, 213–232.

Weber, E. U., 2010: What shapes perceptions of climate change? *Wiley Interdiscip. Rev.: Climate Change,* 1, 332–342.

Williams, J. T., 1998: *The History of Weather.* Nova Science Publishers, 90 pp.

Williamson, R. W., 1937: *Religion and Social Organization in Central Polynesia.* Cambridge University Press, 340 pp.

6

Creation, the Cosmos, and the Origin of the Universe

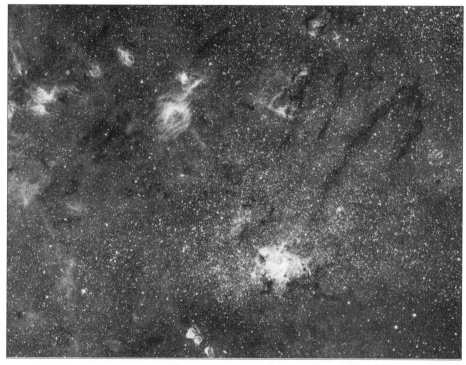

(Spitzer Science Center/Caltech)

An infrared view of the galaxy. As scientists continue to research the origins of the universe, their work often intersects with religious and philosophical thought concerning the origins of life and the human spirit.

The Origins of the Universe: Faith and the Big Bang

By Paul McCaffrey

Up until the 1920s, scientists believed that the universe was static, neither expanding nor contracting. Based on this understanding, they theorized that the universe had probably always existed, and that there was never a precise moment of creation. German physicist Albert Einstein subscribed to this conception. However, around 1915 he introduced his general theory of relativity, a decade-long effort to uncover the mysteries of gravity; with this theory, he revolutionized his contemporaries' understanding of the cosmos. In addition to laying the groundwork for the dismantling of the static model, Einstein's theory contributed to the formation of the big bang theory and related explanations regarding the origins of the universe.

Not long after Einstein announced his findings, a Danish astronomer, Willem de Sitter, analyzed his formulas and determined that for general relativity to function, the universe had to be expanding. Others found further evidence supporting this view: In 1922, Alexander Friedmann, a Soviet mathematician working independently, replicated de Sitter's findings. Meanwhile, at Arizona's Lowell Observatory in the United States, astronomer Vesto Slipher had actually seen the universe expanding in his observation of galaxies (thought at the time to be interstellar clouds of dust known as nebulae) speeding away from Earth.

Despite such input, Einstein doubted the universe was expanding and did not take de Sitter, Friedmann, and Slipher's findings seriously. Still, so that it adhered to the static model, Einstein refined his general theory of relativity, introducing a cosmological constant to his formulas. This adjusted for the perceived expansion and made the general theory of relativity compatible with a static universe. Later, Einstein would characterize his addition of the cosmological constant as perhaps the greatest mistake of his life.

Even with Einstein's revisions, the case for an expanding universe became stronger and stronger throughout the 1920s. In 1927, the Belgian astronomer and Roman Catholic priest Georges Lemaître found further data to counter the static model, though again Einstein was skeptical, telling Lemaître that his calculations were fine, but that his general knowledge of physics was not. American astronomer Edwin Hubble, working at the Mount Wilson Observatory in Pasadena, California, discovered that the moving nebulae Slipher witnessed were in fact galaxies. He confirmed that they were all traveling away from Earth and at a faster rate the further away they were, findings that corroborated Lemaître's calculations. Subsequently, Hubble's law established that the amount of light coming from another galaxy is a function of how far it is from our own.

These discoveries opened up additional areas of inquiry. If the universe was expanding, it must have had a beginning, a point at which it came into being and started to grow. Taking up the question of the origins of creation, Lemaître proposed in a 1931 issue of the journal *Nature* that at one point all the matter in the universe was contained in one "primeval atom," which, at the moment of creation, exploded. "The evolution of the world," Lemaître later wrote, "can be compared to a display of fireworks that has just ended: some few red wisps, ashes and smoke." Thus, the ongoing expansion of the universe is propelled by the residual force from that explosion. Initially called the primeval atom theory, Lemaitre's vision came to be known as the big bang and later the standard cosmological model (SCM).

It took some time for the expanding universe and attendant big bang theories to win widespread acceptance. Though the two men enjoyed a respectful rapport, Einstein thought that Lemaître misused the mathematics of general relativity theory and openly dismissed his scholarship, particularly the notion of the universe having a starting point. Such a concept had potentially theological overtones, perhaps partially related to Lemaître's status as a priest. A moment of creation suggested the possibility of a creator and clashed with many scientists' view of an eternal universe. British astrophysicist Arthur Stanley Eddington summed up much of this opposition when he commented, "Philosophically the notion of a beginning of the present order is repugnant to me. I should like to find a genuine loophole. I simply do not believe the present order of things started off with a bang." He concluded, "The expanding universe is preposterous."

Such criticisms aside, Hubble's insights confirmed that the universe was growing, lent support to the SCM, and made the static model increasingly untenable. As a consequence, Lemaître's theory gradually won more and more converts. Even Einstein eventually came to something of a grudging acceptance of the expanding universe model following a 1931 visit to Hubble in Pasadena, afterward declaring, "New observations by Hubble . . . make it appear likely that the general structure of the universe is not static."

Beginning in the 1940s, the big bang theory endured some competition from the steady state theory put forward by the British astronomer Fred Hoyle as well as his Austrian contemporaries Hermann Bondi and Thomas Gold. Along with his fellow contributors, Hoyle, who had coined the term "big bang" in a dismissive reference to Lemaître's primeval atom theory, shared Einstein's discomfort with the idea of the universe having a beginning. Yet they accepted the evidence that the universe was expanding. The steady state theory postulated that the universe had always existed but that it was nevertheless growing with the ongoing creation of new matter, thus maintaining a constant average density.

Though the steady state theory enjoyed some support during the 1940s and 1950s, additional evidence backing up the SCM continued to accumulate. After Lemaître's initial scholarship, other researchers filled in many of the blanks. The physicist George Gamow, once a student of Friedmann's, working with Ralph Alpher, calculated that following the big bang, the ratio of the two most common elements in the universe, hydrogen and helium, ought to be 10 to 1. Later astronomical calculations found that the universe does indeed reflect that ratio.

While contemplating his theory, Lemaître reasoned that there ought to be detectable traces of leftover radiation from the big bang. Other scientists soon began investigating this potentiality. Gamow, Alpher, and Robert Herman expanded on Lemaître's earlier prediction, calculating that the big bang should have left behind what they called cosmic microwave background radiation (CMBR) of a temperature of around 5 kelvin.

In 1965, Arno Penzias and Robert Woodrow Wilson, two scientists working for Bell Telephone Laboratories in Holmdel, New Jersey, were attempting to adjust an antenna used for radio astronomy. After making some calibrations, they found that no matter where they directed the device, it picked up low-level static. The static, it turned out, was caused by CMBR, which their antenna measured as having a temperature of 3.5 kelvin. The men soon determined that what they were detecting were remnants of the big bang. For their discovery of CMBR, they were awarded the 1978 Nobel Prize in Physics.

Following Penzias and Wilson's contributions, the SCM was all but demonstrably proven. The steady state theory had no way to account for the CMBR. Nevertheless, there was still much to uncover about the peculiarities of the big bang, and scientists continue to explore and theorize about its inner workings. Currently they calculate that it occurred around 13.7 billion years ago, effectively creating time and space. In addition to when precisely it transpired, a central question has been "What propelled the big bang?" American physicist Alan Guth posited a process called inflationary cosmology. Describing the theory, Brian Greene wrote for *Newsweek*: "The centerpiece of the proposal is a hypothetical cosmic fuel that, if concentrated in a tiny region, would drive a brief but stupendous outward rush of space—a bang, and a big one at that."

A major component of Einstein's and Hoyle's skepticism concerning the big bang was their objection to the notion of the universe having a starting point. Though the big bang and its related scientific conclusions do not fit seamlessly with Jewish, Christian, or Islamic scripture, the fact that it implies a definite beginning essentially leaves the door open for divine creation. Thus, it has evoked relatively little opposition in Christian, Jewish, and Islamic faith communities, especially when compared to historical religious responses to the theory of evolution. Indeed, the columnist George Will, reflecting on the insights the Hubble Space Telescope had yielded about the origins of the universe, observed that it "gives comfort to the religiously inclined. For people so inclined, science, especially cosmology, is augmenting, not subverting, the sense of awe that undergirds religious yearnings."

Among many Christian denominations, the big bang received an especially warm welcome. As early as 1951, when support for the theory was not nearly as solid as it is today, Pope Pius XII commented, "it would seem that present-day science, with one sweep back across the centuries, has succeeded in bearing witness to the august instant of the primordial Fiat Lux [Let there be Light],.when along with matter, there burst forth from nothing a sea of light and radiation, and the elements split and churned and formed into millions of galaxies." Not only that, the pope held up the big bang as a definitive indication that God exists, declaring, "Thus, with that concreteness which is characteristic of physical proofs, [science] has confirmed the contingency of the universe and also the well-founded deduction as to the epoch when the world came forth from the hands of the Creator. Hence, creation took place. We say: therefore, there is a Creator. Therefore, God exists!"

In the decades since, the Vatican has maintained that the big bang is compatible with Roman Catholic doctrine and the story of creation found in the Old Testament book of Genesis. "The Big Bang is not in contradiction with the faith," Father José Gabriel Fumes, the Vatican's chief astronomer, said in 2012. He also remarked, "This beauty we see in some way leads us to the beauty of the creator." However, the response among more fundamentalist Protestant Christians who embrace a literal interpretation of the Bible has been somewhat mixed.

Since it establishes a moment of creation and the potential for a creator—or as the American astronomer Allan Sandage remarked in the journal *New Republic*, "The big bang is best understood as a miracle triggered by some kind of transcendent power"—like their Christian counterparts, Jewish and Islamic religious leaders have been receptive to the theory. Some Muslim scholars also suggest that the Koran references a potential big bang as well as an expanding universe. They highlight a number of verses, among them, "the heavens and the earth were a joined entity, and We separated them" (Saheeh International version 21:30); and "the heaven We constructed with strength, and indeed, We are [its] expander" (51:47). In the former verse, the "We separated them" is seen as potentially describing the big bang, while some readings of the latter passage have been interpreted as describing an expanding universe.

The response to the SCM among religious communities is perhaps not as uniformly positive as Will suggests, but varies depending on a particular faith's view of creation. Unlike Christianity, Judaism, and Islam, not all religions envision a definite beginning or a divine architect who set creation in motion. Some faiths embrace the notion of an eternal universe that has always existed, and they avoid the concept of a single creator—or any creator at all. Such beliefs echo those of Einstein and other early dissenters to the theories of the expanding universe and the big bang. In several respects, the SCM is seen as somewhat less compatible with the concepts of creation in certain branches of Buddhism and Hinduism, though given the diversity of these faiths and their scriptures, there are also significant areas of overlap. In Buddhism, for example, there is no traditional deity or presumed creator and the universe does not have a beginning, though this is not always seen as an unbridgeable contradiction with the big bang. Hindu texts have varied accounts of the universe's creation, with some suggesting it is eternal while others hint at something akin to a big bang.

Whether and to what degree the big bang conforms to the cosmogonies of the various faiths of the world depends on both the religious texts in question and their interpretations. Contradictions are common. The emergence of the big bang theory illuminates how similar inconsistencies can develop in the realm of science. In crafting his general theory of relativity, for example, Einstein unwittingly under-mined his vision of a static and eternal universe. His conception of creation—or the lack thereof—did not agree with the general theory of relativity, and soon Le-maître and others, building on Einstein's scholarship, rendered the static model obsolete. Though these and subsequent discoveries have added to our knowledge about the origins of the universe, many mysteries and contradictions remain. "We are approaching a scenario for the creation of the universe that is compatible with the laws of physics," Alan Guth explained to Brad Lemley for *Discover* magazine in 2002. "That raises the question: 'Where do the laws of physics come from?' . . . We are a long way from being able to answer that one."

The Testimony of Faith to the Ultimate Origin

By Hans Küng
Translated by John Bowden
Tikkun Magazine, March/April 2010

Science can neither confirm nor refute what the two accounts of Genesis proclaim as their clear message: in the beginning of the world is God. So it is not "in the beginning was the Bang," but "in the beginning was the word, the will, and there was light; there was energy, matter, space, and time."

Creation of Space and Time from Nothing

Here we are speaking only in an inauthentic way of a "before" the creation of the world. What was God doing before he created heaven and earth? Augustine, in chapter 11 of his Confessions, already gave a precise answer to this question, which he regarded as impertinent. He was brief and terse: the question was meaningless; the question about the "before" was superfluous. Why? Because the world was not created in time, but with time; to this degree Einstein agreed with him. So only the creator is "before" the cosmos, only eternity is "before" time; here Augustine goes further than Einstein and addresses God: "Furthermore, although you are before time, it is not in time that you precede it. If this were so, you would not be before all time. It is in eternity, which is supreme over time because it is a never-ending present, that you are at once before all past time and after all future time." Thus from a theological perspective the act of creation is a timeless act; it comes about through time. And time is created time, created time-space, created space-time.

Now what does it mean to talk of creating the world "from nothing"? In the Bible, as I have said, this is only a later notion, the fruit of Hellenistic reflection. It does not mean the nothing becoming independent, as it were an empty black space before or alongside God. Nothingness must not be confused either with the "vacuum" of modern particle physics, whose "fluctuations" perhaps stand at the beginning of our universe, and which is in no way a nothing, but a something. What is meant rather is absolute nothing, which excludes any material cause in the act of creation. Creation "from nothing" is the philosophical and theological expression of the fact that the world and human beings along with space and time owe themselves solely to God and not to another cause.

But God does not owe himself to any cause. One may not even call God *causa sui* (cause of himself), as Descartes and Spinoza did. He is not caused at all. He is by definition the uncaused reality, because it is eternal and perfect: Id quo maius cogitari nequit—"that than which nothing greater can be thought" (Anselm of Canterbury, Descartes). The Bible does not philosophize about this. But it does express the conviction that the world is radically dependent on God as the author and sustainer of all being yet also remains independent of God. Christian theology has maintained that creation continues: creatio continua. For our present understanding, only in this way is the coming to being of the world as an ongoing process in time possible as a process that does not exclude the origination of new structures but includes them.

Creation from nothing and ongoing creation must thus be as a unity—both are the condition of the possibility of physical process generally. As U. Luke wrote in *Kosmologie* (Vandenhoeck and Ruprecht, 2004): "Creatio continita and creatio ex nihilo would simply be two names for one and the same creative activity of the eternal God, itself timeless and at the same time appointing time. And this one and the same creative activity of God would not lie beyond in a singularity billions of years away, but would be strictly present to us, beyond our control, but nearer to us than we are to ourselves."

What Is the Meaning of Belief in Creation Today?

In images and parables of their time, the biblical accounts of creation answer simple basic questions that also arise for human beings of today and that science cannot answer with its method and language. What are answered in the Bible are not purely theoretical questions but elementary existential questions:

- What was at the beginning? The good God, who is the origin of each and all.

- Is anything else (star, animal, or human being) God alongside God? No, there is no God but God.

- But aren't a good principle and an evil principle obviously fighting one another in world history? No, God is the good God who is not in any competition with any evil or demonic counter principle.

- Isn't part of reality of a lesser quality: matter as compared to spirit, sexuality as compared to spirituality? By no means—the world of the good creator God is fundamentally good, and thus also are matter, the human body, and sexuality. "God saw all that he had made and it was very good" (Gen. 1:31).

- What is the goal of the process of creation? The human being—not isolated but in the midst of the cosmos—is the great goal of the process of creation. According to the Bible, it is not first a redemption but already the creation that represents God's gracious concern for the world and human beings. The preservation of the world can be seen as continued creation and evolution.

We can ask ourselves: Is it pure chance that modern science could develop in particular against the background of the Jewish and Christian doctrine of creation? Two basic insights that the Quran also stresses were beyond doubt helpful presuppositions here:

- The world is not God; it is created and not holy in itself; it has been at the disposal of human beings.
- The world is not chaos but ordered, cosmos; it may be used, built on, investigated by human beings.

So what sense can it still make today in respect to the beginning of the world not only—scientifically—to speak of a Big Bang, of models of the world and theories of the cosmos, but also with full justification—theologically—to speak of a God who has created the cosmos, as countless people from the Hebrew Bible on—Jews, Christians, and Muslims, but also many others—have confessed time and again?

Belief in creation adds nothing to the instrumental knowledge that science has so infinitely enriched; it does not offer any scientific information. But creation faith gives us an orientating knowledge, particularly in a time of rapid scientific, economic, cultural, and political revolutions and therefore of uprooting and loss of orientation.

Belief in creation adds nothing to the instrumental knowledge that science has so infinitely enriched; it does not offer any scientific information. But creation faith gives us an orientating knowledge, particularly in a time of rapid scientific, economic, cultural, and political revolutions and therefore of uprooting and loss of orientation. It allows people to discover a meaning in life and in the process of evolution, and may provide them with standards for behavior and an ultimate security in this unimaginably great universe. Even in the age of space travel, when they reflect on the amazing results of astrophysics and as always look out at the starry night sky, people will ask themselves: What does it all mean? Where is it going? Does nothingness explain anything? Is reason satisfied with that?

The only serious alternative—one that pure reason, like so much else, cannot prove because it transcends its horizon of experience, yet for which there are good reasons, an answer that is thus completely rational—is that the whole does not come from a Big Bang but from an origin. It comes from that first creative ground of grounds that we call God, the creator God.

Even if I cannot prove it, I can still assert it with good reason, in that enlightened trust in which I have already affirmed the existence of God, which is so rational and so tested for me. For if the God who exists is truly God, then he is not just God now, for me here and today, but God already in the beginning, God from all eternity. Only in this way, it seems to me, does the universe become plausible to us in its existence as cosmos, in its mathematically ordered, highly complex, and tremendously dynamic nature. And in the face of the magnitude of our universe and the complexity of science, many scientists have shown feelings of amazement, of reverence, of joy, and even of terror and thus have also asked whether this universe does not embrace more than the apparent—a question that cannot be answered by science but only by a rational trust that has its grounds and that we call faith.

So believing in the creator of the world today does not mean believing in some myths, nor does it mean imagining God as creator in the way in which, for example, the incomparable Michelangelo as an artist painted him in a completely human way on the ceiling of the Sistine Chapel. Here all notions come to an end. Nor does believing in God as the creator of the world mean deciding for this or that one of the changing models of the world that great scientists have worked out. And this is not because here the issue is one of presupposing all models of the world and the world itself. Even an eternal world of the kind assumed, for example, by Aristotle would be compatible with belief in God. This was the view of Thomas Aquinas, though on the basis of the Bible he was convinced that the world had a temporal beginning. That the eternal God is before all time does not mean a temporal but an ontological priority.

Today, to believe in the creator of the world against the horizon of scientific cosmology means to affirm in enlightened truth that the ultimate origin of the world and human beings does not remain inexplicable; that the world and human beings have not been senselessly thrown from nothing into nothing; but that as a whole they are meaningful and valuable, not chaos but cosmos, because they have their primal ground, their author, a creator, a first and last security in God.

Once again it must be emphasized that nothing compels us to this faith. We can decide for it in complete freedom. Once we have decided for it, however, this faith changes our position in the world, our attitude to the world. Anyone who believes in God as the creator can with good reason also fully affirm the world and human beings as God's creation. The person can, above all, respect *human beings* as our fellow human beings (and not as lesser beings), but also respect and cultivate non-human nature, particularly the *animals,* as our *environment and the world with which we live* (and not as our born enemies, not as material to be used at random).

It is not although I am God's creature, but because I am God's creature, and because my fellow creatures and my environment are God's creatures, that I, my fellow human beings, and also—for all the difference—animals receive a dignity that has to be respected. The "fill the earth and subdue it" of the creation story (Gen. 1:28) cannot be understood as carte blanche for unscrupulous exploitation and destruction of nature and the environment, certainly not in an age when we soberly contemplate the "limits of growth." Believing in the creator God allows me to take my responsibility for fellow human beings and the environment and the tasks imposed on me with greater seriousness, with more realism and hope.

This article was adapted from chapter three of The Beginning of All Things, *by Hans Küng, translated by John Bowden. Eerdmans, 2007.*

Hans Küng is president of the Global Ethic Foundation in Tubingen, Germany, and professor emeritus of ecumenical theology. Among his many books are Global Responsibility; A Global Ethic for Global Politics and Economics; *and together with Rabbi Homolka,* How to Do Good & Avoid Evil.

Science on Faith

By Elaine Howard Ecklund
Chronicle of Higher Education, February 2, 2011

Over the past few years I have asked hundreds of university scientists whether or not they engage with religion in their classrooms. The majority say they do not, and they refer to the idea of "nonoverlapping magisteria" (NOMA), made famous by the late evolutionary biologist Stephen Jay Gould. He believed that science and religion are two totally separate ways of discovering truth. Religion, he said, operates within the realms of purpose, meaning, and values, while science operates within the realm of empirical facts—and the two should respect but never interfere with each other. In other words, the proper relationship between science and religion is no relationship at all.

But does the concept of nonoverlapping magisteria work on a college or university campus? And if not, what are the alternatives?

I've surveyed nearly 1,700 scientists and interviewed 275 of them in depth. While many are completely secular, nearly 50 percent say they identify with a religious label, and almost one in five attends services at a house of worship more than once a month. Even among those scientists who are not religious, many see themselves as spiritual. Yet almost none of the scientists—religious or nonreligious—talk with their students openly about how to respond to religious challenges to science—such as opposition to the teaching of evolution in public schools—and few of them formally teach their students how to connect the facts of science with its moral implications.

Whether or not Gould intended to further divide science and religion, many scientists have interpreted NOMA to mean that they should not talk at all about the connection between science and values.

Yet my research shows that while the idea of nonoverlapping magisteria may provide scientists with a theoretical framework for dealing with religion, it is a framework that is not easy to use, especially with students in a university environment. Scientists in academe have a pedagogical imperative, which makes their life's work somewhat different from that of scientists working in industry. University scientists must think about how to translate science to a broader public: the very students in their classrooms and research labs.

Talking with these scientists, I have found that many of them simply don't know what to do when their students bring up issues related to religion. Academic scientists want models that involve more than just asking students to compartmentalize their thinking. They want to know what aspects of religion are acceptable to talk about in a university context, where they should direct students to find resources about the relationship between religion and science, and where in the university it's acceptable to talk about religion. Many of them believe that in educating young scientists—who need to be equipped to deal with such topics as human-embryonic-stem-cell research and global warming—religion can no longer be isolated from scientific scholarship.

According to my findings, a sizable minority of natural and social scientists—about 20 percent, some religious and some not—now think that although the scientific method ought to be value-neutral, religion can meaningfully intersect with the implications of their research and the education of their students. A scientist's faith might motivate her to fight global warming, for example, or to decline research grants from sources that support nuclear proliferation.

> *According to my findings, a sizable minority of natural and social scientists—about 20 percent, some religious and some not—now think that although the scientific method ought to be value-neutral, religion can meaningfully intersect with the implications of their research and the education of their students.*

These academics also see religion as potentially helpful in understanding the purpose and meaning of their scientific work. They think their students ought to understand ethics and values based on religious teachings alongside value systems derived independently of religion. And they believe that students must learn how to connect scientific facts with what Gould called the "spiritual and ethical questions about the meaning and proper conduct of our lives." That is, students need to be able to wrestle with the ethical impact of scientific findings.

One social scientist I spoke with, who described herself as a cultural Jew, feels that college students have to learn to "take responsibility for the ways in which their beliefs and values affect other people," and that they must understand how other people's beliefs and values affect them and their research. She strongly believes that scientists in the academy ought to begin to have "discussions and debates about how we might better address the kinds of things that religion brings up."

So how should scientists on university campuses talk about religion? "Best practices" for such discussions should develop in stages.

First, academic scientists must acknowledge religious diversity. While scientists have an elaborate vocabulary for the subjects they deal with in their own fields and subfields, those without a religious identity (more than 50 percent) have limited experience, knowledge, or interaction with religion and religious people. (Thirteen percent of scientists were raised with no religious tradition, and those who were raised in religious homes were religious in name only.)

Scientists need to understand that different religious traditions intersect with science in distinct ways. Just as not all biologists study the same biological systems, not all religious people have the same beliefs or apply their beliefs in the same way. (For example, many Christians have no problem accepting evolution, while certain Christian groups reject it.)

Academic scientists have a particular intellectual responsibility—in the face of public conflict between religion and science, as well as because of the increasing diversity of their own student populations—to deepen their understanding of religion.

Second, we need to acknowledge the limits of science. Scientists should be willing to discuss what science is and what it is not, which is very much in keeping with Gould's idea of nonoverlapping magisteria. Philosophers of science and scientists themselves have discussed what they call scientism, a disciplinary imperialism that leads scientists to explicitly or implicitly assert that science is the only valid way toward knowledge, and that it can be used to interpret all other forms of knowledge.

Scientists who want their colleagues to do more to advance the public transmission of science—particularly those who think their colleagues are already doing a poor job in this regard—mention rejecting a form of scientism that has no room for meaning and morality. Teaching science, one chemist told me, can't be about just "distributing facts" to students, "because it's not really that difficult to find any sort of fact you want nowadays. [Our best students] can go learn about a topic pretty quickly on their own, but actually thinking about the discipline and what you're supposed to be doing in science is a very difficult problem."

Science at the university level, he says, must involve teaching students to think beyond their own research—which means teaching them how to apply science, how to communicate it to a broader audience, and how to think about it from "some sort of moral and ethical standpoint."

The third stage is a willingness of scientists who are religious to talk publicly about the connections between their own faith and their work as scientists. These "boundary pioneers," as I call them, can show students that it is possible, under certain conditions, to view science and religion as compatible. And they can provide colleagues with a model for how to discuss the ways in which science and religion interact. These individuals must be well-respected scientists, yet outgoing and savvy enough to connect with nonscientists.

Francis Collins, director of the National Institutes of Health and an evangelical Christian, is the most recognized example of a boundary pioneer, among others who are less well known. For example, one woman I interviewed, an atheist, talked about a blog, to which she frequently referred her students, that was written by a scientist who is a Christian. She thought the blog demonstrated possible ways of thinking about the relationship between science and religion.

Perhaps the best place for such conversations across boundaries is campus interdisciplinary centers. They could provide ideological and structural space as well as financial support. One social scientist I interviewed, who had no religious background but finds himself occasionally "tapping into spiritual power," said the lectures given at an interdisciplinary center on his campus and the discussions it sponsors helped him to realize how central religion is to many people's lives—and how much those in academe have generally ignored it.

Several scientists I've talked with hope that, more and more, this kind of dialogue will involve those in the physical and biological sciences. Such an initiative would be a forceful step toward advancing the public's understanding and acceptance of science.

Elaine Howard Ecklund is an assistant professor of sociology at Rice University and director of its Program on Religion and Public Life. Her most recent book is Science vs. Religion: What Scientists Really Think *(Oxford University Press, 2010).*

Let's Get a Big Bang Out of Science

By Richard Malloy

U.S. Catholic, January 17, 2011

Far from being a threat to faith, modern science is an invitation to get better acquainted with the force behind the universe.

"How can you believe in evolution?" a Christian woman accuses me. I explain that I don't believe in evolution. I accept evolution as a scientific theory in the same way I accept the theory of gravity.

In 2006 *National Geographic News* reported that only 14 percent of Americans thought evolution is "definitely true." Around 30 percent reject the idea entirely. Only people in Turkey have a lower rate of acceptance of Darwin's discoveries.

Americans are becoming more and more scientifically illiterate. We often fail to distinguish between different kinds of knowledge. Scientific knowledge, by definition, is always revisable, but that does not mean it is untrue. All scientific knowledge is theoretical. A theory holds until someone comes along disproving the theory and offers a better explanation. Truth for science means "that which has not been disproven." The "law of gravity" is "just a theory" in which we have a whole lot of confidence.

Those who resist science are not defending our faith. The bishops at the Second Vatican Council in *Gaudium et Spes* affirmed the "rightful independence of science," warning against the attitude "that faith and science are mutually opposed."

In just the past few decades we have learned more about the universe than all the humans who came before us. The 13.7-billion-year-old universe is expanding at an accelerating rate, and the fossil record demonstrates evolution. Without evolution the vaccines and pills so many take would be little more than snake oil. Without science, all our technological gadgets, from TVs to computers to cell phones, would not exist.

Evolution means humanity's place in the universe may be more, not less, significant. We are the creatures most responsible for the care of life on this planet. We will save or destroy the earth.

Our global choices will determine the quality of life for future generations. Mere opinion, fuzzy beliefs, or rigid, uninformed ideologies are inadequate to meet such challenges. In the 21st century we need good, accurate scientific and theological knowledge. Any sane and responsible religious institution and its adherents should study and disseminate all kinds of knowledge.

The teachings of science do not contradict the truths of faith. Actually, scientific discoveries can bolster faith. Science tells us what and how; faith ponders why and what does it all mean.

From *U.S. Catholic* 76.2 (17 January 2011): 17–19. Copyright © 2011 by Claretian Publications. Reprinted with permission. All rights reserved.

The discoveries of physicists in the past century have been simply stunning. Albert Einstein took us beyond Sir Isaac Newton's equations, revealing the centrality of the speed of light as an absolute by which we can understand the relationships of matter and energy ($E = mc^2$). In 1927 Georges Lemaître, a Belgian Catholic priest, relied on Einstein's insights to develop the big bang theory. Edwin Hubble demonstrated that the universe is expanding. Fritz Zwicky discovered that some 95 percent of the universe is made up of "dark matter" or "dark energy," while only 5 percent of the universe is what we think of as ordinary matter.

In 1955 Hugh Everett articulated the many-worlds hypothesis, applying the quirky mysteries of quantum mechanics to large objects in the universe. Many physicists think our world is just one of countless others. In 1998 Saul Perlmutter and Robert P. Kirshner stunned us all by showing the universe isn't just expanding, it's accelerating. Sir Roger Penrose and Stephen Hawking formulated equations explaining the mysteries of singularities and black holes.

The teachings of science do not contradict the truths of faith. Actually, scientific discoveries can bolster faith. Science tells us what and how; faith ponders why and what does it all mean.

The disorienting notions of quantum mechanics show that physical reality is governed not so much by absolute laws, but by processes of predictable chance. A whole host of scientists (Heisenberg, Planck, Bohr, Schrödinger, Born) theorize that we cannot know for certain how matter and energy "are" at any given moment; we can only know the probability of something happening.

Scientists agree on these facts: The big bang occurred some 13.7 billion years ago, and 4.6 billion years ago our solar system formed. The moon is 240,000 miles from Earth. The sun is 93 million miles away. Light travels 186,281 miles per second and a light year is the distance light travels in a year.

The Milky Way is so big that at light speed (6 trillion miles per year) it takes 100,000 years to leap from rim to rim. The Andromeda galaxy, our closest neighbor, is 4.6 million light years away. The closest star to us is 26 trillion miles away. The stars within 220 light years of the sun encompass only 1 part in 10 million of the total number of stars in our Milky Way galaxy. There are more than 100 billion galaxies in the known universe.

Science yields even more curious revelations. The universe is incredibly calibrated and tuned. Had the big bang been an iota of a fraction stronger, nothing would have formed. A big bang a fraction of an iota weaker, and gravity would have collapsed, pulling everything back into a black hole. With just excruciatingly infinitesimal minor changes in creation, human persons would never have evolved, much less survived.

If we can imagine all of cosmic time compressed to one year, with the big bang as January 1, dinosaurs don't show up until November 25. All of the recorded human history occurs in the last seconds of December 31.

We live in a vast, pulsating universe: trillions of stars, billions of galaxies. Scientific theories concerning black holes, string theory, and the multiverse radically reorient our comprehension of the majesty and mystery of the universe and thus our awareness of the awesomeness of God. Our imaginations expand as we learn what scientists know. Thus science affects our religious meanings and cultural truths because we are aware of realities unimaginable to those who came before us.

The whole notion of space-time as the context within which we exist and novel ideas about the meanings of past, present, and future marvelously open us to fascinating new conjectures about who God is and how God operates in and through physical realities. Teilhard de Chardin and John Haught contemplate a God who exists not so much in the past or the present but in the future, calling all forward in time to culmination.

We Catholics should rejoice in the astonishing realities science reveals, and we are called to relate other ways of knowing to the ways science knows. To know by love and faith are also legitimate ways of knowing. Remember: Science answers the questions "what" and "how"; the questions "why" and "what does it all mean" are above science's pay grade.

One cannot "experiment" with 50 marriages and then pick one for 50 years. The joy and peace that come with 50 years of marriage are based on the logic of love, not science. By faith we know God, choose to be loyal and committed to the ultimate mysteries revealed in Jesus Christ, and live in communion with the community of disciples, the church.

As believers we want to know what science teaches and integrate that with theological approaches in order to explore the meanings of life and love. Science can tell me how Teresa evolved; scientists can't explain why I fell in love with her and not Maria. A doctor can treat cancer. He or she cannot explain why your child died of leukemia while another child survived. Physicists can reveal a vast universe; they cannot explain why or how God created and keeps in existence all there is. Science cannot do an experiment to explain why God loves us.

Still, all these scientific discoveries portend bright promise for the future. For eons radio waves existed. It is only in the past hundred years or so we've been able to harness their power. Who knows what the conjectures of string theory may reveal and how those revelations may be placed at the service of humanity? Dynamite can be used to build dams and bridges; it can also be used to blow up Times Square. To answer questions of worth and value, good and evil, we need to go beyond science to philosophical and theological methods of knowing.

We exist. We are here and now, whatever "here" and "now" ultimately mean. Life is a gift, and gifts imply givers. Let us praise the giver. *Deo gratias*.

And the Survey Says:

1.   I think religious faith and scientific knowledge are compatible ways to look at ourselves and the universe.
     95% Agree
     3% Disagree
     2% Other

2.   Learning about scientific theories, such as the theory of evolution, can actually help us to learn more about God.

95% Agree
3% Disagree
2% Other

3. Science has caused me to question my faith.
    17% Agree
    69% Disagree
    14% Other

4. I haven't thought much about science since high school.
    3% Agree
    94% Disagree
    3% Other

5. I accept evolution as a legitimate scientific theory.
    95% Agree
    3% Disagree
    2% Other

6. I accept climate change as a legitimate scientific theory.
    83% Agree
    5% Disagree
    12% Other

7. Science classes in Catholic schools should include lessons on:
    93% Evolution
    40% Intelligent design
    30% Creationism
    20% Other

Representative of "Other":

Only evolution should be taught as science. The other two may be taught as social phenomena.

1. In the dialogue between faith and the sciences, I am most bothered by:
    57% Catholics who represent their faith as being opposed to scientific knowledge.
    46% Fundamentalists who give faith a bad name.
    35% Militant atheists who abuse science to bash religion.
    28% Priests and other church leaders who do not bother to keep up with current developments in science.
    14% Other

By Father Richard G. Malloy, S.J., author of A Faith That Frees *(Orbis, 2008) and vice president for mission and ministry at the University of Scranton in Pennsylvania. This article appeared in the February 2010 issue of* U.S. Catholic *(Vol. 76, No. 2, pages 17–21).*

Physics of the Divine

By Zeeya Merali
Discover, March 1, 2011

A group of scientists are embarking on a controversial search for God within the fractured logic of quantum physics

When he describes his line of work, John Polkinghorne jests, he encounters "more suspicion than a vegetarian butcher." For the particle physicist turned Anglican priest, dissonance comes with the territory. Science parses the concrete: the structure of the atom and the workings of the brain. Religion confronts the intangible: questions about ethics and the purpose of life. Taken literally, the biblical story of Genesis contradicts modern cosmology and evolutionary biology in full.

Yet 21 years ago, in a move that made many eyes roll, Polkinghorne began working to unite the two sides by seeking a mechanism that would explain how God might act in the physical world. Now that work has met its day of reckoning. At a series of meetings at Oxford University last July and September, timed to celebrate Polkinghorne's 80th birthday, physicists and theologians presented their answers to the questions he has so relentlessly pursued. Do any physical theories allow room for God to influence human actions and events? And, more controversially, is there any concrete evidence of God's hand at work in the physical world?.

Sitting with Polkinghorne on the grounds of St. Anne's College, Oxford, it is difficult to regard the jovial gentleman with suspicion. Oxford has been dubbed the "city of dreaming spires," and Polkinghorne is as quintessentially English as the university's famed architecture, with college towers and church spires standing side by side. The bespectacled elder statesman of British science walks with a stick and wears hearing aids in both ears. But he retains a spring in his step and a quick wit. ("He will charm you in conversation, as long as you get him in his better ear," a colleague says.)

Polkinghorne's dual identity emerged early. He grew up in a devout Christian family but was always drawn to science, and in graduate school he became a particle physicist because, he explains modestly, he was also "quite good at mathematics." His scientific pedigree is none too shabby. He worked with Nobel laureate Abdus Salam while earning a doctorate in theoretical physics from Cambridge University, where he later held a professorial chair. One of his students, Brian Josephson, went on to win a share of the Nobel Prize in Physics in 1973. Polkinghorne himself joined Nobel laureate Murray Gell-Mann in research that led to the discovery of the quark, the building block of atoms. But in 1979, after 25 years in the trenches,

Polkinghorne decided that his best days in physics were behind him. "I felt I had done my bit for the subject, and I'd go do something else," he says. That is when he left his academic position to be ordained.

Even as Polkinghorne changed careers, science seemed to be making God's role in the world increasingly irrelevant. In 1988 his Cambridge colleague Stephen Hawking addressed the issue head-on in his wildly successful book, *A Brief History of Time*, concluding that the universe could have been created without any need to invoke a Creator. A year later Polkinghorne countered with *Science and Providence: God's Interaction With the World*, in which he framed the concept of divine action in a way that could be tackled by physicists. "I started with the statement that I believe that God acts in the world, but he is not a show-off conjurer who violates the same laws of nature that he made," he says. "My question was, Is there a way of describing God's actions that is consistent with science?"

As a priest with a past, Polkinghorne discussed the question with old friends. "Gell-Mann thought I was crazy," he says with a chuckle. But Salam, a practicing Muslim and one of the physicists to mathematically unify two of the fundamental forces of nature—electromagnetism and the weak force which governs radioactivity—identified with Polkinghorne's quest. Even the most strident atheists from the old crowd enjoyed the debate. Steven Weinberg, who shared the Nobel with Salam in 1979, is a regular sparring partner. "Whenever we meet," Polkinghorne says, "he's always the one to put religious matters on the agenda, and though we don't agree, we always discuss things."

This spirit of respect persuaded another physicist and theologian, Bob Russell, to support Polkinghorne in his search for a physics of the divine. Russell, who founded the Center for Theology and Natural Sciences to foster interaction between science and religion in California in 1981 (before Polkinghorne was ordained), eventually teamed with the Vatican Observatory to launch a Divine Action Program. That group has been meeting with Polkinghorne and others to discuss religion and science ever since. "It's often assumed that scientists are intrinsically atheist," Russell says, "but science can be a spiritual experience. For some, it is about reading the mind of God."

Reviewing the evidence at Polkinghorne's birthday conference at Oxford last July, Russell concluded that the best place to seek scientific support for God is in quantum mechanics, the physical laws describing the subatomic realm. Soon after quantum theory was developed in the early part of the 20th century, physicists realized it had some peculiar properties. For people seeking a place for God in the physical world, the most important of those properties is the uncertainty principle, which states that you can never predict the outcome of a quantum experiment with certainty; you can only calculate the probability of getting a particular result.

As a result of the uncertainty principle, quantum events are starkly different from those in the familiar, large-scale world. When you toss a coin, you could in theory make a foolproof prediction (heads or tails) if you knew every piece of information about the flip—the speed and height of the toss, the movement of all the air currents in the room, and so on. At the quantum scale, in contrast, equivalent events are intrinsically indeterministic: The universe simply does not contain enough information for you to predict a result. This fundamental indeterminism has been repeatedly confirmed in the lab. For instance, physicists have shown that two identical radioactive atoms will decay at different times. There is no way to explain why they behave differently or to predict the precise time of decay.

Russell notes that the known laws of physics do not force a quantum experiment to yield a certain result but allow a choice of outcomes. Perhaps God makes that choice, he argues, swooping in to manipulate the outcome and influence an event in the physical world. That interpretation not only allows a place for God but addresses a philosophical mystery that long bothered Einstein and many of his followers: Is there some deeper determinism that controls the outcome of seemingly random quantum events?

A major criticism of Russell's view of uncertainty as God's tool for shaping the world is that quantum events usually play out only on the subatomic level. There is no clear evidence that messing with the decay of atoms or the bouncing of electrons can affect human behavior or change the course of history. For instance, a midsize asteroid contains about 10^{40} atoms. An unthinkably large number of quantum events would need to be fixed to steer all of those atoms toward Earth in a way that would have led, say, to the extinction of the dinosaurs.

Polkinghorne pondered this problem for decades before finding a work-around in the byways of chaos theory, a branch of mathematics that describes the underlying order in large, seemingly unpredictable systems, from weather to economics. Through the machinery of chaos, a tiny change in starting conditions can lead to vastly different outcomes over time. One common metaphor for how this might work is the so-called butterfly effect, the idea that a butterfly flapping its wings in Los Angeles could trigger a series of events that ends with a hurricane in China. Polkinghorne sees room for God in the deep mysteries of chaos theory and the limits of prediction. A divine intelligence in command of chaos could manipulate a vast number of quantum events with just a few well-chosen controls. The results could then grow large enough to have a meaningful impact on human lives.

Among other researchers, though, adding chaos to the argument did not help. Paul Ewart, an atomic and optical physicist at Oxford, describes himself as "pessimistic" about finding God hidden within the uncertainty principle, with or without chaos to lend a helping hand. From a scientist's perspective, the difficulty is that this model of divine action is by definition hidden from view, making an experiment to detect it almost impossible to devise. It would be like proving the reality of an invisible, tasteless, odorless, silent, intangible tiger lurking in your garden. Short of God's materializing in the lab and shouting, "Look at me!" Ewart notes, it is difficult to think of any incontrovertible proof. "I think we are an infinite distance from understanding God's workings," he says.

Quantum physicist Antoine Suarez of the Center for Quantum Philosophy in Zurich argues that the God seekers are better off pursuing another quantum effect, entanglement. In entanglement, two particles become twinned in such a way that the measurement of one always determines the properties of the other, no matter how far apart they may be. Imagine setting up a pair of entangled quantum "coins" (such as photons with a specific orientation), then giving one to Alice in Oxford and another to Bob in Zurich. When you ask Alice and Bob to flip their coins, they would both get heads or both get tails, even though the results of the tosses should be random and independent. Most physicists accept entanglement as just one more counterintuitive reality of quantum physics. But Suarez claims entanglement tests conducted with real photons in the lab suggest that quantum effects must be caused by "influences that originate from outside of space-time."

In an oft-repeated version of the photon experiment, a pair of entangled photons, A and B, are created by a laser beam. Each photon follows a different path around a table until it hits a "beam splitter," a half-silvered mirror that acts as a crossroads. From this point each photon continues its journey down one of two paths, either short or long—another type of quantum coin toss. In every case A and B will follow the same route, both traveling the long path or both traveling the short one. But why?

Seeking an explanation, Suarez and his colleague Valerio Scarani (now at the National University of Singapore) proposed a way to modify the basic experiment, which had been carried out by physicists in Geneva. Their intent was not to address theological questions but to challenge quantum theory by testing one of its fundamental predictions: that the timing of quantum events has nothing to do with their outcomes. They proposed instead that the outcome might be influenced by the course of events as the experiment takes place. For instance, if particle A hits the beam splitter even a tiny fraction of a second before particle B, its trajectory and outcome might influence what happens to B in its wake, somehow communicating across time. To test the idea, Suarez and Scarani needed to design an experiment that disrupted the cause-and-effect relationship between the photons by making sure that neither one arrived before the other.

Their cunning scheme was based on another famous theory of physics that gives quantum mechanics a run for its money in terms of odd predictions: Einstein's theory of relativity. Early in the 20th century, Einstein realized that time is not absolute; it runs at a slower or faster rate depending on how quickly you are moving. (Your watch falls about 177 nanoseconds behind on a cross-country flight.) Because relativity monkeys around with the rate at which time flows, there is no universal clock ticking away at a set rate that everyone will agree on. Two people moving relative to each other can even disagree on the order in which two events take place. If Alice and Bob are seated on two space shuttles moving in different directions, it is possible to set up a scenario in which they both flip quantum coins, but Alice says she flipped her coin before Bob, while Bob swears he tossed his coin first. According to Einstein, they would both be right, depending on whether you looked at the situation from Alice's or Bob's point of view.

In an analogous "before-before" experiment, Suarez's colleagues in Geneva deployed entangled photons A and B through beam splitters, after which each particle would follow either a short or a long path. The physicists used acoustic waves that had the effect of altering time for the photons—the equivalent of putting Alice and

Bob in those opposite-moving space shuttles. In this setup, a miniature observer running alongside photon A would swear it had been set on its course first, while an observer next to photon B would say with equal certainty that events had happened in the reverse order.

Suarez was sure that by messing up the time-ordering in this way, it would be impossible for the photons to coordinate their paths. He was proved wrong. On every run, the photons still met the same fate. Whatever causes the twin photons to behave in the same way, it must work independently of time. "There is no story that can be told within the framework of space-time that can explain how these quantum correlations keep occurring," Suarez says.

These results have intriguing philosophical implications, he notes, especially for the spiritually inclined. "You could say the experiment shows that space-time does not contain all the intelligent entities acting in the world because something, outside of time is coordinating the photons' results," Suarez says. "Physics experiments cannot demonstrate the existence of God, but this test shows that today's physics is compatible with all major religious traditions. There is strong experimental evidence for accepting that nonmaterial beings act in the world."

Polkinghorne concurs. Although quantum physics itself is a purely material and mathematical description of the world, he says, "the mysteries of quantum objects leave room for God in an explanation of the physical world."

Other attendees at the Oxford events say that attributing quantum matchups to the hand of God is a leap of faith too far. Jean Staune, a mathematical physicist and philosopher at the Interdisciplinary University in Paris who attended the September meeting, puts it like this: The before-before experiment shows that "if an intelligence is directing quantum events, then that intelligence exists outside the material universe. But it doesn't prove that such a mind exists."

This gets to a pitfall Polkinghorne has worked hard to avoid: If you explain away every scientific unknown by invoking God, you end up with a "God of the gaps," one that can be eroded anew every time a new part of the science puzzle is solved. "The trouble is that if science later advances, God will be left high and dry," says Christopher Isham, a practicing Christian and a theoretical physicist at Imperial College London. He questions the merit of trying to validate religious experience by appealing to science. "For me, religious belief is more about mystical feelings about the world, and God is something one encounters in one's self," says Isham, who converted to Christianity at the age of 40. He was asked to act as an adviser on the Divine Action Program when it was conceived 20 years ago but has lost interest over time.

"Most physicists are amateur metaphysicists," adds Nicholas Saunders, a theologian who reviewed Polkinghorne's arguments for scientific evidence of divine action at the July meeting; Also a lawyer with some training in physics, Saunders admits he is "not a fan" of such theories—not so much because they yield bad science as because they lead to bad theology. For example, suppose you accept that God steps in every so often to fix the outcome of a quantum event in the brain—manipulating the motion of electrons to cause a neuron to fire, perhaps influencing your decision

One common metaphor for how this might work is the so-called butterfly effect, the idea that a butterfly flapping its wings in Los Angeles could trigger a series of events that ends with a hurricane in China. Polkinghorne sees room for God in the deep mysteries of chaos theory and the limits of prediction. A divine intelligence in command of chaos could manipulate a vast number of quantum events with just a few well-chosen controls. The results could then grow large enough to have a meaningful impact on human lives.

on whether to become a priest or a scientist. In what sense would your career choice then really be your own? And if scientists ever did manage to uncover mechanisms used by God to influence the physical world, it would become even harder to defend why God does not use this power to alleviate suffering. "It does rather raise the question of why the universe is, frankly, a bit crummy," Saunders says. Discovering God's quantum powers would also seem potentially to give us godlike control ourselves, although Saunders is not too concerned: "It's one thing to understand a mechanism and another to manipulate it."

When I put these dissents to Polkinghorne, his jolly demeanor fades. "We need to find a middle ground where God is not a cosmic tyrant, with us as puppets," he concedes. "The answer has to lie along the lines that God has given humans real freedom, even if they grievously misuse it. But after seeing some of the horrific events that took place in the 20th century, it is hard to say that without a quiver in your voice."

Despite the many critiques that his work has inspired, Polkinghorne insists, in the wake of his birthday meetings, that the challenge to prove God compatible with physics has largely been met. "Physics asks how the world works, and when it answers that question it finds a very deep, marvelously patterned order. But it doesn't explain where that order comes from. I believe that the order is a reflection of the mind of God."

What about says Isham's God-of-the-gaps concern, in which science explains it all, making God irrelevant for good? Polkinghorne counters that, by its very nature, science can never provide a complete picture of the world. "Without the concept of God," he says, "we'll always be forced to treat some things like strange, brute facts."

A God of Creativity

By Stuart Kauffman
New Scientist, May 10, 2008

Complexity pioneer Stuart Kauffman on how we might think our way past the raging science versus religion war to ride out the looming global crises.

With economic and communications globalization, some form of a global civilization is beginning to emerge, perhaps homogeneous, perhaps forever diverse. We all face the challenges of global warming. We face peak oil, that year after which we shall never recover so much oil again—with unknown economic consequences, including hunger and resource wars. And all the while, our diverse cultures are being crushed together.

One response is a retreat into fundamentalisms, often religious, often hostile. This is hardly surprising, as humanity is still split between 3 billion who believe in the Abrahamic God (the majority of whom are Muslim, though a powerful minority are fundamentalist Christians), a billion who, like myself, believe in no supernatural god (though some of these are militant atheists), and the other traditions such as Buddhism. Clearly there is an urgent need for some new thinking.

That is why I wrote *Reinventing the Sacred*, though I am well aware that the very possibility and wisdom of such an enterprise is suspect. For those of faith, it is sacrilegious; those who are not religious remember Galileo recanting before the Inquisition and the millions killed in the name of God, and want no part of a God or a sacred that demands retreat from the truth of the world.

The process of reinventing the sacred requires a fresh understanding of science that takes into account complexity theory and the ideas of emergence. It will require a shift from reductionism, the way of thinking that still dominates our scientific world view. Perhaps the purest and simplest version of reductionism was voiced in the early 19th century by the mathematician Simon Pierre Laplace. He envisioned a "demon"—an intelligence which, if supplied with all the current positions and velocities of all the particles in the universe, could, using Newton's laws, compute the entire future and past of the universe.

This world view has two features. One is determinism, abandoned in part when quantum mechanics began to emerge a century or so later. It is also the "nothing but" view of the universe which, for example, sees a man found guilty of murder as nothing but particles in motion. As the physicist Steven Weinberg put it, the explanatory arrows all point downwards from societies to people to organs to cells to biochemistry to chemistry and ultimately to physics.

Now we appear to be at the frontier of a new scientific world view. Many physicists, from Philip Anderson back in the 1970s to, more recently, Robert Laughlin, are coming to doubt the adequacy of reductionism. I am with them: I do not believe that the evolution of biosphere, economy and human culture are derivable from or reducible to physics. Physicists cannot deduce, simulate or confirm the detailed evolution of the biosphere that gave rise to the organized structure and processes that constitute, for example, your heart. Entities such as hearts, that have causal consequences, are "real" in their own right.

The second transition in our view of science is based on Darwinian pre-adaptations. Were we to ask Darwin what the function of the heart is, he would say, to pump blood; but the heart also makes heart sounds and these are not the function of the heart, which was selected, and hence exists, because pumping blood was of selective value. Darwin's idea of a pre-adaptation refers to a property of an organism—heart sounds, say—that is of no selective value in the present environment, but might become of selective value in some different environment and therefore be selected. An example is human middle-ear bones, which are derived from three adjacent jawbones of an early fish. Did a new function come to exist in the biosphere as part of human hearing? Yes. Did that development have consequences for the evolution of the biosphere? Yes.

Now comes the big question. Could you enumerate ahead of time all possible Darwinian pre-adaptations for all organisms alive now, or even just for humans? We all seem to think the answer is no. Among the problems is the question of how we would list all possible selective environments. How would we pre-specify features of organisms that might go on to become pre-adaptations? There seems no way to do so. We do not seem to be able to pre-specify all of what I will call the "adjacent possible" of the biosphere.

If this is correct, the consequences seem profound. They break the spell cast by Galileo, that everything in the universe is describable by a natural law. If a natural law is a compact description of the regularities of a process, there seems to be no natural law sufficient to describe Darwinian pre-adaptations.

Here we cannot do what Newton taught us to do: state the variables, the laws linking the variables, and the initial and boundary conditions, and from these

> *So the unfolding of the universe—biotic, and perhaps abiotic too—appears to be partially beyond natural law. In its place is a ceaseless creativity, with no supernatural creator. If, as a result of this creativity, we cannot know what will happen, then reason, the Enlightenment's highest human virtue, is an insufficient guide to living our lives. We must use reason, emotion, intuition, all that our evolution has brought us. But that means understanding our full humanity: we need Einstein and Shakespeare in the same room.*

compute the forward trajectory of the biosphere. We do not know the relevant variables—the middle-ear bones, lungs or livers—before they arise. We cannot even make probability statements about such pre-adaptations because, statistically speaking, we do not know the "sample space" of possibilities.

So the unfolding of the universe—biotic, and perhaps abiotic too—appears to be partially beyond natural law. In its place is a ceaseless creativity, with no supernatural creator. If, as a result of this creativity, we cannot know what will happen, then reason, the Enlightenment's highest human virtue, is an insufficient guide to living our lives. We must use reason, emotion, intuition, all that our evolution has brought us. But that means understanding our full humanity: we need Einstein and Shakespeare in the same room.

Shall we use the "God" word? We do not have to, yet it is still our most powerful invented symbol. Our sense of God has evolved from Yahweh in the desert some 4500 years ago, a jealous, law-giving warrior God, to the God of love that Jesus taught. How many versions have people worshipped in the past 100,000 years?

Yet what is more awesome: to believe that God created everything in six days, or to believe that the biosphere came into being on its own, with no creator, and partially lawlessly? I find the latter proposition so stunning, so worthy of awe and respect, that I am happy to accept this natural creativity in the universe as a reinvention of "God." From it, we can build a sense of the sacred that encompasses all life and the planet itself. From it, we can change our value system across the globe and try, together, to ease the fears of religious fundamentalists with a safe, sacred space we can share. And from it we can, if we are wise, find means to avert wars of civilizations, the ravages of global warming, and the potential disaster of peak oil.

Theoretical biologist and complexity theory pioneer Stuart Kauffman originally trained as a doctor. He is now head of the Institute for Biocomplexity and Informatics, University of Calgary, in Canada. A seminal member of the Santa Fe Institute, he is now an external professor. The question that currently occupies him is: if selection operates all the time, how do we combine it with self-organization? His books include: The Origins of Order, At Home in the Universe, *and most recently* Reinventing the Sacred *(Basic Books).*

Bibliography

Asher, Robert J. "Science, Religion and the First Amendment." *The Huffington Post*. HuffingtonPost.com, 4 Apr. 2012. Web. 29 July 2012.

Begley, Sharon. "Red Mind, Blue Mind." *Newsweek* 154.25 (2009): 32. Print.

Chopra, Deepak. "Good News: You Are Not Your Brain." *San Francisco Chronicle*. SFGate, 25 Mar. 2012. Web. 30 July 2012.

Claryton, Philip. "Does the Higgs Boson Discovery Resolve the Religion-Science Debate?" *The Huffington Post*. HuffingtonPost.com, 6 July 2012. Web. 30 July 2012.

Dougherty, Jude P. "Science and the Shaping of Modernity: The Reciprocal Influence of Science and Culture." *Modern Age* 51.2 (2009): 133–43. Print.

Evans, Michael S. "Supporting Science: Reasons, Restrictions, and the Role of Religion." *Science Communication* 34.3 (2012): 334–62. Print.

Fish, Jefferson M. "It's Bigger Than You Might Think: Broadening the Science vs. Religion Debate." *The Humanist* 70.4 (2010): 27–31. Print.

Garofoli, Joe. "Catholics Campaigning Against Contraceptive Mandate." *San Francisco Chronicle*. SFGate, 15 June 2012. Web. 30 July 2012.

Helmut Reich, K. "How Could We Get to a More Peaceful and Sustainable Human World Society? The Role of Science and Religion." *Zygon: Journal of Religion & Science* 47.2 (2012): 308–21. Print.

Hendel, Russell Jay. "Dreams: The True Religion-Science Conflict." *CCAR Journal: The Reform Jewish Quarterly* 59.1 (2012):111–24. Print.

Horsey, David. "When Scientists Predict Calamity, Politicians Plug Their Ears." *Los Angeles Times*. Los Angeles Times, 14 June 2012. Web. 29 July 2012.

Huber, Peter. "Faith Based Models." *Forbes*. Forbes.com, 27 Oct. 2008. Web. 29 July 2012.

Lightman, Alan. "Does God Exist?" *Salon*. Salon.com, 2 Oct. 2011. Web. 28 July 2012.

Lindley, David. "Science Cannot Fully Describe Reality, Says Templeton Prize Winner." *Science Magazine*. American Association for the Advancement of Science, 16 Mar. 2009. Web. 29 July 2012.

Macmasters, Jasper. "Newton, Einstein, Hawking: Who Knows the 'Mind of God'?" *The Washington Times*. Washington Times, 20 Feb. 2012. Web. 30 July 2012.

Mervis, Jeffrey. "In the Eye of the Creationist Storm." *Science Magazine*. American Association for the Advancement of Science, 12 Feb. 2012. Web. 30 July 2012.

Ruse, Michael. "How Not to Solve the Science-Religion Conflict." *Philosophical Quarterly* 62.248 (2012): 620–25. Print.

Sarewitz, Daniel. "Lab Politics: Most Scientists in This Country Are Democrats. That's a Problem." *Slate*. Slate.com, 18 Dec. 2010. Web. 29 July 2012.

Thomson, J. Anderson, and Clare Aukofer. "Science and Religion: God Didn't Make Man; Man Made God." *Los Angeles Times*. Los Angeles Times, 19 July 2011. Web. 30 July 2012.

Waldrop, M. Mitchell. "Religion: Faith in Science." *Nature*. 470.7334 (2011): 323–25. Print.

Weaver, Janelle. "Brain Surgery Boosts Spirituality." *Nature News*. Nature.com, 2 Feb. 2010. Web. 30 July 2012.

Wilson, E. O. "Common Ground." *Science and Spirit* 17.6 (2006): 56–60. Print.

Web Sites

The American Association for the Advancement of Science (AAAS)
http://www.aaas.org/aboutaaas/

The AAAS is the largest science organization in the world for the advancement of scientific research and education. The AAAS promotes science policy on a national and global level, supporting scientists, engineers, and the public in constructive communication through education programs, policy forums, and research centers. The "Dialogue on Science, Ethics, and Religion" program works to promote communication between religious and scientific communities.

The American Scientific Affiliation (ASA)
http://network.asa3.org/

ASA members are Christian scientists dedicated to dialogue and research on the intersection of science and religion. The organization publishes the journal *Perspectives on Science and Christian Faith;* holds conferences; and is active in churches and schools in the United States, Canada, and the United Kingdom.

The Institute on Religion in an Age of Science (IRAS)
http://www.iras.org/Welcome.html

A nondenominational organization composed of scientists and clergy working to promote research dialogue between scientific and religious communities. The society publishes *Zygon: Journal of Religion and Science*, which explores a broad range of scientific disciplines and religious perspectives.

The National Center for Science Education (NCSE)
http://ncse.com/

The primary role of the NCSE is to unite scientists, teachers, clergy, and citizens in the advocacy of including evolution and climate science in public education science curricula. The organization provides literature and organizes events in many of the states where the teaching of these subjects is contested.

Metanexus Institute
http://www.metanexus.net/

Metanexus is a term coined by the institute to define "transcending connections" and "transformational networks" in the study of science and society on a national and international level. The society hosts public lectures and conferences, and provides professional and popular literature from a variety of scientific publications on the intersection of science and the humanities.

Society for Science and the Public (SSP)
http://www.societyforscience.org/

The purpose of the SSP is to provide vision and leadership in the engagement between science research and public education. Many of the programs funded by the organization target children and young adults with a variety of regional events and conferences.

UNESCO: United Nations Educational, Scientific, and Cultural Organization
http://www.unesco.org/new/en/unesco/

UNESCO is an agency of the United Nations dedicated to promoting peace and cultural understanding through a wide range of research and educational programs. Among its many roles, the organization advocates for the positive use and development of science to meet the most critical humanitarian problems. In addition, the Web site presents a wide body of information and literature on cultural and scientific developments in a diverse range of countries and organizations.

Index

Abel, Neils, 79
Adam (biblical patriarch), 121
Allenby, Braden R., 133, 138
Alpher, Ralph, 172
Alston, William P., 132
Alvarez, Luis, 81
Anderson, Eugene N., 146
Anderson, Phillip, 195
Aristotle, 179
Arroway, Ellie, 149
Ashbrook, Jim, 45
Auletta, Gennaro, 115

Bachmann, Michele, 72
Balestra, Dominic, 19
Ball, Jim, 151–152
Barbour, Ian, 114
Bartholomew I (patriarch), 148
Begley, Sharon, 34
Bekoff, Marc, 151
Belden, Dave, 95
Benedict XVI (pope), 112
Bennet, Max, 57
Benson, Herbert, 37
Berling, Judith A., 146
Berry, Thomas, 150
Bhikkhu, Buddhadasa, 155
Bingham, Sally, 152
Bloome, Sharon, 156
Bohr, Niels, 52, 99–100, 185
Bookchin, Murray, 134
Born, Max, 185
Bostrom, Nick, 112
Brooke, John Hedley, 108
Brown, Donald, 150
Brown, Jerry, 152
Bryan, William Jennings, 88
Bunge, Marcia, 121
Bush, George W., 64–65, 77, 157

Butler, John Washington, 87
Byrd, Randolph, 37

Campbell, Marci, 39
Carnot, Nicholas, 80
Carson, Rachel, 119–121, 129
Chardin, Teilhard de, 186
Chidanand, Swami, 156
Chivian, Eric, 126
Churchland, Patricia, 56
Cizik, Richard, 126, 151
Clinton, Hillary, 73
Cobb, John, Jr., 150
Collins, Francis, 6, 182
Copernicus, Nicolaus, 3
Crichton, Michael, 128, 134
Cromartie, Michael, 157
Crowley, Paul, 113–114
Curie, Marie, 78, 80, 82

Dalai Lama, 154
Darrow, Clarence, 88
Darwin, Charles, 87, 101–102, 104–
    105, 129–130, 195
Davidson, Richard, 32
Davis, Percival, 90
Dawkins, Richard, 6, 123
de Broglie, Louis, 79
de Lanerolle, Nihal, 52
Delay, Tom, 161
de Lesseps, Ferdinand, 81
de Quincey, Christian, 95
Derr, Thomas Sieger, 130
Descartes, René, 56, 176
de Sitter, Willem, 171
DeVous, Phillip, 157
Dewey, John, 18
Dowd, Michael, 104
D'Souza, Dinesh, 42
Dyson, Freeman, 132–133

Ecklund, Elaine, 113
Eddington, Arthur Stanley, 172
Edgar, Bob, 153, 158
Edison, Thomas, 80
Edwards, Denis, 113
Einstein, Albert, 6, 24–26, 78–79,
    98–99, 114, 171–172, 175–176, 185,
    190–191, 196
Eratosthenes, 78
Evans, Ray, 134
Everett, Hugh, 185
Ewart, Paul, 190

Falk, Darrel, 22
Falwell, Jerry, 152
Faraday, Michael, 78–80, 82
Farnham, Timothy, 149
Favorite, Andy, 83
Favorite, Mary, 83
Fermi, Enrico, 79–81
Ferrick, Tom, 123
Fisher, George, 150
Foltz, Richard, 154
Foster, Jodie, 149
Fox, Stephen R., 130
Francis of Assisi, Saint, 121
Frankenberry, Nancy H., 92
Franklin, Benjamin, 81
Friedmann, Alexander, 171
Fumes, José Gabriel, 174

Gabel, Peter, 95
Galilei, Galileo, 3–5, 78, 80–81, 195
Galois, Evariste, 79, 81
Galton, Francis, 37
Gamow, George, 172
Gauchat, Gordon, 66
Gazzaniga, Michael, 56
Gelbspan, Ross, 152
Geller, Uri, 110
Gell-Mann, Murray, 188
Gingrich, Newt, 72
Goodenough, Ursula, 148
Goodman, Ellen, 133

Gordon, Catherine, 37
Gore, Al, 133
Gorman, Paul, 147, 158
Gould, Rebecca, 148
Gould, Stephen Jay, 6, 180, 182
Grazer, Walt, 149
Green, Arthur, 95
Greene, Joshua, 57
Grewal, Daisy, 49
Grim, John A., 146, 150
Gushee, David, 127
Guth, Alan, 173, 175

Hacker, Peter, 57
Hadash, Shir, 152
Haeckel, Ernst, 129
Hahn, Thich Nhat, 146
Hall, Daniel, 38
Hansen, James E., 64, 126
Harris, Sam, 123
Haughey, John, 115
Haught, John F., 113, 186
Hawking, Stephen, 185, 189
Hefner, Philip, 107
Heisenberg, Werner, 185
Herman, Robert, 173
Hitler, Adolf, 133
Hoesch, Bill, 21
Holder, Robert, 67
Houghton, John Sir, 151
Hoyle, Fred, 172
Hubble, Edwin, 171–172, 185
Huckins, Olga Owens, 119
Hummer, Robert, 38
Huntsman, Jon, 72

Inhofe, James, 161
Ironson, Gail, 35
Isham, Christopher, 192–193

Jacobs, Mark, 153
James, William, 97–98, 100, 132
Jefferson, Thomas, 72, 74–75, 81
Jenner, Edward, 80

Jesus, 186
John Paul II (pope), 69, 113–115, 131, 148
Jones, John E., III, 17
Josephson, Brian, 188

Kaptchuk, Ted, 39
Keehan, Carol, 69
Kellert, Stephen, 149
Kenyon, Dean H., 90
Kepler, Johannes, 9
King, Martin Luther, Jr., 158
Kishner, Robert P., 185
Kitcher, Philip, 109
Kleinschmidt, C., 165
Koonin, Eugene, 102
Krause, Neil, 39
Krauthammer, Charles, 71
Kristeller, Jean, 40
Kurtz, Paul, 123, 125

Laplace, Simon Pierre, 194
Laughlin, Robert, 195
Lazar, Sarah, 33
Lemaître, Georges, 171, 173, 185
Leuba, James, 63
Libet, Benjamin, 58
Lomborg, Bjørn, 136
Lonergan, Bernard, 113
Lovelock, James, 135–136, 138–139
Lubchenco, Jane, 149
Lugo, Luis E., 131
Luke, Urich, 177

Madison, James, 74
Marcy, Joanne, 155
Marsden, George, 113
McBride, Sister Margaret, 70
McCain, John, 73
McKibben, Bill, 152
Meyerson, Emil, 26
Michelangelo, 179
Morris, Henry M., 89
Morriss, Andrew P., 120

Müller, Paul Hermann, 119
Narayanan, Vasudha, 156
Nernst, Walther, 80–81
Neuhaus, Richard John, 130
Newberg, Andrew B., 31, 36
Newton, Isaac, 9, 78–80, 185, 195
Noah (biblical patriarch), 121
Novalis, 25
Nsar, Sewed Hossein, 154
Numbers, Ronald L., 104

Obama, Barack, 67, 69, 71, 73, 77
Occam, William, 93
Oliver, Rachel, 121
Olmstead, Thomas, 70
Onians, John, 56
Oppenheimer, Michael, 165
Owen, Amy, 33

Pachak, Pha, 155
Paul, Ron, 65
Pauli, Wolfgang, 79
Paul the Apostle, 121
Peay, Austin, 87
Penrose, Roger, 185
Penzias, Arno, 173
Perlmutter, Saul, 185
Perry, Rick, 72, 76
Persinger, Michael, 32
Peter, Saint, 82
Peter the Apostle, 78
Piltz, Rick, 64
Pius XII (pope), 173
Planck, Max, 149, 185
Polkinghorne, John, 20–23, 188–190, 192–193
Pope, Carl, 157
Prieskorn, Kathleen, 69
Priestly, Joseph, 81
Ptolemy, 3

Raghavan, Ramesh, 69
Rahner, Karl, 113
Rappleyea, George, 87

Raulston, John, 88
Raven, Peter, 127
Ray, John, 151
Resnicow, Ken, 39
Robinson, Marilynne, 42
Romney, Mitt, 72
Roosevelt, Theodore, 81
Rupp, George, 150
Russel, Bob, 189–191

Sagan, Carl, 16
Sahai, Suman, 155
Salam, Abdus, 188–189
Sandage, Allan, 174
Santorum, Rick, 65, 72
Saunders, Nicholas, 192
Scarani, Valerio, 191
Scherlinder Dobb, Fred, 157
Schiavo, Terri, 69
Schmidt, Gavin, 138
Schrödinger, Erwin, 185
Schwartz, Richard, 156
Scopes, John, 87–88
Searle, John, 44
Seligmann, Peter, 127
Shakespeare, William, 196
Sheen, Fulton J., 26
Shimek, Bob, 84
Shimkus, John, 65, 161
Shiva, Vandana, 155
Silva, Bruce, 68
Sirico, Robert A., 157
Sivaraska, Sulak, 155
Skell, Philip, 102
Slipher, Vesto, 171
Sloan, Richard, 35
Smith, Dan, 152
Smith, Walter, 41
Snyder, Gary, 155

Soloveitchik, Joseph B., 98
Spinoza, Baruch, 24–25, 176
Stark, Dan, 84
Staune, Jean, 192
Stoeger, William, 114
Stulberg, Debra, 70
Suarez, Antoine, 190–192
Swearer, Donald, 155

Talmey, Max, 24
Teller, Edward, 81
Thatcher, Margaret, 151
Thomas Aquinas, Saint, 50, 179
Tirosh-Samuelson, Hava, 156
Tirupati, Trimuala, 155
Trivedy, Priya Ranjan, 155
Tucker, Mary Evelyn, 150

Urban VIII (pope), 4
Uttley, Lois, 70

Vankhandi, Swami, 155

Wallis, Nick, 154
Waskow, Arthur, 156
Weinberg, Steven, 22, 189, 194
Whitcomb, John C., 89
White, Ellen, 32
White, Lynn Townsend, Jr., 120–121,
    129–131
Whitehead, Alfred North, 98
Wilson, Edward O., 133, 151
Wilson, Robert Woodrow, 173
Woloschak, Gayle, 106
Wright, Nancy, 149

Zogby, John, 73
Zuckerman, Phil, 128
Zwicky, Fritz, 185